DI034595

By Harry Roskolenko

Poetry: *Sequence on Violence*
           I Went into the Country
           A Second Summary, illustrated by Sidney Nolan
           Notes from a Journey, illustrated by Sidney Nolan
           Paris Poems, illustrated by Zao Wou-Ki

Novels: *Black Is a Man*
           Lan-lan

Travel
Books: *Baedeker for a Bachelor*
           Poet on a Scooter
           White Man, Go!

By Harry Roskolenko

 STEIN AND DAY / *Publishers* / New York

When I Was Last on Cherry Street

Copyright © 1965 by Harry Roskolenko
Library of Congress Catalog Card No. 65-14398
All rights reserved
Published simultaneously in Canada by Saunders of Toronto, Ltd.
Designed by David Miller
Printed in the United States of America

Stein and Day/Publishers/7 East 48 Street, New York, N.Y. 10017

To: A.
F.
I.
L.
D.
H.

and

E.

Contents

§

My Father's Time 1

When I Was Last on Cherry Street 23

A Hothouse of Wanderers 47

To Make My Bread 59

A Furious Year 69

Transgressions, Confessions, and Lessons 81

Where the Lions Never Roared 97

Of Minnesingers and Agitators 1928 111

The Politics of Unreality 125

Those Days Will Not Return 137

Writers' Project 147

Portraits: Characters and Some Gentlemen.... 157

Mavericks and Marxists 163

Voyage From Lilliput 175

Doldrums, Decadence—and Some Bastards ... 187

"When the Bottle's Bloody Empty, Pet" 203

Death Is Tomorrow 219

The Future Begins 233

My Father's Time

§

Of the fourteen children we might have been, the first eight were born in the Ukraine and the next six on the Lower East Side of New York. I was to be the thirteenth. My little Russian brothers and sisters all died in the Ukraine from various infantile diseases, but New York was healthier. It killed only one of us, and that by more mechanical means. My oldest sister, Esther, died at the age of sixteen when a truck ran her down on Lafayette Street on her birthday. We celebrated in the funeral parlor and before a hole in the ground. Most of my tears had drained out of me by then. My mother and my second sister, Edna, cried—partly for me. My older brothers, Mike and Herschel, cried for themselves. The youngest, Bill, did not understand anything about death, at two. My father choked. He was a stolid man, and his eyes terrified me with their sadness.

But this book is mostly about the living—amid the immigrant pain, the panic and the occasional joys of Cherry Street, where I was born in 1907. It was a startling, dramatic human trap right off the East River, impinging on a world of commerce where fishing smacks and schooners tied up, their spars sticking way out into the street, their beautiful figure-heads helping to stoke the fires of my seafaring imagination. Every block between South, Front, and Water Streets had magical warehouses that contained the gifts brought by these

1

far-roaming steamers: spices, wines, hides, teas, coffees —
there were hundreds of wonderful smells. There were strange-
looking crates with large black letters telling of the ship-
ments' origins. Later, these boxes would make little carts
for me to race over the frantic cobblestones. I used to walk
by those amazing warehouses, picking up junk, head high,
nose alert, eyes quicker, sucking in dreams from the sources
beyond my private river. Dreams from the spice islands in
the imaginative places of my childhood, where there was not
a bit of garbage, no poverty, nothing racial, and lots of toys
for everyone. These were places and things beyond the all-
engulfing strangeness of being a small boy, wandering by a
mammoth city's river and trying to resolve some of the terrible conflicts that make growing up so painful.

My father had been many things in Russia — a farmer, a
miller — before putting in almost twelve years of servility as
a kind of batman to a captain in the Czarist infantry. But
when my father fled, via Siberia and Japan, just before the
turn of the century, he was off to a really great industrial
adventure in New York's sweatshops. First he worked in
the slaughterhouses of Wilson and Company, which stood
then where the United Nations is today. When I was born,
my father was in charge of the Judas goat that led Mr. Wilson's sheep to their slaughter on First Avenue.

On Cherry Street, we grew up with our fists — the Jewish
boys fighting the Poles, the Poles the Irish, the Irish the
Italians, and all of them usually against the Jews. When we
were not battling, it was a remarkably quiet street. There
were five, six, and seven-story tenements of railroad flats,
each building replete with the redolence of a hundred different cooking odors and the resounding of ten different
languages. Almost no English was spoken, except for the
exotic varieties we each *supposed* to be correct. Cherry
Street was foreign to the core — a unique ingathering of dress

as well as tongue. It was extraordinarily one-world, however, when it came to the brutal simplicity of how a boy went about getting something he wanted. One never asked for a gift or a toy or an apple from a fruit stand. In the accepted norm, one merely stole—and then was away with the petty spoils, sitting by the river, eating the fruits that fast legs made possible, planning another escapade.

Time and place and people combine in a capsule of remembered motion and violence. In horrifying block-fights, we were companions in thoughtless racist gangs when the Jews of Cherry Street fought the Irish from Front Street. When it was not purely racist, it was often terribly mixed up as to why the Micks were fighting the Sheenies—or we were all cooperating against the Wops. We were, obviously, creating the higher values of man and boy in the comradeship of the good fight and the sharing of busted heads. We loaded our stocking hats with glass and stone and charged away, slugging until a dozen kids were left sprawled and bleeding in the gutters—their eyes half-blinded, their arms or legs broken—and we were gone when the cops arrived with the ambulances from Gouverneur Hospital. When the losers had recuperated, the violence—everything short of murder—was on again.

When we were not busy semi-slaughtering each other, we drowned cats, pretending we were teaching them how to swim. Any cat that managed to crawl out was chucked in again, in loathsome indifference to its panic as we tried to outdo one another in this form of animal mayhem. Only a few old ladies, taking the air at Corlears Hook Park, would scream at us, but we were too brutal to care very much. In any event, it kept us from killing each other.

On July Fourth and on Election Day, however, all the gangs teamed up to make six-story high bonfires. We collected wood for days, foraging around South Street and the ware-

3

houses. Anything that could burn, no matter how costly, was fuel for an enormous celebration of our independent spirits. It would take hours and great skill to pile up the stuff. The base of the bonfire would often be fifty feet in length and width, rising a hundred feet to the pyramid's point—and the boy who climbed up to set it off at the top was the hero of the fire. The cops either looked away or enjoyed the spectacle but would finally have to call the fire department into action before all the adjacent buildings went up in flames.

Horses, horse cars—everything had a horse pulling it—and often there were fat dead horses lying on the mounds of garbage made into snow mountains. And some kids, in ugly bravado, would find broomsticks and stick them up the horses. Once a kid attached a small American flag to such a broomstick, and I angrily shouted as I took the flag off the broomstick, "That's not patriotic—shame on you!"

We never really believed that there were other city surroundings like our own. Cherry Street to us was a small village lost in the hugeness of the city more than what it really was—a do-it-yourself slum cast in its own unalterable image. Our slum poverty was far from genteel. It was alive and deadly in our bones, in our food, in our clothes—in all of life. A penny looked greater than a dollar, and only my father had a few dollars from the slaughterhouse, where he worked 14 hours a day. Once, when I went with him, I cried when I saw the slaughter of the sheep. I accused him of responsibility for the deed because he led the Judas goat. Later, when he was locked into a freezer by accident and was forced to stay there overnight because no one was around to let him out, I felt that God had paid him back for being in charge of the Judas goat. Suffering from frostbite, he was away from work for six months, his right leg a mass of bloody protruding veins. We were told that his leg might have to be amputated. Fortunately it was not, and he changed jobs.

4

As a small child, I was always certain that my father, who was tough-minded and peculiarly noble about work, would somehow make a living for us under any situation; but when he could not work during those six months, my mother created her own earning power. She was bequeathed, by a sympathetic *shamos,* a place for a Jewish newspaper stand outside of his synagogue on Madison and Montgomery Streets, where the horse cars ran. Oddly, the synagogue had been a Dutch Reformed church before the mass of Jewish immigrants began filtering into the neighborhood. (When churches of the Old Testament become synagogues, there is some hope for all of man and his many religions.) However, we were still overly conscious of our differences — too strange to each other, still involved in the ingathering on the new frontier, with the Jews feeling very much alien. My mother, though, always spoke to her Christian neighbors in their own tongues — whether it was Polish or German or Russian. She was a linguist who could not read or write; but talk she did and very well. Actually, she looked Christian herself, in the accepted physical norms. She was blond, had watery blue eyes, high cheek bones, and a Slavic nose. My father was darker, with a small, straight nose, brown eyes (one of which he almost lost once when passing one of our street fights), and a wonderful smile. The smile, however, did not help him when he was attacked as a Jew — he was then merely a Jew with a wonderful smile. He was also very pious, quiet, and dignified. Except with me. I was not exactly his chosen one, and his rage at my wayward ways often got me a good slap and a Yiddish warning that I was a *goyashe yinggach,* on my way to a frightening *Christian bucko* future.

At the age of eight, I felt that my future began much too early in the day. I was elected to help my mother at the newsstand. She woke me at three in the morning saying, "Sleep fast, I need the pillow," and off I went with her, in a coma of

5

sleep, pushing a carriage to Canal and the Bowery to pick up the papers for her stand. There were four popular Jewish papers published in those days: the *Journal,* somewhat sensational; the *Forward,* more socialistic; the *Day,* more literary; and the *Tagenblatt,* somewhat obscure. The satirical weekly, *The Stick,* which occupied only a small spot in the huge racks we put up after we folded the paper, was my favorite. The cartoons were inhuman gems. Men were not men but wizened institutions. Women were short and fat; all buttocks, breasts, eyes, and mouths. *The Stick* satirized all and everything, for nothing human was sacred to the editors as they offered their savage sallies for the discriminating. When a man bought a copy, I saluted him with a boy scout salute.

The customers who came for the morning service at the synagogue started to arrive at five A.M. By then my eyes burned, my head ached, my stomach was upset—but I had to be ready for work. First I scurried about to early-opening stores for pennies to make change, my pockets bulging with other coinage. Though a hundred pennies made only a dollar, I preferred them to nickels or dimes. I was so impressed by the volume of this copper kingdom that when it came time to turn it back to my mother, I made little scenes. I would tot up the profits, with the Indian Chief pennies counting for more. When I found a really old one I'd announce that it was mine, by confiscation. I would also shortchange a few pious old men anxiously going from the service to their jobs. This shortchanging came to about six cents daily, which made my after-school hours more cultural. I would go to the Harry Howard Theater, near Clinton and Grand, where for a nickel two children could see three hours of Fatty Arbuckle, the early Westerns, and serials like the *Exploits of Elaine* or *Tarzan.* When the show was over we were kicked out unless we had something called a "late check," a piece of printed cardboard issued if one came in during the middle of a show. The check then allowed one to remain for half of the next showing. Late checks were picked up by an usher, making his rounds in a hurry, while another usher was fumigating the place with rose water. Since all this was done in the dark, it was very easy to palm off a piece of cardboard torn from a crackerjack box as a late check — and to stay on in this crowded, dismal, foul-smelling arena for a repeat of Hollywood heroics.

Usually my initial entry used up only two of my six cents. For I would stand outside of the movie house as the show began and yell, "Who's got three cents? I got two." It might take me a while to find someone with three cents, a kid who would insist on holding the late check if we came in during a show — after all, he'd paid a penny more than I had. When the boy decided to go to the toilet, I'd demand the late check in the event that he found a friend and never returned.

This was my first vague, private economic planning and training. I felt enriched. I could see a movie. I could buy an ice-cream cone, too. There was a great emotional gain to feeling six cents dangle in my knicker pockets — my pay for standing at the synagogue's newsstand until seven in the morning, still in a sleepy daze, staring at the old men with long black linen coats as they hobbled up, went inside, prayed, came out for a moment's gossip, then went off again. They filled my mother in on all the dark details of their lives. Between belching and buying papers, they told her about being pants pressers, cloak makers, dressmakers, coat makers; men still in the garment industry at seventy. They were sad, half-blind and bleary — but still sewing, waiting to get into an old-age home as soon as they had five hundred dollars for a down payment.

When the Irish Easter Rebellion took place in 1916, I was out selling extras to the Irish in my neighborhood, lugging about a hundred English-speaking papers, a popular one with Mutt and Jeff and the Katzenjammer Kids. I yelled myself hoarse, denouncing the British and praising the Irish now risen, telling the locals about their hero, Padraic Pearse, and I got smacked by a couple of over-enthusiastic Irishmen outside a saloon. They tore my papers, disbelieving my fervor for their cause. They tore off my green tie, slapped my face, and kicked me in the shins. I became pro-British by the time I got home — something that lasted until the next morning; then an Irish schoolmate named Tom told me that his father, in protesting my beating, had himself beaten up the two drunks to celebrate his own conceits about the uprising.

§

Not too surprisingly, I was not always wide awake at school. After leaving the stand at seven, I'd go home, wash my face, eat a roll and an apple, have some milk-white coffee, gather my strapped-up books, and go off to P.S. 31 on Monroe Street — promptly to fall asleep. I would stay partially awake during history and English, sleep during civics and arithmetic and most of everything else. My early schooling was a great numbness of nothing mounted on a yawn.

There was *one* school term during which I managed to stay awake. It was the teacher, a Miss Gola, a grand lady I thought, a beautiful woman, I knew, who smelled of heaven, who had a soft voice and gentle hands, and who seemed much concerned with me. I adored her from near and far. When she leaned over my desk, talking about my lesson in history and making me proud that I was awake, that I was sitting there, I listened madly, believing that she, and history, had found facets in me that no one at home saw at all. When I came home after school, I did my lessons, ate apples and Russian black bread, so that reading and

8

eating apples became one thing, uniting the spirit and the body; and when I dozed early in the morning, between newspapers and customers, or watched the small street trolleys being pulled by the horses, I thought of Miss Gola and history, hoping that soon enough something historical would happen to me—and would come, of course, to her devoted attention.

§

One summer day I made a little red cart, using carriage wheels, a soap box, odds and ends. It was designed to help keep our ice box filled with free ice. It was all very simple, my mother and I had reasoned. All we had to do was pull the cart some blocks down South Street to the Fulton Fish Market, wait for the fish to be taken off the ice-laden boats, then filch the ice. It worked. After using this rather fishy ice for our original purpose a few times, we decided to make lemonade with it, but the fish smell was too overwhelming for the kind of lemonade we made: lemonade without lemons. Instead we used white vinegar and sugar. It had a variety of tastes and smells, but mostly of herring and other fish. We solved the smell problem by going to a real ice depot, run by the Knickerbocker Ice Company between the Manhattan and the Brooklyn Bridges. The venture turned to tragedy one day.

A truck was loading up. My mother crawled beneath its rear wheels for a large chunk of ice which had fallen there. She pushed it out, I grabbed it, and into the red cart it went. She reached after another and the cart was half full. She went for a third, creeping farther, then suddenly moving back. The truck's motor had started . . .

I ran to warn the driver. I pounded on the door of the shut truck, but he was moving by now. I howled and pointed. The gears reversed, and the truck stopped. It was too late. A rear wheel had gone over my mother's right arm, and her brown apron was already pooled with blood. People were running. The driver was under the truck, pulling my unconscious mother out. Questions were being asked. Numb with fear for my mother, I fainted.

When I came to, I was frantic to know where my mother was. A horse cop we knew, one who used to give me candy, had dismounted and was patting my head, pointing to an ambulance with two internes standing on the running-board. I looked at the pool of ice water. My mother's blood and bits of skin were circling in its midst. I began to cry, then ran to the ambulance but was held off by an interne. The horse cop came up to try to soothe me again. Then he lifted me onto his horse, and we started for the hospital.

§

There was no real home now. My father became our mother, as well. Before going off to work at six in the morning, he had the porridge ready, the lunch prepared, the orders for the day given, all of us told to keep the house clean and warned to be orderly Roskolenkos. Actually, the warning was for me. I was errant all around; they were proper and sober and contained, without any sort of waywardness. I was the one who had absorbed the miseries and bizarre meanings of the streets, so that my father's right palm knew my much-smacked body very well.

But the problem of raising six children was soon far too much for my father. We were sent, then, to a day nursery for breakfast and lunch and for three hours after school. There was mush for breakfast, as much as we wanted; soup for lunch with pieces of meat, though we always thought the meat was the result of an accident in the kitchen. But it filled our guts, placated my overworked father, and kept me briefly in order. We were home by the time he got back from

10

work. Then we had a family dinner cooked by my father and two sisters: borscht, with meat, if it was cold weather; or stew, or fish and dumplings. In the summer it was sour cream and cucumbers and cold soups.

My mother's condition was a big secret. The neighbors were gossiping that my mother had lost her right arm. Others said it was her left arm, her right leg. Or *both* arms and legs. We refused to believe them, we told Father. He said they were liars; terrible people for frightening us. She had lost nothing at all. But though she had been in the hospital for months, we had never been allowed to visit her. Obviously, my father was protecting us from something. We held a council and elected my oldest sister Esther to demand that she visit the hospital. Now we would know the truth. Esther was to ask the nurses and doctors. She was to feel for arms and legs – or false limbs.

My father warned her not to tell Mother about riding on a trolley on the Sabbath, and they were off to the fearsome Bellevue Hospital. There she tagged after my father, frightened, thinking about the mutilated and the dead, where they were kept. Soon they were in a room with many patients. Such sick faces, she told us later. Such ill, pale faces; people without the red cheeks she remembered of my mother, who had bed number eighteen.

Tears began running from my mother's sad blue eyes. Esther and my father started to cry, too. Mother was so terribly thin. And her red cheeks were gone. There were lots of questions. Mother was asking most of them. When were we coming to the hospital? It was no longer right for Father to keep us away – she wanted us desperately. We were clean and well managed, said Esther. He would bring us next Saturday, said Father. Wonderful, said Mother, kissing Esther.

Mother was covered up to the neck with blankets so that the outlines of her arms could not be seen. But while Father

11

and Mother talked to each other in Russian, Esther began kissing Mother, touching her face, moving her hands down to hug around the shoulders. My father and mother were animated in their discourse and had forgotten to watch Esther. When she found a void where the right arm should have been, she pulled at the blanket before Father could stop her. There was only a bandaged lump framed into the armpit. Esther cried aloud.

Between the nurse, my mother and my father, and the promise of a white dress, which Mother said she would sew with her left hand, Esther was finally quieted. I was to have white pants, too, in the summertime.

A real arm was a flesh arm; but there was that unique equivalent made of wood, steel, or nickel, manufactured in all sizes and weights, in matchless shades, making a sad or comical show for us. But we saw fabricated arms only in the stores for cripples. They were very costly, and we were poor. Instead of a mechanical arm, my mother merely had us pin back the right sleeve on her dress, folded neatly into the socket. Some time later, through a lawyer, she got five hundred dollars for the loss of her arm. We could buy a lot of ice with that, she assured us, and went right on—armless—about the business of bringing us up, sewing, cooking, washing, worrying, running the newsstand, lilting over on her left side when she walked, praying for us, and giving to charity from the little extra there was.

On Fridays, with ritualistic grace, Mother put a penny into each of the ten battered tin boxes that various Jewish charities left with us. On Sunday, with less grace, but equally as much ritual, I took out a few. When a religious collector of one of the boxes would come and count out the pennies, he'd stare at my pious mother in disbelief and ask, "Don't you give a penny every Friday?" She would assure him that it was oftener, but by the time the old, black-robed collector had hobbled off, picking his nose, we had been accused en masse of stealing.

I took everything in penny-thief fashion. I did not have a bicycle—who did? I did not have one toy—some did. No skates, no pony, no train, no boat—nothing but a worn-out fielder's glove and a broken-down football, which I had found while on one of my expeditions out of the neighborhood. I used to go as far as Delancey Street or Fourteenth Street, seeking, finding, taking odds and ends, accumulating a junk pile containing no item of value. But I was happy to own all of it and kept most of it under my bed or hidden in the secret places of our long railroad flat. One day, painting the flat, my father found all this junk, loaded it into my cart, took it to a junk dealer and got fifty cents for the lot. He gave me the fifty cents, but warned me that I would, soon enough, go to jail for such "borrowings."

Once, when we wanted to play a real ball game, we were instructed by an older boy on how to get the needed equipment. He told us where a fine collection of sporting goods was all too visible in a shop. We broke in one night, took a dozen assorted gloves, bats, balls, and a catcher's mask. Since the baseball season was soon ending, we added a few footballs for good measure.

I became a great football kicker, kicking the ball from one end of the block to the other. It would go as high as the tenement tops—if it didn't break a window first. I was a proud if sometimes a wayward kicker. It was much healthier than stealing or slugging, the horse cop with the candy assured me—for when not throwing spitballs or footballs, we still naturally threw punches. I never started a fight, but when it happened, I slugged away. If there was more than one against me, though, I ran, all my bravado going into my feet. You ran, you fought again, you stole bits of nothing, making magic from horse manure. It was the way Cherry Street went.

13

One day, Herschel, anxious to make a cent, brought up one of his friends on a late Friday night. He announced to Father, "This boy is a *Shabbas goy* — and he'll put out the gaslight for two cents." Only bona fide Gentiles were allowed to extinguish the lights during the Sabbath.

Father looked the nervous boy over, then asked in Yiddish, "Are you sure you're a *goy?*" The boy, just as anxious to split the two cents fee, answered hurriedly in English, "Sure I'm sure I'm a *goy!*"

Father was confused. The boy had understood Yiddish. Father said, "If you're not a Jewish boy, then you're not circumcized." With much embarrassment, Father demanded proof. The boy, with his knickers forced down, was circumcized.

Soon he and Herschel were running for the door, with Father calling out as he slapped each one in turn, "Miserable penny *goyem* — out!"

By the following Friday, Father, to solve the problem once and for all, had rigged up a Rube Goldberg put-out-the Sabbath-light contraption. He used the alarm on the eight-day clock, a clothes pin, and an attached string. When eleven o'clock came that Friday night, the alarm went off, to wind up the string, which turned the clothes pin, which turned out the gaslight — and put us into the beatitude of the Sabbath darkness.

Children's games . . . once, when Mike was playing hide-and-seek with us, we hid in closets, under beds, on the bed — everywhere where the hiding was good in our dark railroad flat. And there we were, Herschel and I, covering ourselves with a *perena* — a feathery comforter, pretending that we were pillows. And there was little brother Mike, soon enough, calling out, "There you are!" Somewhere he had picked up a hammer my father had been using, and with every "There you are!" Mike hit away at the *pillows*. Soon Herschel and I,

14

unable to escape, were yelling, bleeding—and Father came running, the game ending with bandaged heads and a couple of slugs of whiskey down our bellies. Father was remarking sadly, when the crying stopped, "I wonder if either of you will ever be the same . . ." Herschel, who got the better bangs on the head, eventually became a millionaire, and I— the author of this book.

Whatever my brothers were I could not be. They were obedient and because of our obvious poverty and my mother's persistence, they were also, soon enough, dedicated to making money. My brother Mike, and Herschel, only eighteen months and three years older than me, started saving their pennies and nickels from after-school jobs in groceries, ice-cream parlors, restaurants. They were on their way with all the sacred urges for going into business, something my mother lectured us about endlessly: "Your father will always be a slave. He is worn out with work but what have we to show for it? You must earn for yourself—this is America." She had a streak of iron on the subject; but I was impractical, even as a child, and only got a faraway look when she talked about what money could do for me. I looked at the ships in the harbor, soon to be sailing away to the spice islands. I knew, then, that one day a ship would be my home. I couldn't wait to grow up enough to be the man in the boy—and become a runaway sailor.

My first bit of running away came when I was nine, after spending part of a summer in a sweatshop working alongside of my father in a loft on Greene Street. He pressed cloaks, and I put them on the racks. I carried heavy bolts of cloth. I pushed carts through the streets, working from seven in the morning to six at night; but I did not complete the enslaved summer. I had other ideas. I was tired of the darkness of the rooms we came home to, tired of the double-tiered beds. I was tired of seeing my father sweat with his undershirt off, showing the marks of the Czarist *nagaika,* the cat-of-nine-tails, still etched on his back. I was fed up with looming tenements, adult European memories, and foreign speech. I wanted to see the world — certainly America. The war was on, and America was officially neutral, though our street was not. The few Germans there stuck up for Germany, but most of us were for the Allies. Right in our midst was a *kasserna,* as my mother called a tenement building that had once been a civil war billet. Whenever I walked by, I saluted the building because it brought America closer to me. And I ran away to see what the land outside was all about.

I rented a bicycle for a nickel, strapped on a knapsack carrying my pots and pans, a few changes of clothes, a tent — and I was off looking for the Lincoln Highway. A taxi driver told me that it began near Prospect Park, in Brooklyn. When I got there it turned out to be a residential area called Lincoln Road. I spent the night with relatives on Coney Island, told them a few lies about going camping, and left for California the next morning before they could inform my parents.

With much clanging and banging (an extra tire was strapped to the top of the knapsack, a tool kit perched over the tire) I rode between large trucks and veered off fat beer-wagon horses, en route to the Lackawanna Ferry and to New Jersey. I saw monstrous tugs and huge ships, too, with colored stacks and pennants: a moving world of names like Hamburg, Rotterdam, Sydney, Cobh. I was going places too, if only with one dollar bill I had saved for the adventure. Down the Jersey roads I fled. By the time I reached Rahway in the evening, my single dollar was a dull dream, already spent on food, and the poor face of hunger growled again in my guts. I went to the local "Y" and was refused a Christian bed, being broke. Another guest paid for me, listened to my adventure-in-progress, wished me luck, and I slept my second night away from home.

I was poorer than a peddler, but I had a dream—any place but the ramparts of Cherry Street. I pedalled up hills, then coasted down, my heart straining. During the mad flight, I met another boy on a bicycle heading for Philadelphia. We teamed up. Once in Philadelphia, he advised me to go to the Brotherhood Club, where I would get a bed and be fed for nothing. I had gone about eighty miles from home.

In the Club's restaurant, a man spoke to me about the foolishness of my trip; California was far away, especially on a bicycle. It was far better to be a sparrow riding the top of a freight train than a lion on macadam, he said. Whatever he said sounded odd; the language itself was peculiar. But he patted my red cheeks and said I was a real American doing things the hard way. He told me he was an Englishman, that he had been gassed in the war. He had been all over France before being released. The gas, he said, did strange things to him. Not having seen a real soldier before, this one was a hero by my standards; and I marveled at his world of action. When I got sleepy, he patted me again and advised me to sleep in a room near his own.

I was awakened during the night by him. He said quietly that it was safer for me to sleep in his room. He was my new friend, after all. I gathered up my gear and followed him. I had to sleep in his bed, he said. I didn't understand, but my muscles ached; so I climbed in and went to sleep again.

He woke me up again by touching my body in a way that frightened me. I pushed him away, perplexed and sickened, and headed back for my room, bolting the door behind me. In the morning, when I explained to the manager of the Brotherhood Club what had happened, he called the police. The police called the man a pervert, a word that I did not understand. When it was explained, I still did not understand. Why should a man bother a boy? There were women for things like that, I told the police innocently.

17

That day, half in rage, still perplexed, I reached Portland, Pennsylvania, where a Cherry Street friend, Morton, was summering on a farm. I told the usual number of lies about my trip but found myself content, at his invitation to stay awhile, not to pedal right on to California, still a good three thousand miles away. I learned, soon enough, to milk a cow. I saw live chickens in their walking-about state . . . for when my mother bought live chickens from her kosher butcher, she tied them up near the hot stove. By Friday they were slaughtered for the Sabbath meal. Now for the first time I romped in the grass, went swimming in the rocky creek, walked in the woods, heard the birds sing, climbed trees, and listened to the largeness of nature.

Then one morning, Morton's father read something in *The Forward,* the New York Jewish paper about me: the police, it seems, were asked to be on the lookout for a boy and a bicycle. He wired my father. I was put on a train with the bicycle and the knapsack, met by my father at Pennsylvania Station, and slapped a few times. The bicycle was returned to the owners—and I was returned to the sweatshop, finishing the summer at three dollars a week in pay.

§

In the Fall my father made his year's stock of wine, whiskey, mead, and *kvass.* It was a silent, sealed ordeal on a Saturday night. The window blinds were pulled down, the keyholes were filled with paper, incense was burned to camouflage the smell of grapes, and alcohol dripped from the copper coils of my father's still. He sat through the first part of the night patiently, listening at the door for imagined government agents, and then he dozed off and on through the long whiskey night waiting for the resultant alcohol. My father, on what seemed to be an industrial scale, worked the grape-press and the still, where the alcohol dripped off the

18

end of a match. I often wondered, as I peered into the kitchen from my upper bunk, how many drops made a gallon. I would count several hundred drops in fifteen minutes and back to sleep I went. An hour later I would be up again, watching Father at the honey vat, making the mead. When Sunday noon came around, the blinds were lifted, the paper taken out of the keyholes, and the results of the night's work stored in various closets. After that, every Saturday, we were dutifully given a small glass of whiskey and all the mead and *kvass* we wanted.

In my own way, and for my own pleasures, I tried to become as inventive as my father. To make a raft for river travel, Morton and I laced twenty-foot logs together, using rope and old cable wire. What the crude raft lacked as a yacht was made up for by the stentorian nautical terminology used aboard it. We "aye, aye, sirred" all over the decks as we floated among the condoms, dead cats, dead rats, old vegetables, and sewage of the East River. Those of us who could dived in and swam, those who couldn't stayed on the raft to marvel at the swimmers kicking about in the nude, coming up for air through the garbage. We used barrel staves and poles for oars as we pulled and pushed toward the Battery, hiding from the police boats, so we liked to think, as we went toward the harbor and the open sea. We never reached the sea, of course. The harbor police would haul us back and give us splendidly serious lectures on our chances of drowning. Once, when I was pushed in fully clothed by one of my fellow navigators, I suddenly learned to swim. I had to . . . but when I reached home, soaking wet, I got another minor beating from my irate father. That I could swim and not drown in an emergency did not impress him; for by now he had lost any sense of humor he'd ever had about me.

Of the local bullies there were many. There were some polite ones who cursed provocatively before smacking you.

Others did it without warning. But we had massive allegiances when the bully was also the hero. Heroism was anything that required muscle, daring, and the rest of the juvenile mythology. Smulick, aged eighteen, was such a fellow. Husky, with six fingers on his right hand, he was looked upon as extraordinary. His face was twisted, his mouth running at a slight diagonal. He had only two eyes, though we might have expected three. He had been in jail, which engendered our respect. At night, he would hang around the beer saloons waiting for a drunken Pole to come stumbling out. Smulick would follow the poor Pole, who would be singing sentimental Polish songs, to a dark spot, clout him one and roll him, taking whatever change had escaped the bartender. If Smulick ever hit you, you dropped to the sidewalk and played dead. His questions were a demand. You brought what he wanted, whether it was an apple or a girl on whom he could demonstrate his sexual prowess; he had all sorts of appetites.

Various of his cultural attainments he was happy to exhibit to our growing eyes and bodies. First we had a short semester in auto-eroticism. Following that, he taught us how to lure girls into dark cellars, using the accepted medium—candy. There, as we grouped around him and the girl, Smulick would carry out his slum version of a youthful black mass—himself as the chief exorcisor of the simple rituals. But such orgies as we witnessed were fairly useless to us at nine. They were exhibitions for our future, explained Smulick, who was having his future now. A few girls lost their virginity to him in a terribly painful way. But if one of us protested, frightened and disgusted by his antics, Smulick delivered the protestor a beating for his moral attitudes.

My private introduction to luring had been quite innocent on my part. It was a girl named Peshky, prettier than her

name, who had been raped by her father and now was quite
open about her almost professional ways. "If you give me
your fountain pen, I'll talk dirty for you," she said to me
one afternoon. I was not that interested. I wanted the pen
and not her dirty words. I had my own dirty words, and they
cost me nothing. She pleaded. I held my ground. The pen was
mine. But when she added, "Come into the cellar with me,
and I'll show you my ass," I found myself down in the dark
cellar, fumbling in the blackness against calcimined walls,
hearing the rats running, the cats after them, and I after
Peshky. When we reached a place that she knew very well,
she grabbed the pen and ran. I caught her and grabbed the
pen back. Then she began taking off her clothes. She insisted that I do the same. I was embarrassed and refused,
but she was stronger and she undressed me—and then started
in playing her erotic little games. Later she offered to give
me a watch-fob. She said, "My father gave me the fob so I
wouldn't tell my mother. You ain't a man yet . . . and my
father did all the dirty things to me. I wanted to cry, but he
said he'd beat me to death if I did. So you take the fob and
I'll take the fountain pen. And anytime you want to play
some more, we'll play some more, especially if you introduce
me to the horse cop who gives you candy . . ."

She had given me a few clues to her favors, but I left
them there with my nine years. Right then I was more interested in making other kinds of discoveries—of the city
and its overwhelming secrets. I wanted to be free of school,
of the newspaper stand, of fights and aimless companions—
and just walk about the city. All that I needed was a few
cents and some food for strength to roam the endless magic
of my city. People were everywhere, walking along with the
many horses and the few cars. I joined the horses along the
gutters. I hitched rides. I walked through all the parks.
Central Park was too simple, hardly wild enough. But I

liked the golden statue of General Sherman for the nice horse that he sat on. The rich were riding horses in Central Park, and I had moments of envy. In any event, I preferred Van Cortlandt Park at the end of the subway, the vast fields wandering off into hills and woods. On Saturdays men ran cross-country races there. I watched with more envy as they followed in line, one trying to beat the other. I decided that I must do that one day. I would be a marathon runner: strong, tall, wiry, agile, with all the qualities of the athlete-hero. Unfortunately, I was short and stocky, though strong and very fast.

I would leave in the morning and skip school, with an ideal program for the day sketched in my head. For lunch — I would tell my mother as I left the newsstand — I was to visit a friend. I kept that up for several weeks by going to the museums. Art was not important — and I spent little time looking at it — but the Museum of Natural History was real meat for me, worth all of my sleeping days at school, even to the intoxicating Miss Gola. On other days, when I managed to have a few more cents, I would ferry over to Staten Island, walk about its then-primitive places. I knew all the bridges of the city as they laced the rivers. Often I would piss into them — in some sort of vain contempt for all the surrounding filth and the prison that I was escaping . . .

After a month of such glory, letters came from school addressed to my father. I tore them up, defying the school authorities. I was learning more than they could teach me. I could tell the difference between a garbage can, which I thought of school as, and the enormous beauty of the self-lectures I gave myself as I walked through the city's encyclopedic streets and buildings, its parks gracefully taking me from slum interiors. If this was hookey, I was at least getting the most from my own non-scholarly ways.

When I Was
Last on Cherry Street

§

My exercises in free motion and enchantment ended abruptly late one afternoon. I was, as usual, but with a companion this time, playing hookey, walking around the wine stalls under the Brooklyn Bridge. Big barrels were being moved. Bums who begged for wine were allowed to move a few barrels, putting them on trucks with the help of pulleys and chains, and getting a handout of wine in exchange. They drank it and started dancing. They looked to us like earth-bound eagles now, moving their arms about, flaying away, heading for Fulton Fish Market—and fish.

It was after three and we started for home. At Market Street we went into a candy store for a cent's worth of mixed drops. As I paid the old lady, she looked closely from me to my companion and suddenly screamed, "You stole from me! You took all the cash from the box yesterday!"

We fled. She looked terrifying, a hag with the word "police" screaming out of her mouth. I was still frightened when I reached Cherry Street, and home. I lied about where I had been, of course, pretended to go over some homework, and was shortly back in the streets, playing a crooked game of cards for marbles. A few minutes later a huge hand, like a great iron clamp, was pulling me up. A detective stood above me, saying that the boy I had been with was accusing me of stealing.

The boy was among us now, and I went for him, but the iron clamp went for me; with my face slapped a few times, I quieted down. The neighbors gathered. My mother was called and soon all of the street was on its way to the police station. I was accused, booked, questioned, and two hours later told that I was innocent, that my ex-companion was guilty, but that I, being wayward, was on probation for three years. I was to report every Wednesday afternoon to a special school with my weekly school record in hand.

I felt the pain of the lost — my glorious freedom had ended; my school-street-prison looked all the more narrow and harrowing. The siren-figureheads of ships in the harbor were more beckoning than ever.

§

When the United States finally entered the war, the Cherry Street boys became the heroes of the scrap iron pile. We collected everything now for patriotic purposes, our petty stealing going for God and for country. Silver foil could be used for this and that; the shells of nuts, we were told, were useful in gas masks. We collected iron, zinc, lead, steel, paper, and twine; the junk that had gone under my bed now went to the nation. And every week the whole of it would be deposited at the police station, a move that made the police look more human than they had when they were themselves taking bananas, apples, and candy from the poor stand-keepers. (I was forever expecting an Irish cop to come to my mother's newspaper stand to take a Jewish paper; one finally did, but he soon put it back, shaking his head at the odd language.) Now, however, with so much patriotism evenly distributed, the cops were our friends; for no matter what we took to the sacred junk heap, it was considered noble at its worst. When we began to look for spies, we reached the

24

zenith of our determination to protect Cherry Street from the possibilities of a Hun invasion.

We found our first spy very quickly; an old German who lived at 364 Cherry Street in a filthy, bundle-laden back house flat. He ate rats, we began saying. We did see rats running around and never a sign of food in his hands when he came by. He never bought a thing at the grocery store and never went into the cellar saloons along with the other men. He acted like a recluse, which was spy enough for us. And since there was no quarantine against our terror, every long mustache that curled up was an enemy to its last hair. The old recluse was monstrously guilty of such a mustache; so we acted.

First we paraded in front of his flat, carrying posters of rats, Germans bayoneting Belgian babies, Germans raping women, Germans dropping huge bombs on children, all in keeping with the historical notes of the times. Then we smashed his door down and moved in to accuse him, cowering amid his junk, of starting the war. When the police came, they won the war for us. The poor old man was taken away. He was accused of rape, not of spying. It was a matter of a little girl, we learned. Among his papers we did find a dishonorable discharge from the Imperial German Army dated twenty years earlier, as well as a Prussian helmet, which I kept. Each spy-hunter also got a nickel from the police sergeant, and each spent his reward at the movies.

There were other ways in which our ennobling war efforts counted. We sold War Saving Stamps. We wore camphor bags around our necks to ward off influenza and measles, especially German measles. And we marched and marched again. The parades were enormous. We shouted and cheered and celebrated for everything. In the parades were horses, horse manure, police bands, patriotic societies, clubs, unions, politicians, hacks, swindlers, pickpockets, bums, whores, nurses, soldiers, sailors, airmen, and us. We bowed to kings of great nations and presidents of small countries. We saw Clemenceau, Lloyd George, Woodrow Wilson, Black Jack Pershing, the aviator Rickenbacker, and several Roosevelts.

Armistice Day, however, was something even sweeter to us—the non-fighters. We raided a candy factory on the corner. Up the elevator we went to the fifth floor. After picking the lock, we ransacked the place, and carted out all we could carry (they were red, white, and blue candies made in the form of little fish). Piled high with candy boxes, we made our way up to Times Square to join the hawkers selling flags, buttons, pictures of all the great men, and we sold our fish candy. Really, we almost gave it away (since we'd stolen it anyhow) especially to the pretty girls. Actually, that candy theft was my last *job;* for as we were leaving the candy factory, I had a terrible scare. There, just as I was closing the door, I saw a bearded old man. He looked more like Moses or one of the prophets—and he was prophesying me no good at all. His index finger was pointed at me and he was intoning a mystical lecture on my larceny. I was so frightened and impressed that I almost never stole again. Whether or not it had been essentially a religious experience, Armistice Day, after that, had a private moral meaning for me.

Armistice Day did not really bring peace all over: there were smaller wars and revolutions. The Russian Revolution of course, occupied most of my parents' concern. Like most workers on the East Side, my father voted for the socialists, but he was confused when the word *Bolshevik* started to be heard. He had listened to Trotsky once during the few months that Trotsky lived on Vyse Avenue up in the Bronx, and my father said that Trotsky talked very well but that his programs were not easy to understand. My mother merely

said that we were all now good Americans — and to understand *that*. There was a good living to be made if one only
had ambition. Since Father no longer had any, ambition must
be up to the children. She would see to it.

When the "boys" started coming back from "Over
There," those who had syphilis and clap along with their
medals were just as proud of one as of the other achievement.
They were not only victorious soldiers — they were men
now. They brought back German guns and helmets, along
with perfume and French postcards. The postcards became
the main attraction for us. It started with a girl named Rose,
aged thirteen, whose brother had come back with dozens of
such cards, each one dirtier than the next. Rose would bring
them to the stoop when our parents were not about and show
them to us one at a time — with the back of the postcard
toward her, as modesty presumably forbade her having a
look.

But look we did, and admire and examine minutely for
detail: it was a complete visual sex experience for me at the
age of eleven. A plump girl named Rachel, a few years older,
saw the postcards one day and took it upon herself thereafter
to portray some of the more innocent aspects of the cards.
She would go to the top of the stoop and lift up her dress to
show herself front and back. Then she would run like mad
for her flat, where her mother, who was thought to be a
whore, was either away or occupied at whoring. Whoever
caught Rachel as she ran had her as best he knew how — for
that was the game she had thought up.

But her game ended disastrously, long before she might
have joined her mother's profession. She gave herself in
order to be popular . . . and she gave herself one night to
thirty men in a gang shag. We heard about it when she died
of it. We were horrified that men could participate in such a
thing — and that its victim had been Rachel.

27

For Rachel had been many things to us, all dealing with our sexual emergence. She made the French pornography come alive in her acting and mimicry. She played upon our hopeless age with an astonishing amount of dramatic bounce and verve. She would scribble out the words to all the dirty songs she knew and pass them out to us like calling cards. She wrote descriptions of girls who were ruined, of girls with red garters above their knees, of girls disporting, girls cavorting, girls making the boy in us become the man in us. It was always there, like sin; and we sauntered, half in shock, half in concept of pleasure, through Rachel's unholy domains, feeling her bottom, her emerging breasts, and her reckless trinity — so that her death robbed us of a great female companion and tutor.

§

After Rachel's death we became Boy Scouts, in an insecure search for some kind of purification. We thought we would find it by sleeping on rocks, blankets spread, pup tents up, fires blazing, on the Palisades; and in listening to the birds, seeing squirrels, finding trails, picking flowers, climbing trees, swimming in the streams; and in the *Long Long Trail* singing that wound on way into the night. By morning we were wearier, hungrier, and more tired; each of us with a cold, our noses running, our eyes rheumy, our hands burned from poking about the fires for our meals. Whatever we prepared fell into the flames: meat, bread, flapjacks, potatoes, cereal. Our scouting was a mess and for a good reason: we were not properly controlled. Oh, we had a Scoutmaster. A man with a thin mustache, he took our dues — and the troop had over fifty members — but he kept the money. And there was always the girl with him on those overnight hikes, hiking in his tent for the night. But we passed all the tests in time, going up to Eagle Scout as we became expert in nature and

28

animal studies, first aid, construction—and the rest of the pure things that we were after so anxiously. We also eventually learned enough about economics to know that we were being robbed. When we complained to the officials of the Educational Alliance on East Broadway, where the troop met, out went the master, his girls, and our desires for any more outdoor manliness.

My mother's right arm amputated, my father's leg frozen —and now death hit us. My sister Esther, while crossing Lafayette Street, was hit by a truck of the Hearn's Company, for whom she worked as a salesgirl. Islanded in the middle of the street, panicked by the sudden rush of trucks, she was ground down when she tried to dash across. She lived for a week . . . and when I came home from school one afternoon, a boy in front of my house was saying, "Your sister's dead, she's inside dead."

I began to cry and tremble. The boy cried along with me. Her body was lying in the front room. She looked paler, smaller, stiller. My parents and our relatives were grouped about her. She seemed to be alive, a smile on her face, her hair neatly combed, her hands together; and I expected her to awake for supper later. In my dread of death, I could not imagine anything else. It was the *long sleep* in my frontier books about the Indian wars. Esther's body was gone, but the spirit was in the room and would be around forever, I had learned from the rabbis. The good remained and went to heaven after the Messiah came—and so Esther would be there, I was assured by the professional mourners—the men in stockinged feet, all of them glassy-eyed, and smelling of alcohol. They cried easily at so much per tear drop. They made loud prayers, drank all the liquor, and promised me much, especially a long life. Everything became mixed up in death; hallucination became reality. Death meant red lips and a wonderful pallor, then my mother shrieking. I was

29

thinking, then, that I could no longer become a soldier—for soldiers bled to death. My sister, too, had bled to death, and my mother was screaming, wailing, crying to God for mercy and understanding, to put life back into Esther's body: "She was so young, so beautiful, so pure. Life had just begun. It is not fair, God, to take the young. They have not sinned. They have hurt no one. I have kept her pure. Is this the *Goldena Medina?*"

Her cries finally forced my father to join her, and his softer tears and his melancholy voice joined the intimate terror. I went into the kitchen where the whiskey was. An old man, one of the professionals, was filling up a glass. He gave me one. I sat on a stool and cried with difficulty. The whiskey tumbled out of my hands and made a pool around my feet.

There was no doubt about it, I assured myself; Esther would return by tomorrow morning just as the birds began to chirp, when the sun came up and everything in the world was alive again. But the funeral came the next day in the rain. Around the freshly dug pit the shrieking began again. The ground was thrown back and a rabbi was cutting a corner of my father's vest to remind him of his daughter's death; and then I knew that the birds chirping in the cemetery were angels of death, that all the bright flowers and the green things were just bright flowers and green things alive unto themselves, and that Esther could not see them nor smell them any more. She was really dead . . . and I was stunned into insensibility.

§

I got a small reward—of sorts—from her death. I was turning pale, not eating, not caring; and when the summer came I was sent for a few weeks to my Uncle Kalman's farm-cum-boardinghouse at Accord, New York. Uncle Kalman was a remarkable man. He made all things grow. All the green things of the earth somehow came from his hands. The milk came from his hands—and his four cows. If he cut down a tree, it became part of something else. He was making little shacks for his boarders that summer and a great huge icebox. I became his helper immediately. I milked cows and got kicked. I sawed wood and got cut. I hammered nails and got banged. I got butted by his goat, and his horse swished its tail into my eyes endlessly. When I tried to ride bareback (there was nothing like a saddle for this work horse), I got thrown into a pile of manure. I emerged with pain from every attempt to return to the soil. My father had grown up on the land, but my land, its flag and its heart, was only on Cherry Street, where nothing but tenements grew in black and gray colors.

In Accord, in the green singing world of the country, Uncle Kalman labored in a vineyard of his own making. He had a hundred acres, most of it under cultivation. He hated the city, the crowds, the tenements and the shrill sounds, though he came down on the holidays to see us. Then we got hard white cheeses with black pepper sprinkled in their midst, as well as eggs, butter, and tomatoes.

And so we ate the fruit and the cheeses from Uncle Kalman's mighty labors. Under five feet in height, he was built like an ox—and worked like one.

When I was there he was almost seventy and had outlived three wives, all buried decently. His fourth, whom he forced to have her hair shorn, doted on him with her forty-five young years. She died when Uncle Kalman reached eighty, at which time he thought of taking a fifth wife, but apparently decided that might be overdoing it a bit. At ninety-eight, he was mourning the death of a cow when his own heart stopped beating.

§

I left the Boy Scouts to go in for less athletic idealism. A group of us formed a club called *The Harding Literary & Social Club,* and soon we had a letter from President-elect Harding thanking us for using his name to perpetuate his rank and station. The club, however, achieved even less than the president, though our scandals were fewer. But I met four or five boys my age who had a distinct influence on me for the good. They read the good books and helped me be more selective in my own reading. Soon I was deep in Thoreau, Emerson, Wilde, Pushkin and Byron. Poetry was always just a bit ahead as a favorite. (Later, after the Teapot Dome Scandal, when I was at sea, Leon, the most intellectual of the group, wrote me that he had written President Harding and broken off diplomatic relations with him. There was no reply, unfortunately, wrote Leon. "The President decided to die rather than answer me . . .")

Leon at twelve wore eyeglasses, and this alone made him superior. He was a Canadian, and his speech, we thought, was grand. He was also really brilliant, we agreed. He knew long difficult words we had never heard before. His little lectures got us involved, beginning with Nietzsche. We listened to the verbal mystification about the *Uber Mensch* with awe, agreeing that we could use some of that. I got everything wrong, with ease. Philosophy was difficult even for Lou, the one who ran the fastest, had the nimblest muscles, and was as scholarly as he was athletic. I was third in intellectual standing. I was the poetic listener, given to long silences, terribly in awe of both Leon's and Lou's abilities to talk about Socrates and the cup of hemlock that he was forced to drink—and I cried at his death scene. It was easier to cry when tragedy hit men of the mind rather than the heart, we decided. For they were the scholars, the teachers, the dreamers, and they had made the books; without them, what was there? Books of all sorts were ours in random reading—much of it pursued so that we could show off and talk with pride about something one or the other of us had not read.

We showed off in other ways, too, and began to write our own stories and articles. Leon, later to become a literary critic, wrote an essay on the need for using the universal language, Esperanto. It hit us with all the force of our nationalistic confusion. Why a babble of tongues, especially on Cherry Street, when Esperanto solved the problem of communication? We gave Leon the highest mark, bought him a handball for a prize, then beat him every time he played the game with us.

My own little literary creation, a poem about King Arthur, I worked out with Morton, with whom I had stayed during my run-away-on-a-bicycle attempt. Morton was a sad boy who never smiled, and who worked when he should have been playing. His father had a factory that produced cigarettes for the rich—smokers who wanted their names engraved in gold on the cigarettes. They came long, short, white, black, Russian style—filtered even then. In the machines they looked like miles of spaghetti being filled with tobacco. After the names were stamped on in gold, they were cut to size, and they piled up at the end of these crazy machines, where Morton stuffed the lot into boxes.

When his father died, Morton quit school to run the factory, working all hours. It was then he became a romantic, aching to run away, talking about King Arthur's legends—for the king was not involved in keeping crazy machines going. And my poem, with Morton's puffing assistance, was a take-off on King Arthur in irregular rhymes, with a girl named Sue cast as the romantic female lead.

The writing school formed by us, which we called the *Lo-Le-Ha-Mo School* after the first two letters of our names, became so involved in production that we copied furiously from unknown books and presented each work as an original creation. We changed names, altered situations, but kept the basic story going. Eventually, we had many writing school applicants, each paying a quarter down for his initiation dues. One joiner was a peculiar character named Charis, much older, who looked like Smulick in some ways. He talked very intellectually about communism, socialism, Marxism, anarchism, and said that he was for all of those things, though he preferred Kropotkin. Kropotkin, it seemed, had just died, and Charis was his chief mourner on the block. Charis, who never worked, and he was twenty by then, talked about the decentralization of industry; about having the brain worker join the agricultural and the factory worker in a sort of nineteenth-century togetherness. It all sounded vaguely sinister.

When we took in our last member, an illiterate Negro named Charlie, we were, we assumed, practicing intellectual anarchism. But Charlie was old, Charlie was happy, and Charlie told us all the Biblical stories in a very colorful way. Charlie said that Noah could fish and catch a mountain at the end of his line; that King David liked jazz and that he had played a Biblical saxophone; that Jonah was just an old-fashioned liar. Charlie was a talking member — the best — but when he joined up, we reached the end of our extensive membership. Charlie died one day from overeating watermelon, and we went to a very sad happy funeral made by a relative of his. For we loved him more than our families as the always happy happy man.

There was a strange murder committed that summer that shocked us into a new kind of reality. The murderer was Frank, a student, aged sixteen. Pimply, cross-eyed, friendless — we would have none of him in our ball games, our writing school, our joke sessions, in any of our playing or our serious times. He was a boy in exile within our midst, given

34

to morbid silences, alone with his fancies and desperations; for we hardly realized our cruelty at all.

One night he murdered his father and mother, bludgeoning and stabbing both in the back yard flat behind our flat — and he killed himself with the big knife, which the police found still in his hands. We blamed ourselves for the triple murder, for not talking to him or taking him in. To Leon, it was a classical Greek tragedy brought into our midst, to be remembered for whatever it could mean to us at twelve.

That summer, too, the horse cop of my candy days shot one of the boys; Tommy, the toughest of the street fighters among the Irish, bled to death on the corner of Cherry and Montgomery. He held up a grocery, had run when the horse cop had ordered him to stop, had kept on running until the third bullet hit him in the middle of the back, and he fell calling out, "Mother! Mother! Mother!" his blood running into the gutters and into the manure pile that made his pillow. When the ambulance finally came from Gouverneur Hospital, Tommy was very dead — and this ended the frightening summer of death for all of us.

I ran my first race that summer in order to get into another stride of meaning. I merely joined a mob in shorts one Sunday in Van Cortlandt Park, jogging along cross-country style, following as best I knew how, taking the lead for a few hundred yards in a show of bravado, then slipping back, way back, so far back that I seemed to be standing still as we went over and away into the small green hills of the park . . . and I learned, when the race was over, with no one giving me water or a lemon or an orange, which all the others got, how grueling indeed running was. I finished last. I was tired and lame, but I was happy that afternoon. To rid myself of pain, I lay in a creek for an hour. Then someone gave me some liniment to rub away my aches, and at least I smelled like an athlete.

When I was not the awkward sprinter, I was still excitedly looking out to sea. Often I would drop in on Captain Robert Huntington at the Seaman's Church Institute — to ask questions about navigation, and I would stay for a lecture on dead-reckoning and piloting. Outside was South Street, the ships, the harbor, the Statue of Liberty . . . and I saw myself, full of liberty one day, sailing past it. In preparation, I'd hidden a knapsack of clothing under a couch at home.

§

There were real athletes nearby, strong boys with fists who could box and whom we envied for their agile movements and their lean, trim strength and stances. They shadow-boxed for our clumsy company; and we, in turn, played handball with them against the walls of P.S. 147 as they waded successfully through the amateurs as lightweights. My favorite, who almost made it all the way to the championship as a professional, was Sid Terris, whom I could beat at handball. He was taller, thinner, older, and tougher than handsome Ruby Goldstein, who almost made it, too. They were our local heroes, although I never saw one of them in the professional ring. It was enough that they accepted our worship, were Jews, that they talked to us, and never bullied us; and whenever they won a fight, it was a holiday around a dirty poolroom on Monroe Street. There we gathered, en masse, to listen to the sounds of victory as the boxers paraded skillful shots on the pool tables and increased our normal state of envy to heroic proportions. And not only did we worship them — but the girls, especially one beautiful one called Stella, made it obvious that great athletes made great lovers. And Stella established a liaison with an as yet unknown boxer, who soon got her greatly pregnant for everybody's discernment.

36

But the times were pregnant with more than bastards. Prohibition made new professions. The terms *gangster* and *bootlegger* had become socially current. They were the Irish and the Italians, we were told by our parents – not the good Jews. It was always someone else, not us and ours, who engaged in these illegal adventures. Late at night, trucks parked along Water Street. Hurrying men were seen lifting cases of Canadian whiskey and rushing into the warehouses lining the street. Occasionally a fire would wreck the operation – enormous conflagrations that consumed the whiskey – or guns would end a whiskey-toting gentleman. Later the detectives would question us; and we, with unusual innocence, never knew anything at all.

§

My mother was a terribly holy woman, her religious fears and lamentations were constant and unending. My father was a bit less so; occasionally, when he bought me a suit on the Sabbath I was warned not to tell my mother that money had passed hands and a transaction had taken place on Saturday. It was sinful, of course, though not to me. What was wrong about getting another blue suit? It was always blue serge, with knickers, black stockings, and black shoes to complete the picture of my half-blond, blue-eyed, ruddy self.

Buying the blue suit was a cultural bargaining process on Canal Street off the Bowery, as my father studied prices and fabric and engaged in Eastern European rhetoric and fancies. The storekeeper, alert to my father's past, recreated visions of the Ukraine as if it was right off the Bowery, making all the right overtures. It began with a round of illegal schnapps and a general statement of trading values. My father drank the schnapps, wished the owner much prosperity and health, and listened for a price. It al-

37

ways came eventually. The suit was thirty dollars, though it was worth, said the owner, at least eighty.

"Feel the material—real wool from Scotland. You don't know where Scotland is? Well, then, from England. You don't know where England is—what kind of a Jew are you? That's where Shylock wrote Shakespeare. You don't know who is Shakespeare—or Shylock? All right, then, twenty-eight dollars for the English, Shakespeare, Shylock Scottish woolen suit. What did you say—are you *masugah?* Four dollars for the suit? A real crazy yiddle. Here, have another schnapps—and let your Bar Mitzvah boy have one. Prohibition or no prohibition, schnapps is like tea, bread, herring —and a woman . . . so let's make the price, and this is the last schnapps, too. Twenty dollar straight. Okay, okay, eight dollars and go, go, go . . . and I wish your boy *mazel.* He will need it in this crazy world, what with Bolsheviks like you all over Canal Street! Soon we'll all go to hell!"

My mother, loud with prayers, and sustained by my father in lower tones, was convinced that I, certainly, was going to hell. My errant *goyishe* ways were hardly becoming to a boy about to become a 13-year-old man, via Bar Mitzvah. I was a *nahr,* said my father. I could not learn the ritualistic verbal tokens for my coming manhood. I felt anything but religious. I hated the old rabbi who came daily for six months to teach me enough Hebrew so that I would not sound like a fool when that Saturday morning came, and I, standing before the Ark, took out the Torah. The rabbi had bad breath, decayed teeth, old clothes, and his beard was scraggly —not trimmed like my father's neat gray goatee. The old man belched at the beginning, middle, and end of every passage; and I yawned back. Most of the time I was thinking of a marathon race which I was to enter a few days after my Bar Mitzvah, and wondering whether I was training enough by running twenty times around Corlears Hook Park daily, a bare five miles.

38

I had been taught a speech by the old rabbi: about two hundred words of gracious promises to God, my mother, father, and Judaism. With this finally memorized, there I was, one Saturday morning, beaming with a cherub's joys, brightness engraving the tumbling air within the synagogue on Montgomery Street. It was a holiday for me and my words, bringing me to a state of grace . . . and there were cherubs all over the synagogue to help me through the unfathomable stages to godliness. With every word there was an echo from the worshipers — their strange lilting voices, hushed and penitential, inflected mystical sadness, pain and fear . . . and their answers were healing tokens for my spiritual absences . . .

§

A week later, I was running the marathon. I stayed with the adult leaders through streets and alleys, over dirt roads and paved roads and hills — but not for too long. I made it for five miles; but then the boy in me became only too evident as I slogged along, wandering off the course, crashing into passing runners, and getting in the way of pedestrians as I was outdistanced by all. I stopped at water hydrants; and I was yelled at by spectators and cops, by officials and small boys. About five hours after the start, I arrived . . . and there was no one to greet me and my terrible pains. My thighs and calves were totally muscle-bound. My chest ached with deadly persistence. I had paused at least a dozen times. I had walked when I could no longer run. I had jogged and half-dozed, and finally, totally dazed, I had arrived. I managed to clean up and get home way past dinner time, looking as if I had gone through a cyclone machine. I smelled of sweat, rubbing alcohol, and cloves — unguents used by runners — and merely to move, step by step, was extraordinarily painful. But I was home, if hardly the hero of the marathon.

39

We now lived on the second floor at 176 Monroe Street. The door to our flat had all sorts of locks, six of them, to make it difficult for thieves; and it was a trying operation to get through to the hot, airless trap that was made up of the five tight boxes of the flat. As I walked in, crippled by the running, I knew suddenly that I was going to lose this home forever.

I went over and stood near the towel rack washing, to be ready for the first course of my dinner, the summery soup called *chaaf* and *smetana*. Immediately, there was violent language from my father. I was crippled, he said. I was a terrible example of a Jew, he said. I was a *goy*, he said. My two brothers, my mother, and my sister went along with him —to run something as stupid as a marathon! Why didn't I study at school? What about that after-school job with the printer, Zamkin, on East Broadway? I replied that I worked enough from three to seven in the morning at Mother's newspaper stand; that falling asleep at school, unable to learn, was normal under such conditions . . . but when I ran, I was living and running with extreme joy.

My mother suddenly called out comically, to halt the father-son drama boiling up, *"Ah klug tzu Columbus!"* I laughed, wondering what a curse on Columbus had to do with me.

My explanations didn't help my father's temper. He picked up a heavy soup plate and spun it ten feet through the air at me. It landed on the left side of my head. There was blood all over my face. My mother cried and so did my sister. I did not. Enraged, I pulled madly at the wooden rolling towel rack. It came away and I hurled it at my father. It hit him on the mouth—and he was bleeding too. . . .

I ran wildly to the day couch, pulled out the knapsack that contained shirts, underthings, red running tights, and my prayer phylacteries, a grab-bag for an envisioned, hurried departure. Suddenly I could move again. With my family in pursuit, I got to the window and out onto the fire escape. I raced down to the first flight, my brothers behind me. My father took to the stairs, hoping to catch me on the street.

I dropped fifteen feet from the first floor to the street but my brothers held back. I saw my father coming around the corner, still bleeding from his mouth, as I ran toward South Street. I had committed an evil thing by hitting him —and now I was dooming his affections, his eager paternalism, his melting anger. I was en route to a self-exile that would last for almost seven years before I saw him again.

Now I was running down South Street, hugging my knapsack, blood and tears streaming, with a cop asking me if I had run away. No, of course not. I began to walk then. I *was* running to something—myself. When I reached the Seaman's Church Institute, I asked for Captain Robert Huntington. I was ready to become a captain, or at least an ordinary seaman. I slept on his leather couch. I could become a cadet on a Grace Line ship in the late fall, the Captain told me. But how was I to live now? I could work on Lake Ontario as an ordinary seaman for the summer and return in October.

I was on my way the next morning, riding trucks to the Catskills. I slept in a barn that night, having dined on bread and water all day. I vomited on the hay and moved my portable bed to another part of the barn. I vomited again. Disgusted, I decided to swim. My red running trunks were with my few shirts and my phylacteries. I placed the fearsome phylacteries deep into the hay, made a quick prayer as I disenfranchised myself, spiritually, of my Bar Mitzvah —and ran out to disport in a nearby stream.

I was in the heart of New York's Jewish vacation playland, the borscht belt, ready for another baptism—a job. Before noon I was working for a Mr. A. in his country store. He

41

sold papers, picture postcards with red cows, Feen O Mint and Ex Lax to the adventurous clerks and the pliable stenographers who ate themselves, pound by pound, into two weeks of extraordinary gluttony — and came in occasionally for condoms to activate another reality. The store was a hangout for them between their fantastic meals or their sessions in the deep woods while falling in "love" as they went shopping for the give-all to their end-all search — marriage.

Near the catch-all country store, Mr. A. had his icehouse. At five in the morning I was lugging two hundred pounds of sawdust-covered ice down to the store. On hot nights, the more reckless of the suitors would bribe me with a dollar for the key to the icehouse. How they made love on the sawdust, ice, and tarpaulins mystified me. On cooler nights, they would "buy" the key to my room over the barn. And since my pay was only twenty dollars a month, I did not feel dishonorable in accepting extras. I worked eighteen hours a day — sweeping the huge store, doing hundreds of essential chores, and tending the post office that was attached to the store. I sold country medicines, what-nots, and myself, especially to Mrs. A., an amazon among amazons. It was attempted seduction on sight, and there was a lot of her to look at.

I was asked to draw her bath as she walked about in her thin chemise, enormous of breasts and buttocks. Then she plunged into the large tub. Later I would clean up the apartment over the store, with Mrs. A in the nude, flouncing about with elephantine grandeur.

Her husband was six inches shorter than she, very thin and very nervous. In their lovemaking, she giggled and he strained . . . and she was immense to see, visible from my perch in the barn. If I was an amateur voyeur, age thirteen,

42

they were professional exhibitionists, at least. Often, in the narrow room of the post office, she would sidle up to me and squeeze by with a long pause, just enough, presumably, to excite me. I had seen her naked in private, as well as in "public," but I was too morally afraid to reach out and touch her. Besides, I was busy cleaning spittoons, calcimining stones on the driveway, washing the side of the house, cleaning three outhouses and filling in the freshly-bored holes in the backboards made by overly excited young men. It was a small Balzacian world, only too droll from icehouse to outhouse.

Hardly enriched, I left Mr. A's exploitation and Mrs. A's vast fruition. My second job, still in New York en route to becoming an ordinary seaman, was that of a shill; and I barked for several weeks at the Walton County Fair, advertising eye-lifting and soft-talking Kewpie dolls as prizes. I ran a wheel, fixed it when we needed a winner to hold the tar-soap and manure-smelling farmers before our stake of hallowed earth, and I re-fixed it when we could afford lots of swearing losers. We took their dollars and their dimes. We hollered and harangued in the midway adjacent to the shimmering belly dancers and other exotic creatures of the midnight march to agricultural erotics . . . and then I met Annette.

She was crippled slightly, and I fell in love with her out of pity. She was twelve, blonde, blue-eyed, and walked with a limp. But her smile was more fascinating to me than the weaving belly dancers in the next stall. She made me feel pure and I thought only lyrical thoughts of stainless emotion. I gave Annette a Kewpie doll, bought her ice cream, and presented her with my copy of Oscar Wilde's *Picture of Dorian Gray,* my "purest" book. For weeks after I left the fair, we wrote longing, loving letters. We lamented life's cruelty that

43

had parted us—that I was off to be a sailor. We had looked into each other's eyes . . . and oh, the pity of it!

§

At last I was indeed a sailor. On a coal barge called *Chantal of Montreal*. It ran, off schedule, its two sails flapping ignominiously, from Oswego on the American side of Lake Ontario, to the Canadian ports of Napanee, Belleville, and Trenton. It hardly resembled the big three-masted schooners still anchoring off South Street; but there I was, suddenly awash, hired on the moment as I climbed up a broken ladder connecting the barge to the rickety dock.

The other members of the crew were four tough French Canadians, two of them brothers. As the youngest and the meekest and the most uncertain, I was tried at everything. One day I was a small cook with a large can opener; a second day I steered as we were hauled by a huge tug to Napanee; a third day I was up in the towering rigging, mending an unmendable sail. I had long needles, tallow and a sailor's palm (a protective half-glove), and I made unusual stitches in my airy tailoring shop. When Captain Yves, a laughing man who was always several jokes ahead of me, saw my stitching later, he suggested that I make him a suit: "If I don't steal one in Oswego. You know, that's how we get our clothes . . ." And that's exactly how they did: going through back yards where clothes were being aired.

A week later, in Oswego, I went along on an evening raid for suits. (The Canadians never raided on the Canadian side, out of patriotism.) A few streets off the docks, I looked on as Captain Yves and his brother, 18-year-old Jean, went from yard to yard taking enormous delight in their ghostly larceny. They marched away looking like second-hand stores in flight; suits, coats and work clothes draped with scarecrow effect over their shoulders. They sang boldly as they

44

went and I remember especially the sad ballad of an Irishman who killed his sweetheart:

> I am an Irishman by birth,
>   my name is Michael Lee,
> I fell in love with a pretty girl
>   in the town of Napanee;
> I fell in love with a pretty girl,
>   Maggy Howee was her name,
> And then I cruelly murdered her
>   and I owe it to my shame . . .

I went along on other raids, too, but for the folk singing, not the stealing.

We in turn were fair game for other daring people. One afternoon, a young woman came by to sell us subscriptions to magazines. Oddly, when one of us agreed to sign up, she insisted that the transaction take place down in the foc'sle. She came back laughing, holding two dollars, with Jean soon saying, "If it's not the clap we'll be reading soon, we'll all be scholars. Don't you want to be a scholar, Harry? She's better than Mary. Come on, Jewboy!" Mary was the local whore.

Occasionally, I was the *Jewboy bastard* to Jean. We wrestled together often for sport, and I'd pin him back easily, having learned how to use muscles to make the difference between life and death on racist Cherry Street. But now the *Chantal of Montreal* was my substitute home, quartering me in anger and loneliness. Tears made my anger nobler, and my lost home became some fixed image of grace, to which I could never return. I had a home with four sailors on a barge lost in November's ice and rain; and we sat in the galley, drinking coffee and tea, waiting for an order to load more coal for Napanee. It was too late in the year to get on the Grace Line as a cadet. When December came, the snow

45

and ice locked us in at Oswego alongside an old wharf, near a park, where in the warmer weather the sailors had taken the whore Mary for walks to the bushes. Now, in icy barren white, we were wintering; and when the sailors talked and the talk drifted to religion, I became the inevitable Jew bastard in their endless conceits about a Christianity they never ever practiced. I had, without doubt, killed Christ at least . . .

Finally one day there came an order to load coal. The ice-breaker had come through, and there was an open channel to Napanee.

"Hey, Jew bastard!" went provocative Jean, "Let's get busy loading the goddamn coal. Hey, Jew bastard!"

Normally, I ignored Jean's racial sallies. I would think of Annette in Walton, my heart covered with love, insulating myself against the sixty racist dollars that was my suffering, monthly pay. But suddenly I was a fist again, smashing away at Jean for calling me a Jew bastard, and he went down. Then Captain Yves and the other two sailors were at me, kicking, punching, grappling . . . and very soon I was thrown ashore, knapsack and all, with the wages due me fluttering in single dollars to the dock. I picked them up without bothering to count and walked away with what I hoped was dignity in my movement. Within six months I had lost two homes; I had been accused by my orthodox father of being a *goy;* but I was a Jew bastard to these sailors. It was all somewhat perplexing.

A Hothouse of Wanderers

§

Later that winter, I sailed on the *James Magee,* a 10,000-ton oil tanker to the Gulf of Mexico. I was an ordinary seaman, age eighteen, I had said, adding five small years to a lot of fine lies. I was husky, short, and stocky. When not too well examined, I passed for a man. The deception was worth $57.50 a month.

The tanker was a hothouse of wanderers many years older, and I listened in awe to all sorts of sailors: to an Englishman who said he was of royalty, who had lots of fine suits and who talked a great deal of heady nonsense to prove that he could, if necessary, make a living as a sailor. On the next trip he was arrested for smuggling dope. There was a dark Puerto Rican in the gang, a wiper. He had syphilis and was a mass of boils and pimples. He sneered at me for my nautical naivete—what I'd picked up on board the Oswego barge turned out to be pretty limited. I was the butt of all the sailors as I looked for the mail buoys on the blue-green Gulf of Mexico as we were approaching Tampico. There would be letters waiting for us on them, I was told. I even looked for sky hooks to attach a heaving line to, and the roaring laughter of Spik, the Puerto Rican, and Prince Hal, the regal Englishman, made me feel like the goat I was.

My watches were from noon to four and from midnight to four. In the darkness of my midnight watch, I was up in the crow's nest, on the lookout for floating debris that might damage the tanker; for whales suddenly coming up to spout; for other ships sailing too close; and I would sound bells every half hour, mostly to show that I was awake and not lost in fantasies about the sea. I loved most the playful, arching, diving porpoises as they sprang from the fore-foam of the tanker. They were always ahead in the sea, looking back, sometimes tempting me to jump in and join them so that I would get away from the endless talk of sex that Spik and Prince Hal intentionally aimed at me.

They had been, they said, with thousands of whores all over the world; with girls from along the canals in Amsterdam to St. Pauli's in Hamburg; from Bombay's Trimbak Parsham to Colpetty, a suburb of Colombo. It was a Baedeker for whoring; and Spik would, with weird pride brag that he'd had the clap fifty times. They were whorestruck, sex-strained sailors who jibed at me for my innocence.

On my noon watch, I took the wheel for two hours though it was illegal for an ordinary seaman to take a turn at the wheel. It was the quartermasters and the able bodied seamen who were supposed to steer. Later I was *soojy-moojying,* washing down the white-painted bulkheads, chipping and painting the ballast-laden tanker, which rode just a few feet above the water. I would be perched over the side in a bos'n chair, staring into the sea, forgetting to paint; and the Bos'n would urge me, most kindly, to try painting while I was dreaming—that I could get some fine shades of color that way.

Then came the massive oil docks at Tampico. Pumps, derricks, tanks, oil lines, fire engines—bulking into surrealist agglutinations. What machinery! It took but a few hours to pump out the water ballast and eight hours to take on 3,000,000 gallons of oil; then we shipped back to New Jersey. But during the loading, the men unloaded their dreams—and

48

to the whores went most of the fifty members of the *James Magee's* crew.

It was a Norwegian sailor, Karl Petersen, who took me to the shanties in Tampico; and it's a little difficult to say, but it was there I experienced the ultimate gift of the whores, a tiny bid toward erotic maturity. Petersen actually had other ideas for me. We were merely shopping for trinkets; he wanted to buy a ring for his girl in Narvik, I wanted a silver pin for my sister. Besides Petersen did not spend money on dry female rot; and he said, in defense of our common morality, "Vid des vimen es lake slippen mid rootten vood. Ve goo church — safe muney . . ."

I remembered the episode with the magazine subscription girl who had visited us on the barge, *Chantal of Montreal,* and that I had not, as yet, taken out a subscription. Nor did I intend to now. Was I frightened? Was I too moral? Was it an expected disease? Was it merely some normal reaction at thirteen? Whatever it was, we were really shopping for trinkets . . . But the trinkets turned into whores, after all. Despite Petersen's sermonizing, he was a sailor. And one who turned out to know the way, across muddy streets, to the shanties — and to Juanita.

§

I am writing now more than forty years after the event. I am, not oddly, back in Tampico, having made the trip, via the deep South and the racial hot war, to get another view before America explodes accidentally inwardly and outwardly. I am playing on the beach at Tampico, remembering the past, telescoping 1921 into 1964, to bring myself into sharper focus — more than forty years older than the boy who went ashore with Petersen. There is nothing much to tear down now . . . for the disenchantments, at middle age, are too many for all of us. But it is now summer, 1964. . . .

49

Restless, I get up and plunge into the Gulf of Mexico. It does not chill. The water is almost hot as the past dives under the water with me. It unwinds, floats, stretches to the under horizon. I try to lose myself in the depths, and I dive to where the fish are. They run, rippling through my past, then tearing through it, and bits and pieces float up to the top with me. A wave hits my head and I happily go under again. The sensual sea takes me back to the whore, who smilingly spreads across the Gulf, engaging me. She is like all the women I've known. Should it have been otherwise? I reach into their marveling depths — and out of myself, I go.

What a practical whore! But then, what a small boy I was. The awkward incapacities of not knowing the beginning, the middle — and the end of it all. Had I see a woman nude before? Childish play. The erotic, inventive games. But the Mexican whore had created more than illusions. I was instructed gently, much as if I were a student horticulturalist exploring the soil before seeding it. When I got back to the ship, I was questioned without end about my first experience. The questions were filthy. I was embarrassed. Did I screw or did I fornicate? I knew all the tender words — and I had read the Bible. I said that I had *lain* with a whore. It made it more classical, less painful to my conscience. But for the week that it took the tanker to get back to New Jersey, I was tied to the foc'sle's fancies, derided for my shyness, made unequal by the older men, and given to brooding about my sexual folly.

Now, on the beach at Tampico, I see a long line of waves breaking over me. Ritual and romance, rot and fever, politics and poetry, wars coming and going — the endless threats to the man of middle age.

What had happened to the idealist who had taken from Plato and Marx — and found a way to live in this woe-laden, warring world? What had I really believed?

My own private Platonic dialogues told me that virtue lay in knowing women well. I had known them uselessly as the child observer; then as the man complete unto himself; then as the poet inducing all the frames of fancies, and lies. Had not Nietzsche said about virtue, "And which of us poets hath not adulterated his wine?" I had, too often. And he had said, "We also know too little, and are bad learners: so we are obliged to lie." Ah, my lies!

Once, as the poet, I had gone into the energetic lies of our time as a vagrant child of dialectics; not Plato's but Marx's. It was another form of whoring, using the morals of the Marxist gutter. It was not a theory of knowledge to bring in the Ideal City. And though Plato, in his time, had said that self-control brings virtue, I remembered that in the end knowledge has but one thing left of it — its moral memories. And my memory was lying with me on the beach . . .

The Gulf lashes up and I find myself, and my visions stuck, mouth to breast, in another time, another country; the water, like a woman, activating everything sensual in me. I was the occasional intellectual type, I say to myself as I come up from under a wave. I once had quite intelligent ideas about man and his many societies. I had joined some worthwhile causes, given my youth and my blood, my days and my nights. There was another maturity. The City was a place of terror and horror; and man, its best kept animal, roamed in it as if it was an African jungle, keeping himself from death by abnormal processes.

And, I remember what the practical whore had said to me — at the time vexed and provoked, eager to surrender, touching her, seeking her, seeing her, finding her like the wave that was riding over me now — and she had said, "After this, you must find love. After me, who am like your mother, there will be many. I am like your mother now . . ." She said it with the soft lilt of an accent. Then she had said, "And you will soon be fourteen, fifteen, then sixteen, then seventeen, and you'll vote one day like a good Americano. Viva Presidente Harding!" And we had saluted much, after that. I was no longer a boy some hours later.

She had also said, "And when you are older, you will be a First Mate, then a Captain of the ship." I had become a Second Mate, in time, but never a Captain. The whores had not flowered overly in my international gardens, even when I sailed. I learned about love, about the painful yet wonderful strategems of love. Love was like the Gulf now, holding me, creating all the wonders in the body; the top of mountains, alone, and the enormous pulse of the sky; the deserts, alone, and the woods and the jungles; the world of nature that made the world of man, and woman, the parts that came together.

And the Mexican whore had said, "I have this cross on my breasts to excite you, Americano. I have these black stockings on to excite the boy, Americano. You will always remember both, Americano." I remembered both.

Yet, what was her name? I had called her Juanita; or I had given her that name. I could have called her Ruth or Deborah, in some Biblical imagery. And we talked of poverty, the oil docks and the horrible shacks near the tankers; how much they resembled my own home, near South Street, where I first saw the ships that soon enough turned me into a sailor. I stroked her breasts again; and I stroked her thighs, thrusting myself, feeling the mountains become valleys, the skies become seas.

Now more than forty years later, I left the beach and wound my way back to Tampico on my motorcycle. Where would I find Juanita? If I found her, probably now seventy years old, I would rid myself of my symbolic fetishes, I assured myself. Expel the whore in the heart of a man, and you'll be free, but free of what? I would be free of nothing.

It was part of the total memory, tied to my heart like every recalled instance of pain and pleasure.

Ah, but she was not down that street! It was running with rain again. She was not down the next street. I parked the motorcycle at a garage and asked for a certain street that suddenly came back to me, an identity from the wandering sailoring years between 1921 and 1927.

"That street? It disappeared long ago," said the fat garage attendant.

"There was a girl who lived there," I said painfully.

"There were many—all bad ones."

"Her name was Juanita . . ."

"Ah, Juanita! There must have been five by that name— all whores."

I was angry. My questions had been reserved, decent, like my memory. I'd had beautiful thoughts but they had been invaded.

"Where did you come from now?" asked the attendant. "Your machine is very dirty. Do you want it cleaned?"

"I came over the mountains from Pachuca and Hua-chinango in the rain. I was here once," I said sadly.

"It always rains in August. Come back in October. May-be Juanita may come back by then?" kidded the attendant.

"Thanks, amigo, I'll walk around anyway and take some pictures."

I walked around and took some pictures. The old dock, where we had tied up, was still there but much refurbished. The tankers were there, too. I choked inwardly, feeling some acid-held sentiments wash through my stomach.

When I returned a few hours later to get my motorcycle, the attendant said, "Have a beer with me amigo? You look very hot."

We had a few beers and talked. Tampico was very rich

53

now. Mexico had grown fantastically, he assured me. "It has now, maybe, more than thirty-five million people. Almost like the United States, no?"

"Just as modern, dirty, and stupid," I wanted to say. Instead, I said, "Not quite, amigo. But you have Coca Cola now so all is right."

He laughed, got me another beer, then said, "And the price of women has gone up, too. We are very rich now. It's five dollars now. What was it then, amigo?"

"A dollar for a whole night in 1921."

"Ah, what a beautiful world. You could get married every night, amigo."

"What illusions you have about continuity," I bantered back.

"You are a smart man." The beer was going down his shirt.

I felt friendlier now, and we forgot about the whores and talked of political things.

§

On the second trip with the tanker, I went as a wiper. I wiped everything in a sanitary burst of over-heated enthusiasm—including pistons that were normally *supposed* to be dripping with oil. I shined brass fittings into mirrors, and I painted, in garish white, the huge areas that housed shafts, condensers, water tanks, pumping engines—all the steaming things that made the 140-degree engine room an eccentric hell of moving parts. It was the filthiest job on man's homemade earth. I was in an eternal sweat, dungarees soaking, eyes inflamed. One of the more exacting tasks was to clean, then blow, the tubes of the boilers. To do this, I crawled through a narrow opening with a chipping hammer and for three days I chipped away at the caked-up boiler. Later I was given a long steam hose to blow the endless tubes inside the boiler. The sludge, under hundreds of pounds of steam pressure, blew back at me; and I looked like a cosmic chimney sweep. It took very little coaxing from Petersen for me to go back to being an ordinary seaman when I signed on for a third trip on the *James Magee.*

I discovered a chest of books on board one day; a hundred volumes ranging from economic history, natural science and philosophy to serious contemporary novels. Since I had found it, the box was unquestionably mine, and I elected myself sole librarian of the tanker. There were other sailors just as bookish, too, and newly discovered subjects began replacing sex as something to talk about during interludes between sleep and work. I dug deep into American and Russian literature of the time: Trotsky's *In Defense of Terrorism;* Dos Passos' *Three Soldiers;* John Burroughs' *Walt Whitman, Poet and Person;* William James's *The Varieties of Religious Experience.*

§

My world was being enlarged, not only through books, but through a variety of freighter trips more interesting than the New Jersey-Mexico run had been. I found myself at last in Europe, the world my parents had fled during the 1890's. I had written to them irregularly, without a return address. And I sent them tokens of affection: sweaters bought at sailor shops; statues of salty old men; pottery that probably broke upon unwrapping; pepper shakers made of silver. I was still sad and contrite about my moment of violence with my father. I was trying to buy back familial love with trinkets.

Wherever we docked, I took as much leave as possible so that I could wander through the cities. In the winter, the ports gave off strange odors that I loved and have always remembered; even coal burning along the docks at Southampton, became jasmine and jacaranda to me. There was something in the English air, despite the ugly vistas at the ports, with poverty gleaming like a huge Christian medal of despair, that was like clean magic — the magic that overtakes a boy who comes in from the sea and is forever excited with newness and expectations.

And there I was, the next day in London, near Soho, walking up the stairs of a famous club to look for the sculptor Jacob Epstein, who had come from my own streets and had taught at the Educational Alliance. He had turned into an Englishman, but he was not at the famous club. Later, I ate Chinese food for the first time in the East End afraid of the bean sprouts, which looked to me like worms. For five days away from the ship, I wandered about London, found dives along the wharves near the East India docks where men smoked opium; I ate fish and chips, kippers, and Yorkshire pudding. I drank five glasses of stout and got drunk for the first time.

A trip later, I was in Germany, sailing on a freighter, the *S. S. Barstow,* up the Weser River to Bremen. There I saw the lost war, the terrifying inflation, the mark not worth the colored paper. Women were offering up their teen-age daughters to the sailors for some ship's food.

And on the next trip, when the freighter was unloading for a week in Le Havre, I took the train to Paris, to wander almost speechless, all over the beautiful city. I sat, beer in hand, one late afternoon at Le Dôme, listening to odd Americans, the expatriates of the heart and mind. Their talk was much too strange. I listened and did not understand either their French or their American speech; but I said, after the beer, that I was an American sailor and everybody laughed. I was bought a beer and asked my real age. They were talking about a man named Tristan Tzara who had created something called *Dada.* One of the talkers was a Japanese, his hair in bangs, who was called Foujita.

In 1947, when I was a correspondent in Tokyo and was arranging to bring a Foujita show to New York on my return, Foujita recalled the afternoon at Le Dôme. He had bought me a Pernod and introduced me to a model called Kiki ("of the wonderfully beautiful body and a fine voice," Hemingway once described her). In 1922, when she posed for Foujita, she was all of Montparnasse; comely, strident, Bohemian, as she sang, danced and partied — kissing everyone, talking madly, laughing like a great female clown — the mistress and model for Kisling, Soutine, Man Ray, and Foujita. She was also part owner of the Jockey Club, then the center of post-war experiments in art. In 1950, before she died, I was to see her again. She was thin and wasted and drunken. She dragged a herring on a string, from café to café, pushing the stinking herring into the faces of the diners to make them give her a few francs, trying to dance again, and ready for death . . .

Paris, when I was first there, had briefly introduced me to many provinces of art and the imagination, and I marveled at what a man could do. But I had done little with myself. At sixteen, I had no ambitions worth categorizing. I was about to become an able bodied seaman with every ocean, lake, and river in the liquid world open to me. The waters of the world were my enforced home, wave on wave, between the sky and the deck. And of all the things non-human that I loved, there was the cavorting porpoise diving through the green fore-foam. But sailors picked up stories and myths of the land-bound world, and the reader and the listener, growing in my bones, was anxious to stay ashore for awhile.

To Make My Bread

§

I was ashore, islanded, and housed, temporarily giving up the foc'sle for a room in a boarding house on Fourteenth Street off Third Avenue. The room was at the top of the house—a round room, all circles, that I thought of as a tower in the clouds above the rocking, hurtling trains of the Third Avenue El. The house itself was built over a Max Busy Bee—a restaurant filled with flies and Bowery bums. Every time I raced through the Busy Bee to my "tower," I was panhandled. I'd give the bum a cent, or maybe two cents, or maybe nothing. I had been taught by my mother to "Give when you have nothing to give . . ."

What I had was certainly not much, but a *sort* of job. Actually it was four part-time jobs. I ran four different elevators. One of them was in a building on Fifth Avenue near Scribner's bookstore; I ran it from 8 A.M. until noon. At 12:30, having eaten, for economy's sake, two bananas and half a loaf of raisin bread, I hopped over to a building on West 47th Street, next to a diamond and jewelry mart. There I filled in two more hours by relieving two operators going out to their lunches—of steak, they always assured me, once they'd discovered what my own noontime diet was.

In the mornings, through Scribner's window displays, all the authors of the period bore in on my consciousness, if only through the clean glass: Michael Arlen, Theodore

59

Dreiser, Willa Cather, Edgar Lee Masters, Harold Stearns, Vachel Lindsay, and Amy Lowell. Over on West 47th Street, I heard exciting stories about the trading of precious stones. (Some years later, in 1947, I represented a jewel merchant from that building. Between roving journalistic assignments, I was in Coober Peedy, the Australian opal mines — and in a single week I made $5,000 in commissions.)

The third elevator had me on East 53rd Street, in an apartment house of the wealthy — and sometimes slightly disorderly. Silk dresses and ravishing perfumes, top hats and gallant talk — as these people swept into the wide elevator I would stand stiff in my blue uniform, keep my face reserved, and ask politely, "Your floors, please . . ." But sometimes the men — or the ladies — had had too much to drink. Then I would be asked to find their keys, to let them in, to put them to bed, to wind the clock, to leave a message somewhere, to get them tea or coffee or pills and whiskey. I was once even asked to help a poor old millionaire remove, with gentle force, a woman who was becoming too demanding of him.

It was much more fun when I occasionally took over the service elevator. For the Irish maids were coy, kissing, loving, and laughing. They gave me bits of dinner and bits of themselves. They made it possible for me to piece together at least one real meal before midnight when I went off to my last elevator job, at another apartment house half a block away. Here the maids were fatter and older, not as kissy, but just as considerate. They fed me, early in the morning, on steak or caviar or whatever was going at that hour in the various apartments where brokers or industrialists were visiting their well-kept women.

My total wages from these four jobs came to eighteen dollars a week. At three in the morning, I was dazed with fatigue, hardly able to read a book. And I had left the sea just for that — to study and prepare for captaining my lonely self.

I decided to quit all four jobs, to get a single one, and to go to high school at night.

The high school was right up the street on Irving Place. Nearby, the Irving Place burlesque house provided rapture or contentment for young boys, old men and middle-aged salesmen. Fourteenth Street, then, was the focus of a different sort of culture, too. There was Lüchow's, the great restaurant, which enjoyed mysterious diplomatic immunity during Prohibition, and where H. L. Mencken went for his beer and belched murderous discourses on the American scene. I occasionally found a copy of Mencken's magazine in the garbage—and through reading it had come to know of Sacco and Vanzetti, of Shaw and Sinclair Lewis—the related and the unrelated. On Fourteenth Street, many of Mencken's barbed images somehow stood out in strident relief; for it was then the center of both Leftist dalliance and Tammany Hall frolicking.

Going to night school meant imposing scholarly discipline on myself and I moved from the noisy tower room to a quieter one on Second Avenue at Nineteenth Street. It was a dismal back room from which one viewed a single pale tree that had not grown a green leaf since Adam. After some months of silence, I finally wrote to my sister that I was back from the sea—a secret not to be divulged to my father, for I still imagined his feelings would be violent. It was now four years since I had run away. I wore long pants. I shaved every week. I looked serious. I had seen much of the world; but both of us were crying when my sister Edna and I finally met, one Saturday afternoon.

We talked for hours in my room. She had been supposed to be married soon, she said. She was less blond, high of cheek, beautiful. She wanted to become a librarian, but books and literature did not count to my mother, who was driving to get her married off "to a fine businessman." The fine

61

businessman was kind, but he was a butcher. This was too much for Edna, who preferred a more scholarly profession, one "dealing with books instead of blood and salami—bank books—a banker!" The marriage was soon off—and Edna talked on about how rich my brothers had become. They went off on weekends, rode horseback and played golf. That was their new world. My mother was proud, my father was silent—and that was his world. Edna said she would call again next Saturday, "Because you look so lonely. Have you any friends?"

§

I studied Spanish, typing, bookkeeping, and English; I didn't really know why. I hadn't picked any of these subjects —an old lady at the interviewing desk made the academic decisions for me. I was there nightly, ambitious though bored, trying to adapt my mental reflexes to the debits and credits of bookkeeping. In a sudden revolt, I quit the course and shifted to one billed as "architecture." I would rebuild New York, starting with Cherry Street. I would give the city the best of Paris' broad avenues with their grand buildings, and there would be some of the lovely light-yellow houses I had seen in London's Upper Wimpole Street. The new New York would be flowery, tree-laden, quiet—and garbage free. I made secret blueprints that no builder could have ever read or used. My talents were strange, the instructor commented. He didn't think I would ever be certified to practice architecture. It was a dream, private and splendid.

Since I was not learning too well or too fast, I fell in love often—it gave me an emotional "home." First I found Peggy, a would-be dancer from Second Avenue and Eighth Street. Peggy had lovely legs. She flirted with all the students. I held hands with her, walked her home, kissed her stiffly in the dark hallway, and talked purposefully to her about social problems; but our minor affair ended when she got a bit part in a chorus and quit school for the odds and ends of Broadway.

Then came Bessie, with whom I went to Loew's on Delancey Street on Saturday nights. Bessie was tall, sumptuous, willing, and reckless. Bessie loved love, even on the dirty roof of her building on Forsyth Steet. It was always a problem of place. We could not go to my room, for I would have been thrown out by my religious Russian landlady. And love on the roof meant alarums and viewers, with Bessie's brother seeking her out late at night. The vulgar intrusions violated my emotions as well as my embraces. But while I shied away from the roof for romance, Bessie welcomed it as an exhibitionist. She was big-breasted and big-rumped, and her language shocked me. When I actually visited her home, I discovered that her younger unmarried sister was pregnant, that Bessie herself posed for pornographic postcards, and that her sorrowing parents were resigned to their two loose daughters. I left her.

To succeed Bessie there was Hanna on Cannon Street, a Canadian girl who sat near me in typing class and volunteered to help me, though she hardly was as good at touch typing as I was. But my heart jumped at the keyboard every time she touched one of my fingers, which I used randomly to strike keys and spell out, "Now is the time . . ." And come to my aid she did.

After a week of touching "instruction" I finally walked Hanna home. We dallied on Second Avenue, stopping to read the notices of the laughing and sad Jewish theaters, sandwiched among vegetarian restaurants and gypsy tearooms. On Allen Street, I bought Hanna halvah and dates, and we listened to the Turkish and Arabic music that spilled down from the one-flight-up Middle Eastern coffee cafés. The stores below, run by Greek and Syrian Jews, sold wares from the bazaars of Asia Minor: copper, brass, and overly-colored bedspreads with overly-large women embroidered on them. The embroidered women, scant of dress, danced amid men smoking hubbly-bubblies. Sex, it seemed, was not a Puritanical thing in the Middle East—and I decided to sail there one day. Hanna and I bought polly seeds, littering the walks as we went onward, leaving the world of ouzo, raki and retzina— all of it spicing our imaginations.

One night we walked up the one flight. We drank bootleg raki and watched a huge girl, all buttocks and belly, go through a languid dance. She wore gold bells on her ankles, and bangles around her middle; and she clicked castanets as she whirled and twisted, her navel bellying in and out with magical movements. There was a gross demonstration of approval from the sweating Syrians and Greeks who watched, while the few tourists seemed mystified rather than enchanted by her exotic splendors.

Overly enthusiastic, glowing with Middle Eastern delights, we tried our own version of it later. She had invited me into her home for the first time; her parents were out. In the darkened living room, a red-tasseled chandelier created all the Middle East atmosphere we needed. I was used to Russian rhythm and bounced when I should have bellied. Hanna, however, went at it like a houri. Exhausted eventually, we sank to the couch and began talking about, of all things the *Sturm und Drang* of Goethe's *Sorrows of Young Werther*. And then, Hanna suddenly began disrobing. I abandoned my Puritanism to help Hanna lose her virginity.

She cried as she washed away the stains of her vanished virtue. And she talked of marriage with wonderful clarity, accenting the subtleties of a "home" to me, the wanderer. I could, of course, go into business. I could join her father in a fur shop. I could study law. I could be most anything . . . and soon we were acting "married" again. Her parents came in and found us going through another chapter of personal *Sturm und Drang.*

I was called a rapist in Yiddish, Russian, and Canadian English by her father. Her mother whacked me with a broom. At the door, her father threw me out, and her mother threw the broom after me—despite my protests that "I want to marry Hanna tonight." Hanna stood crying under the red chandelier, unable to enter into the crisis at the door. It was all very sad, for Hanna never returned to school. My typing got worse.

My job, then, was somewhat bizarre. I was both a normal office boy and an employee *extraordinaire* of an organization called The Inter-Cosmic Institute of Inventors. Thomas Edison, Henry Ford, and a great Hungarian inventor named Nikola Tesla were listed as paying members, though none of the three ever attended the meetings held in a floor-through loft turned into offices and showrooms downtown, where a few hundred eccentrics gathered monthly to discuss dubious inventions while their patents pended.

After a month, I had my own invention and a model; a combined salt and pepper shaker shaped like a Y. My specifications to the Patent Office claimed that this Siamese twin was a great time-saver, since both salting and peppering were accomplished in one speedy shake. When I finally received an answer from the Patent Office, it stated, in government prose, that my invention was thought of at least once a day throughout the United States and its Possessions—and to try for something rarer.

The inventors' organization employed the varied labors of five people. The most important person was Mrs. Baringprone, a stoutly aggressive woman who really ran the show because she had inherited this inventive loft from her bankrupt father. She was married to George Baringprone, a quick-talking, mustached, handsome salesman who had created something he called the Rookman System to dupe would-be patentees. Then there was a Czech engineer named Vacker, who had deserted his wife after making the Olympic soccer team in 1920, and who now gave most of his engineering talents over to an odd collection of patent-seeking females. Finally there was a Mrs. Allinson, who did the books, but who was mostly concerned with her overly-plump daughter, Thelma, whom she was preparing for a dancing career on Broadway. Mrs. Allinson was near-sighted and Thelma danced as a Pavlova in her vision; to the rest of us, she was just fumbling, fat Thelma.

My job often took me to the Public Library. There I traced claims and patent specifications before we took the costly application to the Patent Office in Washington. Our collection of inventions was rare indeed, and we exercised all the prudence we could to discover the real value of the strange models that were piled all over the exhibition rooms. We had a cycle that ran without wheels, levitating on huge balloons that catapulted the rider toward heaven. There was a typewriter that made organ music — the model, when typed on, played "America I Love You" in very slow cadences. There was a really eccentric reducing machine; two large wheels in front, one in the rear — and when it went into action, the reducer was thrown up and down in frantic action. I knew, because I tried out everything when I swept through, with broom, duster and mop, on my monthly cleaning tour the day of the meeting.

To the meetings came heavily bearded Italians, Germans, Swedes, Finns, and Swiss, and I'd watch as the All-American members of the staff pulled working money from the poor inventors. There were dues (life membership was urged); one hundred dollar deposits for models-in-creation; more money for the search at the Patent Office; more fees for the patent attorney, who was, in actuality, the aggressive

66

Mrs. Baringprone. It was a money-taking night — and none of the assembled eccentrics had ever invented a substitute for money. During the latter half of the evening, inventors, one more weird than the next, would take to the platform to talk like broken down science fiction writers. Most of them were as zany as their speeches — they had no nuthouse to go to but the Inter-Cosmic Inventors Society's large loft. I was one of their amateur keepers.

When it came time for me to get paid on Fridays, there was a sense of payless, moneyless terror abroad in the loft. I was often three weeks behind in salary. The Department of Justice wasn't far behind the Rookman System, however, and before long, the larcenous inventiveness came to an end downtown.

A Furious Year

§

It was not the Department of Justice, however, that ended my career with the very earth-bound Inter-Cosmic Inventors Society. It was my own decision; I had not been paid for four weeks, and I had had to borrow small sums to keep alive on starvation staples of cheese, bread and carrots. I left the Society abruptly, carrying off the office typewriter and yelling to the staff that it was worth less than what I was owed. I bounded down the decaying wooden stairs with stout Mrs. Allinson in hopeless pursuit. Instead of pawning the typewriter, I kept it, thinking vaguely that its ownership might hurry up some undiscovered talent.

Broke and hungry for more than carrots, I found an emergency job that would pay me daily. I was hired without conversation; just nodded to. I was to dye laces—in a tin-sealed, airless room containing great vats, chemicals, and a small useless fan that blew toward a transom.

Fifteen minutes after my initial try, I was almost out of my head, dazed with the dye fumes. I flung myself out the door. The manager, a little late in his explanations, said sternly, "Boy, you can't stay in there for more than five minutes at a time—understand? And if you don't quit we'll give you a two dollar raise." Since it paid for meat and room rent, I went along stoically with the dyeing chores in this lace-enshrouded death chamber.

69

Because I still thought I wanted to study architecture, I left Washington Irving High School and transferred to night classes at the Mechanics Institute. I learned that there were styles called Empire, Gothic, Georgian, Roman, and Byzantine; but ours was called Etcetera. Beauty had little to do with real estate: steel had been introduced and was hardening all of us into its form. As far as I could see, it made money, not architecture.

At the dye shop, there was a slant-eyed girl who packed the jabots and waists. She made a quixotic decision for me. "Be smart!" she told me one day. "Get out of that dye-chamber and get a real job. Study law, not architecture. What are you going to build, another Madison Square Garden for Jack Dempsey and the circus? Be a lawyer. You could turn into another Clarence Darrow—or even a Cal Coolidge!"

In 1924, people were buying in style through the newly created finance companies that promoted installment buying, and law was intimately related to installment buying and the recovery of unpaid-for goods. Being a lawyer sounded like a good idea. I figured all I had to do was read the right books to be bright, apply to Fordham, and I would be enrolled.

But before I entered law school, I wanted another try at seeing America. I hardly knew what our country was really like. The frontier was disappearing, and I wanted to see what was still untouched of the mountains, prairies, and deserts. I needed some sort of a wilderness to frame for myself before the American earth was swallowed up in concrete. The Model T Ford was already changing the face as well as the rear-end of America.

I hitched rides on wagons, occasionally in cars, rattling through the gravel and dirt, through the bustling and building of our emerging barbarism. Calhoun had said in 1817, "We are great and rapidly—I was about to say fearfully—growing." Calhoun, even in his time, was forewarning the

70

citizenry. A farmer near Malone, New York, was the kindest American I met on my first crossing. He fed me, housed me, and paid me to work in the fields and the orchards with him, picking vegetables and fruit for several weeks. An Iroquois Indian, high-cheeked and serious—all pride. I was a Jew, all mixed up with wandering angers and emotions, belonging really nowhere.

Once, over a dinner of pot roast and homemade beer, he remarked, "We could have been real citizens earlier if the French had not given us guns. *Our* American history is bloody . . ." and we had more beer on that. His wife, a local white woman, was teaching their two children at home, preferring that to the public school. It was most American, of another time. Whatever I had learned, I myself had read in isolation . . . .

I went on to Buffalo, agape at the big farms, the spacious valleys, and the soft mountains. It was cold along Lake Erie as I skirted Cleveland and waited in the freight yards for a manifest highballing it to Chicago.

I waited in the "jungle" near the marshaling yards of the Erie Railroad, watching locomotives and boxcars, reefers (refrigerated cars) and gondolas (coal cars). I went for a reefer carrying refrigerated vegetables and four talkative hoboes. At each end of the reefer was a narrow compartment; in the summer, ice was put in to keep the car cool; in the winter, a small stove kept the car warm. The trap door on top of the car had to be kept open, or you died of carbon monoxide poisoning if you fell asleep, but an open trap door gave you away to the brakeman and the yard bull—and soon they were after the hoboes, bums, and bindle-stiff sociologists.

When this freight train reached snow-covered Galesburg and began slowing down, the hoboes jumped from it and made for the nearby jungle. Sleepy and warm in the compartment, I took my time, waiting for the train to stop. When I finally

71

clambered down the ladder, a fist caught me on the chin, knocking my head back against one of the rungs. It was the yard bull the hoboes had talked about, their stories of him ranging from myth to reality. Yomo Red went for me again. Red of both face and hair, Yomo was not a gentle man. My bindle, which I had thrown from the reefer when I thought I saw no one about, lay behind him. If I didn't get it, I would be clothes-less. Wildly, I butted Yomo Red. My head went twice to his chin; then I kneed him in the groin, and he fell back across my pack. He lay there gasping and howling, and whatever pity I felt I quickly put away. Had he been able to get up, he'd have beaten me to death. I grabbed my bindle from under him, and dashed for the jungle.

I found the hoboes, now happily jungled, cooking up a mulligan stew—from bummed vegetables, bits of meat, whatever their hands had received at back doors. All of it was in a huge tin pot. They looked up and stared at my bloodied mouth and chin. I had brought no back-door offerings—but I did have a juicy story about kneeing the ape of a yard bull, Yomo Red.

A few days later, via the highway's harder lifts, I was hungrier and colder in snowy, slushy Omaha. I was wetter than the December prairies, locked with winter's furies. I burned with a slight fever—but I could join the U.S. Army and have a home for four years, said a sign at the Omaha post office. All I really wanted was a meal . . .

Wherever I went to keep warm, I was chased. At coffee pots, cafés, truck depots, I was unwanted and unfed, dirty, soaked, alien. I begged meals, mostly for soup, when my hunger was all-demanding. One out of ten joints was about my score. I was a lousy bum, inept at begging; my voice whistled when it should have been keyed for a human response. Once I washed hundreds of dishes at a Greek coffee pot—dishes waiting for someone like me to come along. I got soup, and a cheese sandwich for a bonus.

At the Omaha post office, in a recruiting room upstairs, I decided to "join" the U.S. Army. Sick and feverish as I was, I knew that the marines wouldn't take me. But my physical check showed me *healthy*. I had just been a cold wet bastard in the rain . . . and soon my clothes were dried. I was taken out and fed a steak—and then another—by the recruiting sergeant. In the joining-up process, I bummed him for five dollars—an advance on soldiering. Just before my signature was due on all the papers, I said, "I'm only sixteen, sir . . ."

"Can't you get your goddamn father to sign for you?" the sergeant asked angrily. For every recruit he got a bonus. My "enlistment" was turning into a loss—I'd had two steaks and a five-dollar loan.

"I no longer have a father," I was saying. It was some sort of a truth and it hurt all the more. "I am a kind of an orphan, sir." I was overdoing the remorse, afraid the five dollars would soon be back in his khaki pocket.

"Poor kid—and that's why you need the United States Army. You can become an engineer, fella."

According to the enlistment signs around his office, there wasn't a trade or a profession that couldn't be "learned," but who wanted to become a soldier in order to learn it at twenty-one dollars a month? It was for bums, the undisciplined, the careerless *lumpen proletariat,* everyone said. It was a great future to stay away from . . . I shook my head, and the saddened sergeant shook my hand. He gave me his address for the return of the five dollars in some dim time and said, whimsically, "When you grow up, join the diplomatic corps, fella." With five dollars, I headed for New York. I'd again briefly seen America.

I'd had bits of America hurriedly; the face and the foot in

73

many ways. It was a land without any sort of a frontier; gone, civilized by so many crude hands. President Coolidge had preempted everything for business, and every myth that I had about the land was over the hill. It was a land of immediacy. It said, *make money or die*. The continent, so wide, had narrowed at the heart . . .

Soon I was riding a horse in the Chicago stockyards, a watchman over cattle and men, to keep the cattle trains from running over both. Later, in Cleveland, en route home, I shoveled coal along icy Lake Erie. In Akron I lifted heavy rails in an iron foundry. Each city was a blueprint for labor . . . I mixed paint in a factory, loaded flour on freight trains. It was sweat all the way home; the boy with new muscles, months later, finally crossing on the Weehawken ferry to Manhattan, washing away the dirt of America in a toilet.

What infinite misery the trains had sung for me! It was made in America — made in the night's echo of locomotives whistling their full heads of steam. I'd heard that sound as it wailed steam from a train that left Ottumwa in Iowa one night. I rode the rods, wondering how soon I would bounce off, be minced into bits, then left between the rails with no identity between my skull and my shoes. In those days, the trains were still crying their coal-blackened, early industrial operas. And it is gone now from the land, in the electric Diesel's soundless running of the rails.

In 1952, when Carl Sandburg was visiting me for a drink and a burned-black jungle-style steak, I told him about Yomo Red and Galesburg, where Sandburg was born. He laughed in his loud Swedish way, saying happily, "Everybody remembered the beating Yomo got — it was his first one. . . ." And then he enscribed a book of his, *Remembrance Rock,* for me: "As between scholars, hoboes, seekers in fellowship and in many faiths . . ." I did not know it in 1925, but I had unconsciously adopted a new faith — radical socialism.

America was no longer the land where a government gave a would-be homesteader forty acres and a mule.

§

But do would-be radicals work for the greater aggrandizement of capitalism? Yet there I was, as messenger, clerk, and later, as a librarian, with the great law firm of White & Case, at 14 Wall Street, in the geophysical heart of capitalist enterprise. An employment agency had turned me, for a fee, into a passable Lutheran "in event" of possible discrimination. I was Jewish to some of my colleagues, Christian on my workaday face, and Pantheist to my inner self. It was part of the masked trinity, bucking the various types of discrimination prevailing then against Jews. Though it was a private game to shame the *goy,* I had more than shame for entering into this small-masked disguise. A man must be what he is, Hottentot or Hebrew, I said to myself when I took the job. But a man must also be allowed to work, as well. I worked . . .

I still did not study law. I preferred to go on thinking about fieldstone, brick, marble, slate, and timber — man and the physical poetry of his architecture. Law was hardly working for the poor man; one of the major clients in the plush, leather-chaired offices of White & Case were the Van Sweringen brothers, the railroad tycoons. They had begun the building of their empire in 1916 with the Nickel Plate Railroad and by 1925 they had bought up or into every railroad that ran into Cleveland and beyond; now they were attempting to form a transcontinental line. They had merged, extended, enlarged, and consolidated — and they were endlessly in the courts under charges of the Interstate Commerce Commission. I saw them, short and polished, waxed and worried, Oris and Mantis Van Sweringen, as they talked over legal briefs with lawyers in the conference rooms. They had an air of money and mystery. There were references made to

75

Samuel Insull, who ran vast utilities on other people's money, via the holding company. The Van Sweringens were holding, merging, uniting, and startling a nation still not used to revelations about monopolies. Big Business had a natural home at 14 Wall Street, and I brought volume after volume to corporation lawyers battling for the Van Sweringens against John Sherman's anti-trust law of 1890—fighting the regulations of the Federal Trade Commission, the Justice Department, the Commerce Department—and marching tragically toward the fatal days of 1929.

§

Away from the law office, I ran for fun, at Madison Square Garden. I wore blue trunks, a red athletic shirt, and a floppy number pinned with safety pins to the back of my shirt. Unattached to any club—no one ever made a bid for my membership—I bounded around the track in the Wanamaker Mile against Willie Ritola and Paavo Nurmi, then the fleetest Finns of them all. I was with them, short and stocky, chest out, tearing my lungs apart. I loved the effortless lope of Ritola, who was the taller, thinner and more wiry of the two Finns, and Nurmi, who had more heart and bigger lungs and could have been sued by the Justice Department for his monopoly in winning races. I never won a race though I came in fourth once, for a copper medal. But I had my name on the sacred Millrose Games program . . .

I found a friend at White & Case, a tall law student named Stanley; soon we shared an apartment on West 65th Street. He was as excited about running as I was, and at six in the morning, in good weather, we trained around the flowery, fenced-in Central Park Reservoir, joining the boxers who jogged and the dog-walkers who strutted.

Riding the subway downtown, I read the *New York World,* then the only literary newspaper for radicals. It

76

opened up the American world. Each page dissected the daily scandals of corruption—many of which had begun where I got off the subway, in the narrow-laned Wall Street section, and many of which ended, in legal briefs, in my office. It was all for the making of money. The lawyers made it their business to give a legalistic plush-lining to Coolidge's dictum—"The business of America is business."

Many of my business hours, in those days, were spent in reading things other than the *New York World*. Sitting in the library, Stanley and I, between chores, tried to find our way through T.S. Eliot's *The Waste Land* and Robinson Jeffers' *Roan Stallion*. Edgar Lee Masters' *Spoon River* was easier. And Carl Sandburg made poetry much simpler for me, giving me back poems about the raw material that I myself had experienced. I had, not quite, been the hog-packer. I was now well-dressed—blue-suited and white-shirted. I was an errand boy; I lugged dull, heavy books to bell-ringing lawyers—and I hated them, their clients, and the associations of industrial monstrosity that came to mind. Stanley and I had seen, between our track meets on Saturday nights, Elmer Rice's *Adding Machine* and Capek's *R.U.R.* When the managing clerk, McConnell, asked me for the tenth time what law school I intended to enter, I could no longer invent lies fast enough. I said, "Well actually, I don't intend to study law. If anything, I want to be an architect . . ."

"Then why are you staying on here? Is it merely a job?"

"A man must work," I said, feeling lame but still game.

"Then work at architecture, son. Besides, you've been talking about Sacco and Vanzetti—those two Wops. You're not by any chance sympathetic to them?"

"If I said yes, Mr. McConnell, I'd be fired—right?"

"You certainly would!"

"I'm a radical socialist, Mr. McConnell. Am I fired?"

"You're a *what?*"

"A radical socialist. I believe in law and order, in government and freedom, in progress and happiness and good citizenship . . ." I thought I had covered all the vital points of my limited reading.

"Boy, you just got fired. If you want to practice Fourier's theories, get the hell out of here!"

The next day I was at the Forty-Second Street Library reading, for the first time, François Fourier's theories of utopianism. But I couldn't just go on reading—I was jobless. Reluctantly, I decided to go to sea again. The sea would be an antidote to my poisonous, if brief, career at White & Case.

I told Stanley, and he wanted to join me.

A few days later we were on the *S.S. Republic,* Stanley as a messman, I as an able-bodied seaman. It was to be Germany—Hamburg and Bremen—as a regular service. Almost eighteen, everything I had done since leaving home had been disorganized, directionless, pointless.

I was wrong, of course. All my zany jobs, all my odd reading, was preparing me to become a writer. I knew that I never again wanted a nine-to-five job. Nor did I think I wanted America, which had begun to despoil itself. I wanted Europe and I wanted the sea, which would give me a chance to read. Maybe, one day, I would write something.

As a sailor again, I explored Germany. I saw and heard Hindenburg in Hanover, where the new nationalism blossomed. I heard a man named Hitler snarling like a small mustached dog when I visited Munich on leave. Hamburg was another story. It was open to the sea, not locked in and insular. It was anti-nationalist, cosmopolitan. The communists had rioted there in 1923, and they were a powerful force now. I listened to all the political doctrines, especially to those of the errant Trotskyists, in St. Pauli, on the Reeperbahn, in the sailors' cafés and bars.

Hamburg had known the world's woes; a great fire in 1842, and cholera in 1892 — but now it was richer than any other German city, mightier in its social idealism, and I found myself at home there. Brahms and Mendelssohn, Christian and Jewish composers, had been born in Hamburg. If I could, I would have changed my own birthplace. I identified, strangely then, with German ways. There was strength, if not always direction — and I liked that because I was a *wandervogel*. I loved the look of the sculptured houses, the tapering roofs, the arches of time's best architecture, and I was eye-struck with streets and streams. Then there were the Germans themselves, the defeated people who still knew poetry, and wrote great prose. There was Von Hoffmansthal and Ernst Toller, the radical; and Rilke, who in 1911, had decided to remain German rather than adopt France. There was also Stefan George, who had remained aloof during the first war, and wrote of the Germans in 1916, "It is naturally easier for weaklings to send armies into battle than to govern a people in peace . . ." It was peace for me in all ways, in 1926; and I accepted, between trips back to New York, a peculiar happiness that I felt only in Hamburg.

Transgressions,
Confessions,
and Lessons

§

I jumped ship one night, sneaking off with my two old valises
to settle in and around the Reeperbahn, Hamburg's Pigalle.
I felt awkwardly rich—I had saved most of my seaman's
pay, but not for the whores. I was looking for something
else, with recollections of Hamburg in 1923 when I had
first come as a younger, rawer sailor—a boy, all eyes, taking
in the many sadnesses of Germany's many hungers.

It had been a time of inflation, political putsches, insurrections, Free Corps adventurism. There had been plots and
uprisings. It went with the beer, back alleys, distortions—
a political pissoir all over Germany. You smelled it in the
beer mugs, even in red-controlled Hamburg. Fights, brawls,
knifings, then the eloquent comraderie over another beer—
if you agreed; and in Hamburg, you agreed with the sailors
and the stevedores, who were in permanent opposition to
everything capitalistic . . . and I remembered it as I walked
about St. Pauli, looking for a cheap hotel.

Over the Albany Bar was a small rooming house. Soon I
unpacked and was settled, with a view of the harbor. And
soon I was adrift in Hamburg's many normalcies and
eccentricities.

It was April, with the cold almost gone from the North
Sea's winds of winter. The weather made everything come

wonderfully, colorfully alive in Hamburg. The weather also seemed to bring politics into flower—red and black blossoms as communism and Nazism sprang up all over the city. At the Albany Bar, communist sailors sang offensive songs, which I picked up quickly. Hitler, the butt of one, had received less than 500,000 votes at the last election—and he was hardly a problem in Red Hamburg; but the sailors sang on:

> *Schmier die Guillotine,*
> *Schmier die Guillotine,*
> *Schmier die Guillotine*
> *Mit der Hitler Fetts—*
> *Bumbarassa, Bumbarassa, Revolution!*

This was followed with a mock Nazi salute, and a yell—

> *So hoch mit Scheisse!*

From another corner of the Albany Bar, a more mellowed sailor, feeling his own spring sadness, sang:

> *Ich hab mein Herz in Heidelberg verloren . . .*

The Albany Bar was a rendezvous for rough raptures in politics and girls. It was St. Pauli, the Reeperbahn, and about time to fall in love. Love came with politics; and it was not odd, in 1927, to love a girl if you agreed with her as a Marxist. Anna was seventeen and a Trotskyist like her father, who worked as a stevedore. Anna was a music student and knew English. I heard of Purcell for the first time when she sang, "I Attempt From Love's Sickness to Fly," and I flew, with my now experienced nineteen-year-old conceits, into her buxom arms. She was taller by an inch, blonder—an erotic child who had almost never known the condition of virginity. Anna laughed a great deal, dimpling her rosy cheeks. She gave off the recklessness of youth—

82

radiated with animation of her own. Then her sea-blue eyes would suddenly still into the music she loved, and I would be left with the impression of clouds and distances.

And it became love in her little bedroom when her father was out talking Trotskyism. Pop, as I began to call him, knew that I was sleeping with his daughter Anna. But Pop was concerned with my political soul, rather than my sexual arrangements. With Trotsky, Anna, and Pop, I had politics, love, and even a father, by proxy and proximity.

Pop was fifty; he had been a sailor, had lived in both London and New York for several years. He was a true cosmopolitan, and a fiery Trotskyist. His blue eyes danced in his proletarian face whenever he scored a political point. After his lectures, there was always a question period for me.

I knew and gave the proper answers, of course, but my attention often strayed to his daughter. It was an admixture of Marxism and love, Trotskyism and her music, and Anna overall; for no matter how seriously we talked about the real situation in China, Russia, or Germany, Anna and I ended up less dialectical and more physical. One day, to increase my sense of social values, Pop took me for a walk up the notorious Herbert Strasse, an alley of sexual exhibitionism. "This is what capitalism does to women. Look!" said Pop.

What a foul bunch they were, sitting and beckoning to the never-ending line of men who walked up and down. Some whores were dressed as grandmothers, with little bonnets; others, in baby rompers, exercised a different perversity. There were wrestler-looking types in shirts and shorts, women who looked bruised, had broken noses and large biceps—but who must have had their customers. There were even women dressed up as nuns and madonnas. They looked purer than novices. It was Resurrection and Erection in one. In every degree of distortion it was all for men in every stage of decadence. Even without Pop's accompanying moral lecture, I was sickened by what I saw, shot through from brain to crotch with disgust.

Hitlerian accents were rising and Pop, knowing that I was Jewish, told me about other German extremists. He talked of Wagner's myths and the Wotan-cult; and he read over a poem written by the poet and playwright, Ernst von Wildenbruch, who had many racist followers in religious circles:

> We, of thy blood,
> God of the Germans, approach thee;
> We, lost among alien folk,
> Call upon Thee, Father of All . . .

And there had been the thinker of the Bismarckian day—Paul de Lagarde. A theologian and philologist, he wrote that Germany's identification must come from "the invisible force which lives in everything that grows and thrives in Germany, and to bring out in every single German that divine image which is in him from birth." If that was not Wotan, Wagner and Hitler, Pop said, then it was nothing but the usual Germanic nonsense that normal people did not need.

Pop went on with scorn to another racist, Julius Langbehn, who said, "Blood is mightier than political nationality and mightier even than language; blood affinity inescapably produces spiritual affinity . . ." The lecture went on to Konstantin Frantz, who was a full-blown Nazi in the 1880's. Pop, in completing this seminar in racism, reminded me that only socialism would free man from such stupidity. . . .

Anna listened sadly. I remarked that I had been born a member of the *chosen people,* which was just as racist when my mother spoke about it. It was just as primitive—all bloody memory for a ghetto spirituality. Marxism removed the religious ghetto from the mind, replacing it with universalism, and I had happily adopted that. Man had all of the earth, no matter his birthplace and language—and I had proved it. Nationalism and racism was sickening in any disguise. Pop thought that I was making progress in every direction.

I had been in Hamburg for several months by then, living off my savings. I occasionally went to the opera house, the Schauspielhaus, with Anna. We took the ferry or we walked across the bridge until we reached Kirchenallee, where the German Theater played Sophocles and Goethe was well as contemporaries. Near the slum, Gaengeviertel, we saw the Blue Blouse Theater set up shop in the streets of the whores and the *lumpen*. The actors were basically agitators doing an early version of "living newspaper"; they used soapboxes, sticks and stones for props, and illustrated, with broad accents, the tenor of the political times. They satirized the socialists, Hindenburg, and Hitler's mustache . . . and *that* would provoke street battles with the Nazis. Then, police, the green-uniformed Schupo, would come with rifles and wound a few communists.

Only once did I get caught up in any gunfire. It was one of those insurrections which never got reported; it began in Barmbek, a communist stronghold, and petered out there. I had spent the day drinking with American sailors. I was homesick for New York and my language; and when I left the Albany Bar, I was good and drunk on beer. I was, in my way, saying good-bye. Anna wanted to marry—women always do. We had talked about it for days, and it frightened me. It meant maturity and responsibility, and I was not ready. I'd had over five years of sea time, and I was prepared to sit for a mate's ticket when I got home. But marriage meant giving up the sea; so why sit for a mate's ticket? My mate, if I married, would be Anna, and I'd be sitting in a flat in New York.

I was confused about most things except politics. I would be twenty in a few months; and I saw myself almost engaged, en route to a family, professionless, the boy-wanderer turned man. Yet I would soon be able to vote, to engage in American politics, to help rid the United States of Coolidge, to sponsor a cause worthy of man — Marxist universalism.

I thought a great deal about revolution. I had seen Brecht's agitprop play, *Man Is Man.* Man was stomach, mind, and spirit, in unequal parts. In Hamburg the men I knew believed in something called *Rot Front* — a red front of proletarians against capitalism. Bolshevism, the universal kind, not the national kind that Stalin practiced, became my red banner of rebellion. It went beyond the belly and beer. Materialism, to an idealist, was merely a way to rally the masses. Somewhere Brecht had written satirically:

> *Erst kommt das Fressen,*
> *Dann kommt die Moral.*

Because I was interested in escaping love's little domestic traps, I wandered away from Anna, drunk, seeking other wounds . . . an exchange of pains. I had never sought out violence before, but I heard shooting and went toward it . . .

I walked drunkenly; I was near the Rathaus, and I sneered, surprisingly, at its beautiful Gothic architecture, towering above the Old Wall. Ahead I saw the Bahnhof, then bars, women and streets that danced and jigged. I sang to myself bits of German communist songs, then American sailor songs. I had decided to leave Germany for American visions after months of Hamburg's beer, politics, and private ecstasies. I was approaching the Schauspielhaus. It was festooned in a glow of memory, and it made me sad, voiceless. I thought of love, of the softness of words in Anna's bed. . . .

I went to another bar for more stolidity. Then I skirted by the Outer Alster and walked aimlessly toward the sounds of the shooting. It might be firecrackers, at best. More beer. The place was filled with whores. It had nothing but more noise and ugliness. In a corner men were quarreling; four against four, then five against five, then the numbers became confused. Someone was calling Judge Thayer, who had denied Sacco and Vanzetti a new trial, *stupid* — *"Er ist blöd, dieser Richter Thayer."* After that, it was President Coolidge, who had also denied them an appeal — he was *blöd* too. Sacco and Vanzetti were innocent, I said in drunken acceptance. A man slapped me on the back in praise and bought me a beer. I bought him one — and now a fight had broken out — somewhere close at hand, the police were trying to put down the communists. A man appeared in the doorway, and yelled, *"Die Schupos kaempfen . . ."* It was not firecrackers but rifles I heard. Men were brawling, breaking beer mugs to use the handles as weapons. I did the same and out of the bar we went, dashing off to a small street insurrection.

It happened every night in this area. The delusions of beer. Soon I dropped my broken mug handle. My head was clearing — I had better watch, not participate. I was the foreigner, the natural spectator, not a partisan for communist insurrections.

There were Red Front Fighters in loose Russian blouses with hammer and sickle arm bands. They had rifles and assorted amateur arms. They were at the head of the street now and were moving down, facing the green-clad Schupo. It was a night of *Rot Front,* bullets badly aimed, bricks and glass being thrown — improvised bedlam, sudden attack, sudden retreat, surrender . . .

I started running like all the rest. The Schupo were shooting. I felt a sudden sting — a bullet had scraped my left forearm. It was nothing, just a sharp, bleeding pain, and I kept on running. I fell, tripping over someone lying still. I got up and ran again, to find a dark alley and hide . . . then I got a clubbing and out I went . . .

What a small hero I had been! I was in a small cell in the large police station on Von Essen Strasse. Someone had my seaman's passport. A few hours later, my clothes were brought to me from my hotel in St. Pauli. Yes, of course, I was innocent. I was just an American sailor who forgot his ship, months ago.

"Why did you stay here, young man?" someone asked.

"There was a girl . . . there is a girl," and I lied, poorly, that it had been love that made me jump ship.

"She's not a whore? That's something new—a music student! Ah, so! And now, do you have enough music for awhile?"

I was sent back to the barred little cell. A young clerk from the American Consul came to get me out. It was a matter of form and papers; I was being evicted from the country. The clerk signed a number of papers. He was used to getting American drunks out of jail, to sending sailors back as workaways at a cent a month. In no time at all I was on a beat-up old freighter heading for Mobile, Alabama.

The trip back took almost a month. First the steering gear went wrong, then one of the boilers—and the ship was rudderless and steamless for almost ten days in the Atlantic while engineers worked it over. It was a dead ship, soundless, with nothing in the steam pipes. In this strange kind of mechanical silence, a huge German sailor named Hans—all shoulders, chest and skull—played games with our nerves. He had been taken on through a pier-head jump, to replace an American sailor found too beaten-up to make the trip back. Hans, paid, would also go home to Hamburg as a passenger—and he was strutting, bullying the unpaid others

88

of us. To beat him up would take at least two men, or a capstan bar, and that was murder. He blew in and out of the foc'sle like Wotan himself shouting, *"Ich hab' die groessten Muskeln in der Welt—ja!"* He *was* muscled like steel and granite; he did exercises by the hour, showed off day and night, and cursed us contemptuously for our smallness—and our indifference to race. A Mexican sailor, a wiper, took a capstan bar to slug him, but the Mexican ended in the hospital. Then a Yank from Marblehead, lean and powerful, hit him a few punches, but it ended when the Third Mate pulled a pistol on both of them.

After that pistol incident, the foc'sle was an armed camp. Hans slept with marlin spikes under his mattress and his pillows. The Mexican who'd recovered from his wounds waited openly for revenge. Even when Hans showered, he took along a marlin spike, in case the soap dropped and the Mexican went for him. It finally happened on August 22, when the radio announced the execution of Sacco and Vanzetti, about whom we had argued for days. We expected a revolution in the United States, at least. Most of us believed them innocent. Hans, all Nazi, denounced them: *"Sie sind anarchistische Schweine!"* I translated eagerly and made things worse for him by adding epithets he hadn't thought of.

He stood in the center of the foc'sle, big and belligerent, centered for slaughter, sneering at us with, *"Ich bin ein Riese! Ein National Sozialist!"*

As the Mexican listened I translated Hans into a national socialist giant with the biggest muscles in the world. Hans turned momentarily to admire one of the many photos of himself that decorated the side of his bunk, and the Mexican went into action. He grabbed one of Hans' marlin spikes and clubbed that Germanic skull, laying him out in purest Nazi blood . . . and soon the Third Mate was back. Hans was in the hospital and the Mexican in irons all the way to Mobile.

§

I met Hans again during the Depression, when Union Square was the holy ground for demonstrating against it. There he was, big, beefy, and blue in a cop's uniform; and oddly, we shook hands. Then the demonstration turned into an organized riot. A few women, prepared by the communists, got in the way of the horse cops, to needle them. It was an old technique to get sympathy in the press—to cry "Cossacks! Cossacks! Cossacks!" If the horses did not go wild, the taunted police, with pepper thrown at them, did. But through it all there was Hans, smiling, amiable, asking me to get in touch with him. He was married, had a child, lived in Yorkville, and was a weightlifter in his spare time. A few years later, when war broke out, I saw his picture in *The New York Times*. The F.B.I. had rounded him up along with a group of alleged Nazi spies . . .

§

I wrote to Anna from Mobile, when the freighter finally arrived. I would see her again one day, I said. I loved her, I said. I had five dollars and one cent—the cent was my legal pay, the five dollars a small gift from five sailors—and I was hitching to New York. I had exorcised my hate, and I would now see my father. I had nothing but ideas, and he would not like any of them. God was gone, and Marxism was my religion. Could I tell my father and mother that I was in love with a Gentile? Was that all that I had come home with? Would I ever really see Anna or Hamburg again? I wrote to her for six years until Hitler stopped our correspondence.

When I did see Hamburg again, in 1950, there was no Anna any more, nor Hamburg. It had been bombed out of its past during ten raids by the Royal Air Force in July 1943. They had been called the "Gomorrah" raids by the R.A.F.,

90

devastating the culture and the people from St. Pauli to Barmbek. 100,000 had died in ten days, and Anna was one, gone through magnesium and phosphorous bombs. It was all gutted, desolate, mummified by firestorms. There was nothing I could recognize. The museums, the parks, the fountains, the whorehouses and theaters were only a memory. The Schauspielhaus still stood, but not the Albany Bar. I gutted it, along with Pop and Anna, from my dazed memory. I tried to find a hotel . . .

I did, near the still-standing Bahnhof; but it was a bomb-proof shelter deep in the German earth. After an hour in its subterranean breathlessness, I came out stupefied and waited out the night at the Bahnhof. Hamburg, could not be resurrected, nor Anna. Besides, I was another man in another time. I was married, joyous, writing books, hating Marxism —all of its branches—and I went on to Denmark to escape the nightmare of Hamburg.

§

It was October and rainy with autumn when I reached New York from Mobile. It had been seven years since I had run away. My father and I kissed, Russian style. We made peace. He said that I looked strong, "staark," like a man. I was no longer thirteen, I said. I was sunburnt and road-toughened by the hitch up from Mobile. And I had a job working for a sort of "bootlegger," which I did not tell my father. We talked of many other things.

My answers to his questions were half fact, half fancy, to spare him. We had tea, glass after glass, from the old samovar that was always going. They lived in another apartment. They had achieved the Bronx, with heat and hot water, a toilet within, a bath; and their home was, at last, all-American. It had taken my father from 1895 until 1927, at 67 years of age to get it all. With the help of sons and a daughter,

91

he had gone the full American circle toward the middle of it. My two older brothers had bought a luncheonette from a Greek on New Street—my mother had urged, coaxed and finally forced them into the venture. My father was, despite his age and obvious lack of strength, still wielding a heavy pressing iron in the garment district. He had made his own circle within the circle. He looked aged, haggard, and unhappy, at the end of a harrowing life, as if he had achieved nothing at all, though his sons had. My mother was still stolid and more religious than ever, the *"Balabusta"* reigning over all. She had intense pride as she moved about, the right sleeve pinned up over the armless socket. She kissed me and upbraided me at the same time. I was home again as an occasional sleeping-over stranger.

My two older brothers, Herschel and Mike, were marrying soon—to enlarge on their vision of coming affluence. It was all very American for them; business, marriage, children, Florida when the time and the winter came for it, Turkish baths, and pinochle. It was the Jewish and the American way, from cuisine to clothes. In a few years, they would own a chain of restaurants from Manhattan to Brooklyn. They would join the Masons, give to certain causes, be good citizens and good fathers as they went from seltzer water and lox to Cadillacs and champagne. They were happy, and they were on their way.

§

Mr. M., the "bootlegger," was really a non-practicing chemist who advertised in the *Police Gazette* that he manufactured essences for make-it-yourself gin, rye, Scotch, and cordials. An ounce of essence that sold for five dollars made a gallon of liquor, providing you had pure alcohol. Mr. M's business was in the essence; the buyer had to find his own source for the alcohol. Nevertheless, hundreds of envelopes came in weekly with postal checks. His red-haired 23-year-old sister opened the envelopes, typed out the orders, and made up mailing labels. I worked in the packing room.

Ours was a peculiar status: we were legal and not legal. Cops and detectives came often enough, including men from the post office; and the illicit joined up with the licit in a financial comraderie of take-and-give-back-a-bit. It was my first experience in a paying-off profession, a small lesson in the developing democracy of the unequals.

When I was not filling or mailing the spiritual essence orders, I went on cultural errands for Mr. M., getting him tickets to George White's *Scandals* or to Mae West's polite little orgies that brought the police to Daly's Theater, or to the Dempsey fights; for Mr. M., unlike his sister, had not heard of Eugene O'Neill's plays, *Dynamo* and *Marco Millions;* nor of Hemingway, who had just written *Men Without Women.* Miss M. had. She had also seen the Irish Players in the Village do Synge and O'Casey. She knew, too, about James Branch Cabell's *Something about Eve* and F. Scott Fitzgerald's *The Great Gatsby,* which she gave me to read, one slow afternoon, before deciding that she might be putting on weight. To find out, would I please help weigh her?

We had a large weighing scale, and she climbed on. She was tall, fleshy, and slightly freckled. I pushed the slides about and she weighed 150 sexy pounds.

"But that's impossible, Harry! I must weigh less without these . . ." and she was out of her shoes, weighing again.

"About a pound less," I said, getting a minor clue to other expectations.

"And without my heavy skirt?"

"Another half pound," I said breathlessly, trying to take in more air.

And she was out of her heavy woolen skirt . . . and then came her slip, her bra, her panties . . . There among the essences, our own chemistry went to work. After that, whenever her brother went out to lunch, we had a weighing-in ceremony.

Once I said to her, "You know that book of formulas your brother uses to make the essences? Well, I'd like to see it. He never leaves it after he makes a batch — why?"

"Because you might steal the formulas, Harry. You might leave and never weigh me again. Would you?"

"Why should I leave you? I love weighing you . . . " We were polite about everything, especially our ceremonials.

The idea about getting hold of the formulas had been given to me by a uniform manufacturer next door. He was a wily Frenchman, once an officer under Foch, which gave him a special rank in the trade. His uniforms made doormen look like Czarist generals; his chauffeurs were more regal than royalty. But his ideas went beyond epaulets. If I copied the essence formulas, he said, as we ate our sandwiches together one lunchtime, "We can set up shop and undersell Monsieur M., Harry. We are not so terrible, yes?"

Since we were only "borrowing" I got hold of the book from Miss M. and one day copied out formulas for the newly created Okay Walton Beverage Company. Within a month the Frenchman and I had a going organization, after hours, amid uniforms, sewing machines and tailor's dummies. We duplicated every formula except the one for Scotch essence. It had a mysterious element in it that Mr. M. merely called "smoke." When I queried Miss M. after a long session on and off the scales, she said, "It's in his head, and he won't tell anybody. Is the Scotch coming out wrong?"

"It's not smoky, unfortunately . . ."

I also "borrowed" Mr. M's customers, copying their names and addresses and noting which essences they bought. To all of them, we sent a sales letter as an opener: prices were cut in half. It worked. We sent samples to the

94

doubtful—and that worked. We had a box at the Main Post Office; and nightly the Frenchman and I went there, collected dozens of letters, went back and filled orders C.O.D. As our business increased, Mr. M.'s skidded down.

Then came the postal inspectors. I had visions of prison, but if I merely went out of business, I hadn't really lost anything. Then came Mr. M., to inspect my lack of loyalty to him. The postal inspectors had been loyal to him and had informed on us. He was wrathful and profane. I faced him in the shipping room, denying nothing. Where had I done it? I kept the Frenchman out of the affair. I had mixed, packed, and shipped the essences from my bedroom. Everything was under my bed, I said. "How much of a business can I carry on under my bed?" Mr. M., a cold man, did not laugh. He said, as I reached for my coat, "If I were Al Capone, you'd be dead already, you prick!" He said it ten times over, with variations.

I got out.

Miss M. called me at my room the same night out of habit (the shipping room had eventually not proved bedroomy enough). Her brother did not know about our relationship. She was suffering from conscience. "I gave you the damned chemical formulas, the addresses—and what did you give me, Harry?" she asked pointedly.

I wanted to say, "I gave you *me*. How many boys take to fat, freckled redheads?" Instead, I said, "My share from the Okay Walton Beverage Company's operations will be about three thousand dollars. You can share that with me."

"But I don't want blood money, Harry! It's all yours, do what you like with it. What *are* you going to do with it, anyway?"

"It's learning money. I'm going to read at the library for a year," I told her.

It was Spring, 1928.

Where the
Lions Never Roared

§

It was a uniquely superior place, with all of mankind's learning layered within its walls. The indifferent stone lions stared their blank guardianship from the steps, ignoring the unwelcome gifts of pigeons and sparrows just as they ignored the intellectuals, the cranks, the unattached, the writers-in-the-making, the critics already made — who had chosen New York's genteel library as their semi-permanent home. And always, milling about, there was the careless crowd not quite listening to the overloud opinions of the fast talkers, the readers, and spielers.

It was an eccentric collection of men and women, a circus of shrill commentators. Each haranguer had his brief moment to hold or lose a fickle audience; too soon, the mob would move on to someone else lampooning the country's gelded morals, its literary outhouses, the two-party political system, or President Coolidge as a representative of American culture. It was a time for philosophers, historians, anthropologists, and Marxists to declare that some new sort of world had just arrived. The cop on the beat was no scholar at all and usually dispersed the philosophers.

Within, the library was also a serious challenge to the questing wanderer who sought the universal truths in the library's encyclopedias. It was a rendezvous of self-applied

97

scholarship, a university without teachers, whose courses were all self-elected. Graduation day never came: the time spent in the third floor reading room was the yardstick used by each educational vagrant to measure his progress toward an imaginary degree.

It was my place, both within and without.

Some of the scholars who were also bums, spent time in the sun panhandling for "coffee and"; others, more alert to the folklore of philanthropy, looked about for slightly crippled pigeons and sparrows. When they found a hurt bird, they took it to the great inventor, Nikola Tesla, who was known as a sentimental pigeon-fancier as well as scientist. To Tesla the bird-lover, a pigeon was worth a dollar; a sparrow came only to fifty cents. One day I found a sad sparrow, and off I rushed to Tesla's hotel. It was not the money, of course; I merely wanted to ask Tesla about my former employers, the Inter-Cosmic Inventors Society.

At his midtown hotel, I was announced by a balding clerk, who phoned up to say, "Mr. Tesla, there is a young man here to see you with a small sparrow. It's the right leg, sir. Shall I send the sparrow up alone?"

I had seen Tesla often at the library. He came, paper bag in hand, to feed not to read, tossing crumbled Melba toast at the pigeons. Tall and elegant, in somber suit and bowler hat, Tesla looked incongruous among the bums and the old ladies. He had a superior non-speech look that made him seem unfathomable to everyone else at the easy-talking library.

Now he took my chirping sparrow into his massive hands, and gently soothed the frightened bird's feathers. Then he reached for fifty cents and was about to bow me out in silence. But at the door, I managed to blurt out, "Mr. Tesla, I used to work for the Inter-Cosmic Inventors Society — and you were one of our most elect members. I swept the offices, I dusted the inventions, and I mailed the invitations to the monthly meetings. But you never once came, Mr. Tesla. Nor did Mr. Edison. Why *not,* sir?"

Tesla smiled. But there was no real meaning in the smile. He patted my shoulder and said, finally, with a slight foreign accent, "Thank you very much, Mr. Cosmic Sparrow . . ." and both he and the bird were locked away.

I felt offended; Tesla had been aloof and anti-social, I decided. But then I recalled, from the library gossip, that Tesla was given to more than just social lapses. I'd heard a story that he had once sent a messenger with a letter addressed to Samuel Clemens, 35 South Fifth Avenue. The messenger returned: no such person, no such address. Tesla, irritated, explained to the messenger: "Mr. Samuel Clemens writes books under the name of Mark Twain — find him!" At the time, Tesla's old friend, Twain, had been dead for two decades.

The library had both its geniuses and its crackpots, and if you could tell the difference — then — you were yourself a genius. One of the loudest and most eloquent of our genius-crackpots was Leon Samson. He was completing a book that was to be published as *The American Mind,* a series of impolite essays that were curiously exciting in their capsule-commentary on our political, social, and psychological folk-lore — our overall social infantilism as America came of age.

Samson was a complex martyr of a man. During the War, as a radical student at City College, he had called for a political strike against the War. He stood up during an assembly — short and bellicose — and called on his fellow students to follow him, but he walked out alone. After that, Samson became a permanent loner, seeking to influence radical thought among the herd-minded. Like Ambrose Bierce, his bitterness and vitriol for things American edged him into unmasked contempt — more for radical intellectuals, union leaders and bourgeois-aping proletarians than for the upper classes; for if Samson accepted anyone, it was the aristocrat who lived *above* such conceits.

Samson had a highly charged sense of social caricature. He told me once, "Do you know what Henry Ford says after breakfast? Ford says, 'I'm going to *work*.' And do you know what his overdressed, over-plump, over-pretentious stenographer says after her morning orange juice? She says, 'I'm going to *business*.' What business is she in? She's in the class-hopping, swapping business. She swaps symbols, thinking that *work* and *business* are interchangeable economic forms of social flattery. The poor slob of a stenographer is a proletarian, not a boss. But she makes everything democratic by proxy." It outraged him.

Samson bristled with venom for many things including the Columbia School of Anthropology. He accused Franz Boas, Ruth Benedict, and Margaret Mead "of slumming on the American Indians every summer. They measure Indian penises and call it cultural anthropology." Others in line for his acrimony were the popular journalists who passed as literary critics. Samson spat, his small body shaking with spleen, as he spoke to the crowd facing the two stone lions: "Our American idiom is rich, not in its subtleties, its shadings, but rather in its robustness, its picture sequences and passion. Our American idiom is less an idea than it is an outcry, less a stimulus to thought than a substitute for thinking, and so it blends best with the cacaphony of the street. Journalism is the genius of America. This is as it should be since journalism is the commerce of literature . . ."

A wandering cop would suddenly become a critic of rhetoric and involve himself by shouting at the mob, "All you bums get a move on, now—scram! Whadda ya think this is—Union Square?"

Samson would push himself up a quarter of an inch, and into a final blast: "Ideas are nothing with a cop around . . .

100

ideas are nothing if they are not aristocratic, exclusive, dictatorial. It is only when they are lacking in originality and virility that ideas become democrats . . ."

The cop, baffled though he might be, would soon send all the wayward scholars scattering. Samson and a seedy vegetarian disciple of his named Red-Tie would then head for Union Square, and more talking time . . . That evening, at the Labor Temple on Fourteenth Street, Samson would deliver one of his explosive free weekly lectures.

He specialized in caricaturing the prophets of American humanism, Paul Elmer More and Irving Babbitt. "If Sinclair Lewis has done nothing else," it gave Samson pleasure to lecture, "he has given the American plebs the pleasure of discovery that they are people worth debunking. Babbitt is a name of derision from Harvard Yard to Iowa pigsties. Irving, Irving Babbitt, the apostle of neoclassicism, is just another literary businessman. Another middleman of our literary and business morals—what happy mixers and marriage brokers of the intellect! Unable to breathe the ether of revolutionary ideas, they would make philosophy, art, literature sociable, by putting it into humanistic working trousers . . ."

Up front as a cheering yea-sayer, was Red-Tie, Samson's all-around one-man claque. Whenever someone disagreed noisily—and that was the only way at the Labor Temple—Red-Tie would point a wiggling finger at the shouting naysayer, and yell out, "You bourgeois bastard!" Red-Tie, who came by the name through having worn the same dirty neckpiece for years, did odd bits of research for Samson, like copying out items on anthropology from abstruse volumes. Red-Tie was a short, thin scholar of parts. His pants, shoes and jacket were handed down, like so much of Red-Tie, to make up an unusual Greek salad of a man. He was thirty, but looked older. A natural iconoclast and rebel, he showed his contempt for normal civilization by setting up camp in a cave in Central Park, and living off vegetables he cadged.

As a dialectical defender of his master, he was like a fretful terrier at meetings. His verbal counter-attacks created some magnificent moments of comedy for everyone present; for Red-Tie, spluttering and spitting, managed to misquote every Marxist writer since Marx. In any rhetorical pinch, he returned to, "You're a bourgeois bastard!" *Bourgeois* came out as "bushwah" in Red-Tie's Americanese; but there was no mistaking the *bastard* part of it.

Red-Tie once undertook a debate entirely on his own. It was to be staged with my new friend, Max, in opposition. The subject: "Will Dogs Bark Under Communism?"

It took place at Lew Ney's coffee house on East 15th Street. Across the street was the socialist Rand School, which we denounced for its non-revolutionary academism in matters of Marxism. The debate had a very proper tone to it. Red-Tie, a dog lover, took the position that communist dogs would not bark. As part of the diseased capitalist-hydrant syndrome, dogs, he argued, were oppressed — barking was just the cry of a hungry dog. Dogs were naturally unhappy in a system of dog-eat-dog. With the general largess of communism, dogs would no longer be anti-social in gardens, against hydrants, and on rugs. Instead, they would be taught by Marxist-trained behaviorists to use "dog toilets, thus coming into their own. And with more meat for the working class," Red-Tie wound up in a blaze of conviction, "there will be more succulent bones for dogs!" Exhausted by his acute presentation, Red-Tie sat down.

When it came Max's turn to talk about the future dog, Max shimmied onto the stage like an accomplished dachshund and barked out his presentation. Red-Tie, howling like a dingo, denounced Max as a clown incapable of serious debate.

§

The Library, despite its characters and occasional minor burlesques, was mostly for the serious. I arrived when it opened and left when it closed, thirteen hours later. Downstairs, the growlers and talkers tore apart man's small progressions toward humanism, then much under debate. American humanism was everything to every critic. As Marxists, we were humanist enough — man must control the machines of capitalism, to serve all men. It was all so very simple!

To the library's elite, men like social-creditor Gorham Munson, estheticians Kenneth Burke, Paul Rosenfeld, and Ernest Boyd, and to the Marxists, Sidney Hook and Charles Yale Harrison, humanism was what they were doing — and each was doing a book. I was doing books too, plowing eagerly through assorted things. I read the English poets because they were easy to get to on the shelves. I read Byron completely, preferring *Don Juan* and *The Bride of Abydos*. Some years later, I passed the ancient spot where Abydos had been. There, in the liquid mist, Byron had swum the Hellespont, and I tried to interest the Turkish skipper with whom I was having a drink, in a few classical considerations.

"Byron? He sounds like another Greek! Leander the same! As for Abydos, ask the First Mate. We need more *raki,* not literature," said the Turk.

From Byron I went to the Russian shelves, to read Pushkin's *Eugene Onegin,* the hilarious take-off on many, including Byron. I read on through Keats, Shelley, and Blake, going back periodically to the Russians. I shuttled from idealism to metaphysics in ungraceful stages of confusion and identity. I was all things each day; and I would scrawl my own poetic lines, mostly eccentric and experimental.

I was experimental because I lacked the prosody to be classical; and I wrote strange surrealist things because I had also read a weird book, Comte de Lautremont's *Chants of the Maldoror,* which threw me off balance. To try to add contemporary sense to my reading, I went through all of the little magazines which printed writers like William Carlos Williams, Marsden Hartley, Hart Crane, Maxwell Bodenheim, Mike Gold, Norman MacLeod, Emjo Basshe — mixing up the lyrical writers with the emerging proletarian scrawlers then preparing for a revolution, at least in letters. Soon I was to meet so many of them, for the library was a permanent forum for new ideas.

It was Max who now became my mentor in Marxism, though he himself was a short-term Marxist. He had a relaxed, restless charm, though he could be thoroughly autocratic in conviction. He was Napoleonic in stature and ready to take over the world with his porcupine-prickly wit. He was a scholar who quoted text and source, but not always exactly so; for like many of us, he preferred a phrase's posture and sound to its accuracy. Max could out-talk anyone, for he was extraordinarily verbal, even in the world of magic that went for learning on the stone steps of the library.

When one of Sidney Hook's lesser protégés (we admired Hook because he'd studied Marxism in Moscow) said that Marxism was not contributing to the decline of the West and that American capitalism would last forever, because it was "revolutionary and exceptional," Max dismissed him as a professional fool, and told him: "Don't bother to read anymore. Just hie yourself to the Civil Service and may your normal stupidity be used in the minor demands the government will make on your sad, disorderly mind . . ."

Max's next challenge was presented by the appearance among us of a famous anthologist from Baltimore, then preparing an anthology on Negro culture in America. He was the victim of exceptional thoughts—ones offering up jazz, the blues, and sad poetry as the main cultural achievements of the emerging Negro.

"You are denigrating the Negro!" yelled Max. "If those are the best samples you can offer, you are anthologizing a cultural fraud. But, then, you've done the same hack-job with psychoanalysis—to titillate virginal schoolteachers. Go back—learn something about cultural prudence from Mencken, since you can't recognize the meaningful of anything, including Harlem. Go, man, go!"

We knew all about Negro culture, especially its superficial aspects. We'd learned it from the Savoy Ballroom and Small's Paradise and from the Interracial Club that we had formed in a bring-your-own-booze joint on West 135th Street. Actually, the club was run by a crippled Negro who fancied would-be writers; and on Saturday nights it was open house for us. We brought the hootch, the fiery Italian *grappa,* and girls, both white and black who had radical minds and radical bodies. They listened to us read poetry. We read it with revolutionary vigor to a background of drums. We read it to the girls with an underlined conception of how the rest of the night might be spent. We argued against racism and extolled equality for all—to begin right then. We had small, modest bacchanals, mostly playful, to show that we were, racially, all American. When the *grappa* got going, the girls would go nude and dance out their own rebellion.

Often, Charles Yale Harrison, then finishing his best novel, *Generals Die in Bed,* would come by, and the party would almost burst with battle between Charley and Max— mostly about James Joyce. Max announced reverently one Saturday night that Joyce's "Anna Livia Plurabelle" had more than one thousand learned allusions about rivers in it. Charley's reaction was, "So Joyce has written the last novel? And no novelist has a right to write after Joyce? Well, I'll

105

write, and without saying fuck on every page, especially since Joyce seldom bothered to do it. Max, you're pregnant —with *merde!*"

"Oh, go take a Joycian fuck for yourself!" shouted Max. "That will certainly give you real 'ego-association' Charley. So fuck yourself again!"

"I would if I could, but I'm not my type," retorted Charley, and it sounded very funny then to all the girls who were dancing in the nude at the Interracial Club.

Charley Harrison had been a hero in the Canadian Army during World War I, a member of the Sacco and Vanzetti Emergency Committee, a wonderfully sharp-scented columnist and a successful novelist. He wrote a biography of Clarence Darrow and he could have used Darrow later in a legal capacity, during his spells of brawling with cane and fist. Spun on by drinking and a swollen ego, Charley could be as tender as a bear—hugging you to death. He loved in his fashion, made friends and lost them, made enemies and kept them, including Harold Ickes, Heywood Broun, and Arthur Garfield Hays. Charley had three wives—and went through an analysis by Dr. Edmund Bergler. (Max said to me, years later, "Charley wasn't analyzed—he was Berglerized.")

On Fridays Harrison held open house, and enemies as well as friends (when we could tell them apart) came for booze, badinage, jazz, and polemics. We were Marxist kibitzers, and we talked violently; for there was much around to be savage about in 1929. There was Al Capone's slaughter of fellow gangsters on St. Valentine's day to help us kid the new images of murder, en masse, to come. Art and poetry had turned surrealist; Mickey Mouse had been invented, and the times were animated. Drinking straight gin, bootlegged, Charley said, "Capone's complaining so sensitively. Listen to this, he just said, 'I haven't had any peace of mind . . . it's

106

a tough life.' Between Capone and Hoover, there goes a nation."

Charley's living room had a ballroom's expansiveness for the sudden folk dancer; and after enough to drink, I often did a Russian *kazatzka,* heading for the high ceiling with carving knives as clashing sabers. A gourmet cook, Charley had a lot of fine cutting instruments in his huge kitchen. He would stand over pots in the kitchen for days, preparing for the eaters and talkers who came: E.E. Cummings, Simone de Beauvoir, Henry Treece, Bernard Wolfe, Mel Pitzele, Max, Kenneth Rexroth, Louis Waldman, Isaac Don Levine, Suzanne La Follette, Paul Sann, Harry Van Arsdale, Fred Woltman. They all came through the years to listen to Charley talking disenchantments. Stomached like a Buddha, he had a face like a mad-bad cherub. Never neutral, always the attacker, it was Charley's style of talking, and not his writing, that gave away the flavor of the man. Stinging with anti-views, endorsing private anarchism, favoring almost nothing, Charley hardly seemed the man he really was—an unhappy sensualist dooming himself with his own appetites.

Because Charley piqued easily, it was easy to fight with him, to stay away, sadly, for many years, and to come back, happily—and to laugh like hell again. I did that twice in our 25 years of fury and friendship, and I called for the last time after Charley had had a heart attack. A hospital room was his literary parlor. There was a bottle, pills, flowers, books—and Charley, still able to laugh.

Five years earlier he'd said, over gin, that Norman Mailer wasn't much of a novelist: "He stinks, up and down. He's nothing between hard covers. His heroes are frauds—and that style! He's *drek!*"

I had said, "He's not shit, Charley, he's got power. Since you haven't read his book, you're better than most critics, but you're just as wrong."

107

"Power, my arse!" snapped Charley. "Mailer's copied every racial stereotype from Dos Passos to the Ringling Brothers!"

Soon the splendor of the evening disappeared along with Mailer's first novel, and I disappeared under a fusillade of Harrison's rioting bombast. It took his heart attack to bring me back to him.

Max and I were totally lost when Charley died in 1954. It robbed our calendar of a night in the week—the Fridays that began during the Depression and went on through the years. Charley had fought endlessly for esteem from the literary critics. He had not become a great novelist. "But who has except Hemingway and Faulkner," Charley had said. "And look what's happened to a simple philosopher— Samson!" Samson had gone, long ago, to the madhouse: a lesser Nietzsche to a lesser dream . . .

§

My days and nights were then economical and socially apportioned. The savings of my brief bootlegging interlude gave me more than just "reading money." I was nearly twenty-one. At night I joined Max, and two poets, Anton and Spector, in Village misadventures. Poetry, though sacred and new to me, was easy to profane in the Village, which had all sorts of open-all-night speakeasies and cafe-terias. On Sheridan Square, there was the limelight-lit Huberts, with Maxwell Bodenheim, not yet the lyrical drunkard, and John Rose Gildea, already the drunkard. One night Gildea was found frozen to the street and had to be ice-picked, dead, from the gutter . . . There was Robert Clair-mont, who was giving away $250,000.00 in fifty-cent drinks at a speakeasy in Minetta Lane; Genevieve, a buxom model and dancer, who took off her Roman toga for us to dance and swim in Washington Square's ecstatic fountain; and Ina, a beautiful English girl who had modeled for Pascin, doing similar gamboling through the Grecian nymph-nights. I had not yet, however, had one poem published.

It was Spector who took up my poetry. The bitterest man I ever knew, Spector was a poet who was published regularly. Ezra Pound, then extolling social-credit economics in Mussolini's Italy, had made Spector one of his faraway poet-protégés, and Spector made me his close-at-hand protégé. Spector was savage, brutal and brilliant, an innovator in poetry, and Pound admired his experiments. Spector came from the upper middle classes and loathed them. He could have been rich had he said *yes* to his father; instead he took shoddy jobs to aggravate the cosmic hatred in his poetry. Spector's father, a hard-headed manufacturer, once had a strike pulled on him by his then-behaving son. But Spector could not stand any sort of physical association with the proletariat in his father's factory; when they came near him or shook his hand, Spector was soon heading for the toilet to wash away the proletarian taint. Always impeccable, he bathed too often and changed his white shirts several time a day. Though frightened of women, he married too early — and remained frightened, rudely unawakened to any joy.

Between his joyless poems and his misery-seeking jobs, he wrote explosive class-complaints to poets and editors. To Mike Gold, then the editor of *The New Masses,* a red-conditioned magazine that published Spector, Spector wrote: "The proletariat must learn all the refinements, become superior and delicate, sensitive to language — and not remain hogs at the trough. Right now they are ugly slobs, sullen goons, incapable of revolutionary or human growth — to be shit upon, like the maudlin middle class."

But it was through Spector's intervention that I had my first poem published. I suspected that I was one proletarian

109

he could accept. I had, by then, done everything with my hands; and now, the whirl of the imagination had jacked me up — to whirl with other revolutionary poets. Spector, one day at the library, took a poem from my pocket, wrote a note, mailed an envelope, and soon my first poem, "Head Over an Orange," appeared in a magazine called *Blues,* edited by two southern gentlemen, Charles Henri Ford and Parker Tyler. I was in the great companionship of experimentalists — Hart Crane, Gertrude Stein, Erskine Caldwell, James T. Farrell, William Carlos Williams, Louis Zukofsky, Harold Rosenberg, Samuel Putnam, Ezra Pound, Horace Gregory, Kay Boyle, and Kenneth Rexroth — and soon other poems, with Spector's few flattering impulsive letters, were to appear in *Pagany*, an esthetic organ . . . and then came the revolutionary periodicals. A magazine in Moscow, *Literature of World Revolution*, mentioned me in a critical essay as "one of the promising revolutionary poets in America." Another essay in T.S. Eliot's magazine, *The Criterion*, related me to surrealism. Finally, Louis Zukofsky, the founder of *Objectivism*, printed me in a special issue of *Poetry* magazine — and he called me an *Objectivist*. But I objected to being in any school. I objected to almost everything else too. It was time to talk revolution. The Public Library on Fifth Avenue had done its work. . . .

Of Minnesingers
and Agitators 1928

§

It was summer. The birds came to the Fifth Avenue Library,
and some of the scholars left for seasonal employment in
the Catskills. They became busboys, waiters, cooks, or
athletic counselors. Others, like the poet-painter Anton
and I became hoboes-with-a-mission.

Once when Dr. A. A. Brill, the translator and popu-
larizer of Freud, came up to see Anton's surrealist paintings, the psychiatrist said in shock, "Young man, your work
is dangerously close to pornography." Anton, who'd had a
whiskey or two during the clinical viewing, replied, "Doctor,
the penis is in your head, not in mine."

Now Anton and I headed West to perform as the minnesingers of revolution. In the spreading cities, in the tighten-
ing villages, we discovered some of the sacred standards
of our stolid American brethren. The new industries had
brought cars, roads, radios, weekends, bootleg joys, tweed
suits — and amoral ease. A great boom was over the country;
but we were two doomsday prophets, burgeoning poets prepared to dig for a funeral-in-the-making. We had read all
the contemporary hosannahs to America's spiritual and
economic strength. Installment buying had given the country
temporary relief. But the next stage, we knew, was the twi-
light of capitalism, of President Coolidge, and normal
American vulgarity.

111

"Money is very vulgar," I said to Anton when we left. "Everybody wants it."

"But not to have it is very awkward," said Anton.

A lumbering freight train got us to Chicago for our first talking stop, the Dill Pickle Club off Bughouse Square. In Bughouse Square, among qualified agitators we tested our ascending values. When we collected a few dollars in a hat after a performance, we knew that we were professional enough to go to other areas of political and literary combustion. Anton, peculiarly handsome, had a fine appreciation of the whimsical and the ridiculous. His Agitprop, which we called exercise poetry, was riddled with inventive nonsense. I did Russian dances in praise of communism, and sang out laments with broad Sandburgian accents, for Chicago's newest crop of murders. Murder in Chicago, right then, was not a subject for entertainment, and a week later we headed for the more innocent hinterland.

At North Platte, Nebraska, we helped assemble an itinerant motordrome. A daredevil motorcyclist was to zoom sideways at 60 miles an hour, defying balance and his future. To add more to the present, ten minutes before the cyclist's act, Anton and I went on in ours. We profaned Wall Street, Main Street, and Washington in free verse. We had stuffed our pockets with quotable new and old items. I read *The Man With the Hoe,* a pictorial elegy to sweat. It was basic opportunism—and a dollar bill floated onto the drome. I read it a second time and got a dime.

The motorcyclist was getting nervous racing his engine —we scrambled up the wobbly ladder and left the other performer to roar about the drome. Up the sides, down the sides, top and bottom—wheels, machine, man, helmet and goggles and fumes. It was an adventure in suicide. A few days later the cyclist went over the top, and our quixotic job ended with a funeral.

The land was brilliant with sunshine and circuses. Across the cricket-hopping plains and the tall cornstalks of Nebraska, we offered up low poetry and buffoonery to the farmers at honky-tonk fairs, hoping to shock them into the realization of approaching doomsday. They stared, laughed rudely, and wondered what sort of New York idiots we were. We made occasional dollars. Vachel Lindsay, the folk poet, made a great deal more, satirizing in a jazzier way America's varied mystiques about God, man and politics.

One day, between changing freight trains, I lost Anton. It was a willing girl, he told me later, who had beckoned to him like a fleshily seducing wraith across the tracks. With Anton gone, I was alone, making a noisy speech in Grand Island, my companion involved in other speechless ecstasies. I was saying, to the five gawkers who made up a crowd near the station, "Goddamn the president, he's cutting the taxes of the capitalists and cutting your throats. He won't help you— the farmers. Agriculture is your bloodstream, but to hell with your bloody stream, says Coolidge. Coolidge is anti-union and anti-working class; so damn that little man!"

I'd read it all in the *Daily Worker* a few days earlier. But saying it out loud soon had me on my way to the local jail.

"I agree with you," said the kind arresting cop. "I was a Wobbly ten years ago. But you can't use *damn,* damn it!" After a free hamburger dinner, I was locked up in a kindly way, given a book to read, and bedded down for the night.

At five in the morning I was fed again, driven far out of town by another cop, in a sidecar motorcycle, and lost in the Nebraska prairies. I talked to the birds, damned Coolidge some more, ate raw corn, swam in a stream, washed my shirt, whistled, and fell asleep under a tree, too dizzy at high noon to go on. Butterflies and grasshoppers were my companions, hitched to wings and kangaroo-hopping legs. I walked again, disconsolate and lonely. Occasionally a

113

farmer's haying wagon rolled by, and a waving hand saluted me from under a straw hat. I saluted him, his horse, his hay, and walked on, dusty, thirsty, hungry.

I heard someone calling. I saw arms awave from the windows of a slowing car. It was Anton and a Chicago bootlegger he had met, named Tony. Tony drove a big green car and was out collecting. He was heading for Los Angeles to collect or to kill someone, said Anton. Then he told me, vividly the details of his seduction by the girl at the railroad tracks.

Tony was big, and he was stuffed with welcome cash, which he was very generous about doling out. He bought us steaks at any hour of the long-riding day that we were hungry. He had Canadian whiskey for immediate consumption, and I took steady nips to acquaint my stomach. Because of our ragged clothes, he stopped at a store. Soon we had straw hats, "Because that goddamn sun gonna kill you guys if you have to walk again. Here, kids, try on some pants, too."

Tony loved us at once—our mad talk, our wild poetry, and our tough attitudes.

"If we weren't poets, we'd be gangsters, Tony," I said cheerfully. "But poetry reduces the criminal tendencies in a sensitive man. It purges him and makes him content to be poor and dignified."

"But all that goddamn stuff didn't keep you out of jail last night, Harry."

"It was Marxism and not pure poetry, last night, Tony."

"Tony, are you killing someone in Los Angeles?" asked Anton with a laugh that was more nervous than carefree. "Because if you are, could you let us off in Arizona?"

"I'm just *collectin'*, fellas. Come on, teach me some poetry—in case I ever need to feel purged . . ."

"Okay, Tony," said Anton. "I'll make up the first line and you make up the second. Here goes—'Once there was a man—Capone.' Take over, Tony,"

114

Tony, puzzled, searched for a rhyme praiseworthy enough. When he got it, he spewed out his delight, spitting Scotch all over us: "Who as a gangster is no fuckin' phony!"

"You're another Chicago Rimbaud," said Anton. "You're an extraordinary versifier, Tony. Jesus, what an oblique rhyme!"

After another rhyming session for him, and another free meal for us, Tony stuffed a ten-dollar bill into one of our pockets, and dismissed our thanks with, "It's nothing. I mean, it's *nuttin'* at all. You got me talking like you guys. You're killin' me with the language and that poetry crap!" Tony was a noble kind of Chicago gangster, all heart, whiskey, money and guns.

By Denver, the green car broke down. The main gear was stripped. Tony asked us to wait around for a week, "Until that sonofabitch of a mechanic fixes it, fellas. Come on, we'll make this town turn greener, blacker, redder, pinker— all them Rimbaud poem-colors!" Anton had talked about Rimbaud's contribution, and Tony liked the fact that Rimbaud had been a celebrated gun-runner in Ethiopia and was "a tough bastard—he had four black wives. Imagine that, Tony!"

Tony imagined; and so did we, about Tony's coming "collection."

We said a sad good-bye. More money was stuffed into our loose pockets. We'd meet again in Los Angeles for a ride back to Chicago. We'd meet Al Capone. We'd tell Capone about Rimbaud. We'd recite poetry, too, and Tony was saying, "So long, you fuckin' agitators!"

§

At the Grand Canyon we sneered grimly. Anton spat; I pissed. It was a hole in the ground for rich tourists. A former member of the I.W.W. seeing it had once said, "God-damn that capitalist scenery!" But Hollywood, when we

115

got there, was even worse to our Marxist eyes. It was a cult-ridden repository for every lunacy.

We went to Sister Amy Semple McPherson's million-dollar Angelus Temple to brood on America's spiritual greatness. A halo of brethren-gladness hung about Sister McPherson as she exorcised the devil in her chaste, white-streaming, cross-embossed robes. As her voice, her face, her figure, and her words took her audience to glory, we brooded on as hungry, spiritless malcontents. (Two years earlier there had been a sex scandal . . . for Sister McPherson had gone to the devil at a seaside resort, taking a male organist along.)

Anton and I were turning acidy. Ten oranges a day for a nickel was our diet with Tony and his gangster money gone. We were feverish, expecting some materialistic revelations, like steak and potatoes for us. But when nothing developed besides theatrical chastity on the holy platform, Anton, angered, called out, "Oh, you enchanting wench! Let us commit spiritual fornication . . . ah, Priapus!" And out we ran, with ushers and the devil after us. We sought other playgrounds.

After two weeks on Hollywood and Vine, on Pershing Square, and in the Japanese and Mexican districts, Anton said, "If I wanted to stay, I'd start a cult for nymphs and satyrs. I bet you could find a hundred men with small green horns coming up out of their foreheads, as well as a hundred ladies just as horny. Do you believe, Mr. Roskolenko? Would you go for the pastoral life?"

"Verily! Let's find it . . ."

We caught a bus. Three hours later, we took jobs as fruit pickers in the lush Sacramento Valley.

It was oranges, lemons, and grapes at thirty cents an hour. Soon we were stuffed with vitamin C and tired of diarrhea. We tried other food for strength, but it cost money and we needed that for our trip back. We tried to pull a strike to raise the hourly scale. We argued with ten fellow fruit pickers to join us. They joined themselves in vague answers. More or less alone, Anton and I addressed the three husky brothers who owned the orchards, "Gentlemen, another nickel won't make you poorer! Do you want to see the bones on our rib cages?" I pulled up Anton's shirt and pointed to his normally skinny body. "Do you want him to *die?*"

"You start a union," answered one burly brother, "and our dogs go to work. Are you working, talking, or walking?"

We talked on for that extra nickel an hour . . . and soon two visible wolfhounds were growling. The other pickers went back to the fields, to work. Anton and I stood rooted and argumentative, with my shirt now coming up. I was far from skinny.

The dogs barked louder. We wanted a nickel more, and they wanted to bite. Feeling suddenly stalemated, Anton shouted, "You're a bunch of no-good bastards! Pay us off, and we'll scram out of here!"

Both the dogs and the brothers went for us.

We ran, shinnying up two nearby apple trees. Twenty feet off the ground, I howled down, "Okay, so no nickel, gentlemen. Get those goddamn dogs away. Just pay us and no more talk — okay?"

The dogs were locked up, Anton got a mild poke on the jaw from a brother, and our first strike was over. Paid off, we were two tame poets as we ran from the orchard, heading now for San Francisco to see Kenneth Rexroth, another poet and agitator of sorts, whom Anton knew.

The Valley, hot and artificial, bloomed with unpicked fruits. The land was spongy and acrid. It was a massive conglomeration of fruit, canals, dikes, and human enterprise; but the Bank of America owned most of it, including the men. The nickel we wanted would have come from the

Bank, and we threw stones at imagined fat bankers. The sun was fiery. We thirsted. We walked emptily, the orphans of Marxism rather than the children of Israel. At a canal, fearing sunstroke, we waited in the shade.

A truck came by with two farm girls, and soon Anton was asking them to swim with us. One, a redhead of about twenty, agreed; the other, older and fatter, shook her head, saying, "But we don't have bathing suits. We can't go in nude."

"That's the way Eve went in swimming—and then came Adam," said Anton.

After that it was shrill laughter all around.

"Clothes are for the ugly," said Anton. "And both of you are beautiful. You have ambiance, certitude, and illusiveness. Let's have a fertility rite to fecundity! Let's confront the origin of all mankind!"

But there was no such pixyish fertility confrontation. The redhead waded in, skirt held high; but the fat one sat by the sluice, chewed an apple, tossed the core at the redhead, then said to Anton, "What do all them funny words mean?"

"They mean you're spontaneous. You have inner regard for central cosmic imperatives. So, prithee, lift thy skirts—and go maritime!"

"He's crazy, all right," said the fat girl. She waded in, asking, "Is this cosmic enough?"

"Ah, Samoa in primitive California!" said Anton. "Think what Margaret Mead would say!" Anton and I, disrobing prudently, went in with our shorts on. We were shy satyrs ...

We dried in the orange grove and picnicked on the chicken, bread, and tomatoes the girls had with them. It was all very good.

§

San Francisco was another country, the coast of Bohemian Barbary, thrumming with Mediterranean colors and

118

energies. It made us drunk to walk up and down the hilly streets, looking at the lovely legs of girls. They had calves like ballet dancers, and from their bottoms to their breasts, they fascinated us. Rexroth's house was near North Beach.

He was on his second book of poetry, and we admired his total act of creation: a book between covers. Anton and I had only bits and pieces of scribbled papers, a few published poems, and a hundred envies — and we sat and drank poems and red wine and listened to Rexroth, who was also a mountain climber. That meant more envy. He was also a teller of taller tales, with a special perception for the raconteur's relationship to his naïve guests.

Rexroth, too, was wandering around among political ideas as if he were exploring a literary relief map of the times — testing out communism, socialism, and anarchism. He had just read a book, *The Right to Be Lazy,* but he himself was ambitious and impatient. The anarchist was emerging by the shortest political route — Rexroth, personalized and explosive. He was a man of nature, Whitmanesque to the large black hat. His mind was an oriental garden: he thought a great deal about Chinese and Japanese poetry, which he later came to translate, as well as French and German works. He had a fruitful, surging personality; when he was not charming, he could be rude, with the massive Germanic conceit of an ego straining against all of history. He was the red king of the forest primeval brought up to date in San Francisco.

In 1928, we talked about death as we drank the lively bootlegged wine. I said, romantically, that the land was inhospitable to, in fact was killing off, its minnesinger poets, who were its moral messengers. I mentioned the need for roots, and that I had none; the need for loving, and that I was not in love then; the need for myths, and that only Hart Crane was creating a myth about the Brooklyn Bridge; and the need for living, occasionally, in the American wilderness

119

to purge yourself of every city-killing artifice . . . and Rexroth liked that. We became friends for the next thirty years, with due explosions over the rude awakenings that our varying personalities brought. Once, Rexroth, in an amiable burst at my apartment, said, "You know, Harry, we're two of the most disliked people in the United States—we're uncompromising bastards!"

"Are you trying to flatter us? Who hates us for being 'uncompromising'? The editors of literary magazines? Or poets who ass-lick their way up and down entire editorial boards? Or the Foundation fraternities? Do you fancy yourself as the Bastard Laureate of America, Kenneth?"

Rexroth was hardly listening. His eyes were in my mirror and he was watching himself grow into an uncompromising bastard. . . .

During that first visit to San Francisco, the red wine made Anton all the more surrealist. He constantly recited nonsense epics that annoyed Rexroth's standards of lyricism. He'd sing out something like:

> There was a little feather
> That met another feather . . .
> They never got together
> For the good Lord said—
>   "No ditherly, no ditherly,
>   There is no ditherly feather."

> One little feather cried,
> The other little feather sighed—
> "We'll never get together."
> For the good Lord said—
>   "No ditherly, no ditherly,
>   There is no ditherly feather."

Anton once interrupted a serious remark of Rexroth's by suddenly saying, "Kenneth, the trouble is, your name's

120

not Ezra. How can you be a serious poet with a name like Kenneth? It has the wrong antecedents. Why even Sam, from Samuel, or Abe, from Abraham, would be better. Kenneth is not Biblical or savage enough, Mr. Rexroth."

It did make Rexroth laugh.

Many years later, when I came home from the war in New Guinea, I stayed at his home again. I had a bad case of malaria, and all through dinner with other Rexroth guests, I was heady with fever. Sweating and almost out of my head, I excused myself for bed. I undressed, got into bed, felt imagined loving arms take me, and I fell asleep — burning up. Then I heard laughter. I had mistaken Kenneth's wife's bedroom for mine, and Marie had been in bed all along. At the door stood Rexroth and the other guests howling at my malarial disorder. I bowed out as best I could to find the second best bed. In the morning, Rexroth, an indefatigable autographer of books wrote out a Tu Fu poem in Chinese ideogram, to celebrate my arrival, if not my departure to the second bed.

Anton and I left Rexroth's poetic encampment and made it to Montana on freight trains, to work in the blazing wheat fields. It was five dollars a day for fourteen hours under the sun on the wide land. At night we slept in an open barn, five blankets over us, shivering, talking, planning. All day we followed the combines that waddled through the gold-tipped wheat; as the bound sheaves left the combine, we stacked the sheaves to fill up the trucks that followed. We turned brown and gold, happy with the natural noises of the prairie. The crickets chipped the air, the combines rattled their cutting machinery, and all was soft in the windy wheat that stood like huge wreathes. It was very good.

Not long before, it had been very bad. At Grant's Pass in Oregon, we were pulled off the road by a sheriff to fight a nearby forest fire. If you didn't fight it, you went to jail and so we fought it for 24 hours, along with hundreds of local farmers. We were trucked up the mountains to the flaming timber land. We built trenches, made back-fires, cut down huge trees, to try to contain the blazing, rushing destruction. It was stopped eventually, but we felt stopped, too—all feelingless. Our muscles, chests, eyes, and throats smoked out, we waited until the sheriff paid us our 35 cents an hour. At Grant's Pass Rogue River we lay and slept . . . then I swam, caught cramps, and went down . . .

I was midstream. Anton was on the shore, several hundred feet from me. He couldn't swim, but he could shout. I went under a second time and had visions. How easy death was—you took in water, and the water quieted you. The past returned, pressured back in the brain—and I saw memories, miseries, love, and hate—and the past was drowning me. I saw my Hamburg days, and Anna; my father's many angers and my mother's many softnesses; my brothers, all towering ambition . . . and I numbed. Nature was swallowing me and my uncertainties.

I came up again, my arms stroking; I was swimming through some vast unconsciousness that said, "Don't drown now! You can always die another time. Keep on stroking . . ."

I neared the other shore. A man who had heard Anton yelling waded in to grab me. And there was Anton, too, saying, "How would I have written home that you were dead? How does a poet write a sad letter?" We embraced, Russian style.

We rolled on to Plentywood, Montana, to visit with the Trotskyist labor editor, T. J. O'Flaherty. T. J. was the brother of Liam O'Flaherty, whom we admired for his lyrical naturalism and his Irish novels. But Tom was another sort, boozing away his gaunt rebellions. Many years later he spent a summer at my apartment on East Houston Street, to finish his book *Man of Aran*. Then he went home with his

American ulcers to the bare Aran Islands off the Irish coast to die from laboring over booze. In Plentywood he edited a labor paper as well as a small satirical magazine, *The Wasp*. He was fine when the bottle was opened, then all remorse when it emptied — and there was tomorrow morning. Tom had a poet's warmth, Irish magic, and morbidity; and we watched him empty bottles as we talked Trotskyism and talked about Liam, then offending all of Ireland with his novels.

Some writers wanted to live, and some wanted to die. They lived in the beauty of the mountains, gardens, rivers, valleys — hating nature. Everything was whiskey, bottled infantilism. To answer for Marxism's inadequacies, there was the bottle, to die a little more every day . . .

Once I made up a private list of the boozing, fighting, dreaming men who had created their own carnivals of death. My resemblances to them were few, for I had neither the facility nor the stomach to die like that. I preferred my own non-bottled wildness, the wilderness that I was to find when I began to write odd books about odder places that I traveled to. But there were so many of those embattled men with bottles . . .

There was Philip Kling who could recite Pound's poetry with exalting freshness. I saw him, tall, curly-haired, an actor-poet, justifying his love for Ina — and I heard the cadences:

No, no, go from me
I have left her lately.
I will not spoil my sheath with lesser brightness, . . .

Phil hanged himself one day — an early arrival to Madison Avenue's word factories; advertising was not poetry. Ina was, but she'd left Phil for the English countryside. And Hart Crane, briefly on Madison Avenue, and our most original lyric poet, a friend of Anton's — Crane suicided in

123

the sea. There was Bill Cooper, proletarian, ironworker, who had fought in the civil war in Spain — a suicide, politically, morally, then physically . . . and how the bottle took them all! Vachel Lindsay, the same, via Drano. Charles Yale Harrison, via all the pills he had and some parts gin, by spontaneous combustion. And the Spectors, from inner and outer hatred; the Dylan Thomases, from beer when the lyrical expectations did not balance with love and cash on the American earth. And even Anton, who managed to escape, and live, after ten trips to Bellevue's alcoholic ward . . .

Years later, in my house, Kenneth Rexroth taped an angry, all-indicting poem which celebrated the death of his friends through off-side American ways . . .

But in 1928, there seemed so much for Anton and me to do, to see, and be. This had been our journey, his and mine. It had been brief and ill-balanced, but we were maturing — with comedy and pain — and getting ready for the Depression.

The Politics of
Unreality

§

The Trotskyist garden of mixed fruit, germinated by Pop, in Hamburg in 1927, bore their revolutionary plums early for me in 1929. I had read and heard enough to believe that all that was terribly wrong could be righted only by world revolution.

In the factionalized American Communist Party, a three-way split was exposing the differences between the attractive left, (Trotskyists) the muddled center (Stalinists) and the Lovestone opportunist right wing. Stalin believed in socialism in *one* country—for the Soviet Union; Trotsky said that this nationalistic formula was a betrayal of international Marxism; that socialism could only succeed if it had other revolutionary countries on its side to help it against the large capitalist countries. Stalin, said Trotsky further, was also sacrificing the German communist movement for his own opportunistic reasons; he was allowing Hitler to grow stronger by keeping the German communists from joining with their proletarian brothers, the socialists, in fighting Hitler.

With my revolutionary idealism, I sided totally with the Trotskyists. I was told by their leaders to join the official Communist Party, to bore from within as their secret agent; to spread, quietly and subtly, Leon Trotsky's opposition to Stalin's policies on world-wide political and economic questions.

To spread ideas, Max, others, and I began a theater, the Pro-Lab (Proletarian Laboratory Theater) to make revolutionary converts through the dramatic arts; the theater, after all, was a way to bring home the reality of the times. Max had some experience—a brief interlude with the visiting Irish Players, doing Synge; and I, some briefer participation in Hamburg, with Agitprop plays. Anyone who looked proletarian enough was a natural actor for us. I myself could always play a dock walloper, a miner, or a sailor. My voice, too, was strictly for working class plays.

A small loft, one flight up at 231 East Ninth Street, became our showcase for ideas. We hauled and hammered lumber to make a collapsible stage, sans proscenium, for all our illusions had to be totally visible to our audiences, composed largely of shapeless, sexless school teachers slumming for whatever experience they could find. We built hard benches for their scholarly bottoms, and we wrote rugged plays (admission one dollar) to agitate their gentle middle-class sensibilities. And what plays!

Since we drew upon the ranks of the proletariat for all of our creative bombast, we had declassed kibitzers turn into ravaging actors. Stanislavsky-ridden house painters and postal workers became our scene-makers, and pressers and idle junior intellectuals wrote our Americanized rewrites of Gorky's "Lower Depths." Max and a creative furrier named Alex were our most promising playwrights. They drew upon events reported in *The World* and *The New York Times:* most often, the strikes in the mines of Pennsylvania and Illinois.

Max had never been down a mine, but his inexperience hardly restrained the rigorous style of his harrowing dramas. I remember one bit of dialectical dialogue between a wife, whose husband had just been killed in a mine, and the mine boss:

126

Wife: My husband is dead. How shall we eat?

Mine Boss: Go and dig coal, ma'am.

Wife: I can't. I have six young boys at home. *What shall* I do?

Mine Boss: Have them dig coal and they'll grow up to be men sooner. We need apprentices. Coal means money!

Wife: Coal means death! Coal is a grave! Coal is murder — you murderer!

Alex who lived solely on ham sandwiches, was a bit more tender as a playwright. His work was a mixture of Dion Boucicault, Hemingway and Horatio Alger. In one scene we heard this dialogue between young lovers in a fur factory:

Sam: Alice, I'd climb Mt. Kilimanjaro for you! I'd face tigers, lions, and leopards for you. But this fur factory is a terrible jungle — I can't face those devouring bosses. I'm going to quit Alice . . . But I love you, my darling.

Alice: Stop climbing! Stop facing tigers! What you need, Sam, is a union card, not Mt. Kilimanjaro . . .

Some of the hundred teachers, professors, artists, and garment workers in our audience applauded with revolutionary hurrahs, but most reacted with uncharitable titters. Soon we gave up the Stanislavsky method of acting. (Also, a leading Method-Mummer, whom we had once asked to direct one of our fervent plays, had wanted to be paid, an unheard of thing!)

We hired, for "nothing," Jasper Deeter of the Theater Guild to direct our first full-length proletarian play, *The Greatest Boob in the World*. It was written by Karl Wittvogel, then a German anthropologist, but now an expert Sinologist.

In 1929 the concept of *proletarian culture* was everybody's sacred bull. We assured ourselves we were helping

127

to create a worker's theater. In Greenwich Village, at the old German Theater on Grove Street, John Dos Passos, then loved by the transitory radicals, had his play, *Airways Incorporated*, flying through the proletarian balconies, and we sat there and applauded. Uptown, we saw the Theater Guild do O'Neill's *Dynamo*. New images of America were bursting onto the stage—but, oddly, as if unconcerned with proletarian economics, Henry Ford, in Detroit, was undermining our revolution by bribing his oppressed workers with a two-dollar-a-day raise.

We also watched neurotic, bourgeois entertainment. Ibsen was playing within the gaunt walls of the Civic Repertory, things like *Hedda Gabler* and *A Doll's House,* both plays running wild with symbolism and suicide, with the id and the libido. Psychoanalysis had not been accepted, as yet, by the Marxists, but we knew the symbolism being used in Eva Le Gallienne's citadel of decadence. The Civic Rep gave us plays without miners, plays without furriers, just the sick bourgeoisie dying all over themselves. They were corrupted from within by capitalism, we said.

Our own Pro-Lab Theater may not have been "art," but it was energetic. We killed the English language along with our miners, but how joyful were our dramatized denunciations! One of our best actors was Jake Shakespeare, a lovable wall-eyed character who later did bit parts for Clifford Odets and Elia Kazan. Jake knew all the plays of his acceptable namesake but preferred herring and potatoes to mead and roast beef.

And as much as Jake loved Shakespeare, he loved baseball more. At a crucial World Series game when the Giant player, Bobby Thompson, a Scot, went up to bat, Jake, who had a mighty voice, yelled out through the Polo Grounds, "Lay on, MacDuff!" Thompson layed it on and belted the ball over the center field fence to win the game.

128

As for Jake doing Shakespeare, Jake, all five feet short, completely wall-eyed, did a Hamlet on our Pro-Lab stage that never wert before nor after. Jake occasionally came up with inventive phrases, some of which were paid for by Odets to incorporate in his plays. To Jake, the water in public drinking fountains was "municipal champagne." An "East-West answer" meant no. A "Pro-Anti" was a *liberal*.

Ours was a combative theater, raging with Leftist views, challenging all of capitalist culture, but especially Wall Street.

§

Then suddenly "it" came, and they jumped from on high that week. I saw one body flying downward on Irving Place, and soon the police had a tarpaulin over the smashed body of an investor in Wall Street, which had crashed that day. Soon the apple-sellers appeared in front of the gilded burlesque house, and the bread lines formed. . . .

By a fluke, I got myself a job, working for the City of New York. I was a substitute drawbridge operator on the seven city bridges over the Harlem River. I had once, when one of my ships was anchored alongside the Willis Avenue drawbridge, been taught how to operate its huge machinery by an Irish engineer, Tommy, who had something else in mind for me — Father Coughlin's fascistlike orations, which Tommy was selling me with the bridge. For a month I was at the levers and the gears ignoring Tommy's proselytizing prattling for the talking Father from Detroit. But, Tommy knew his pistons, if not his politics, and I was all eyes as I memorized the bridge's exciting machinery. It was like a stationary ship, brassy with switches, with huge circling gears, and great turn-tables thick with grease and oil. Daily, when not on my real ship's watch, Tommy would take me through dry and wet runs; then he saw me through the Civil Service examina-

129

tion. I passed it and forgot about it when my ship sailed away from the drawbridge. Now I was back. Tommy was gone, retired to a wet old age — to the bottles in Ireland — and the city had a rare kind of a poet-engineer in me.

I was full of free verse, soon enough writing pieces to scows and tugs and cantilever arches and the boozing Irish proletariat. The embottled bridge attendants and oilers, my colleagues, arrived drunk and left drunk. They belonged to Tammany. They were loyal sons, filled with the sweet sustenance of Civil Service — and bath-tub gin.

It took four full minutes for the bridge to open and five minutes for the bridge to close. When a tug approached, downstream, it whistled three times. I blew an answer — for the attendants to clear the bridge and close the gates. When all was clear, I started the engines, and the bridge swung out. The tugs and their tows passed, and I closed the bridge. But there were few tugs towing barges that year, and often I would go all day without opening the bridge once; to pass the ecstatic time, I had my typewriter, and a desk for poetry. It was a lyrical life in the Civil Service. After my daily eight hours on the bridge, I had my subterranean life in the Communist Party, which I had joined for Trotskyist reasons.

At the Party meetings, there were nights of study and instruction in Marxist theory; and there were nights for agitating, organizing street meetings to gather in possible dissidents. Within a year, the branch that I belonged to in the Bronx doubled its membership as we enrolled the angry and the frightened, the employed and the unemployed, as well as some future spies for the Soviet Union.

Meetings were held in a small building on Intervale Avenue, between a grocery store and a hardware store. It was shabby in the accepted style, with folding chairs and a smell of dust, mimeograph machines, and tobacco. It was snotty and filthy and loud with speeches. Everybody snarled and

130

nobody smiled. The walls were plastered with signs an-
nouncing meetings, protests, picnics. It was sickening to the
soul and hardening to the artery.

It was a rendezvous for subjectivity and class vengeance.
Each had his reasons for joining; mine was the consciousness
of being a Jew. I'd had inequality sewn in my heart as a child
on Cherry Street during the wild fighting to keep alive. Communism, Trotskyism, meant equality. It meant an end to
poverty. It meant the beginning of human intelligence in
handling all social problems. Yet, I constantly reviewed my
reasons for being a radical as if I suspected myself for entering into this moral challenge. I did not love all the people.
I loved, then, all the *ideas*.

When a section leader in the Communist Party heard that
I was operating the bridge, he became instantly conspiratorial.
He wanted to know if, during an armed insurrection in the
Bronx, an open drawbridge could be frozen in that position?
Shades of the Kronstadt sailors at St. Petersburg in 1917!
But, if the Bronx must become a drawbridge bastion, I was
the engineer to make it one, I said. Gears could be smashed
if violence was needed, or I could merely sabotage a few
minor things. We played with these thoughts for a few months,
with occasional written reports about my contributions
toward taking over the Bronx some hot night.

The unemployed rioting in the streets — before City
agencies, charities, welfare organizations, emergency centers
for feeding — had now reached beyond one of Mayor Walker's
convivial solutions: that the movies show only happy films.
Work and wages had disappeared. A lady with a fifty thousand dollar emerald ring offered it for twenty-five thousand
dollars as a symbol; and even Babe Ruth took a ten thousand
dollar wage cut for hitting balls into the bleachers. I, however,
was earning almost a hundred dollars a week. I kept my two-
room apartment in Paradise Alley on East Eleventh Street

well-larded for down-and-out friends and comrades. Keys were handed out. Large salamis hung in the kitchen and there was bread and wine. There were records to play, and it was not a year of the locusts there.

One day, the Willis Avenue Bridge almost fell down, and I was the chief comic engineer of the affair. A tugboat pulling two barges blew for the bridge to open; I started the gears going and the bridge swung out wide. Just then a fire truck clanged for the bridge to close—and that was mandatory. A few blocks away a tire factory was blazing. I pulled the levers for the bridge to close. The fire truck went over the bridge but the tug and the barges, unable to hold back against the incoming tide, crashed into the bridge, smashing booms and the pilot house.

Instead of being fired, I was praised by the Fire Department for my keen reflexes, and the City of New York paid out $20,000 in damages to the Sullivan Towing Company. (Later in the Depression, when I was jobless, I was called in as an expert witness in maritime matters on the Harlem River. I got fifty dollars a day for two lovely weeks of watching the City's legal department at work.)

I was on the bridge seven days a week, without time off. After a year of this, I wanted a Sunday in the park, a swim in the summer, a day away from the gears and the boozing Irishmen. I had money but no liberty; and I would roll out of bed, after a night of poetry and propaganda, and an occasional girl, to dress in the wintry dark, take busses and subways, lunch in hand, shifting from bridge to bridge every three weeks. It was painful, clockridden, challengeless. It was a cushy job for an old man. I was twenty-three . . .

Restless, I challenged the City and formed the Drawbridge Workers Union. As its charter member, I called meetings to redress my complaints. I wrote leaflets to try to impress the Irish: I called on them to remember the Irish

Republican Army, Ireland Risen, and the Easter Rebellion. The Irish of New York, however, preferred meekness, whiskey, and seven days of "labor." It was the end of the Drawbridge Workers Union.

Soon I was under charges by the Department of Plant and Structures. I was a communist, they said. I tried stalling. I had only given out leaflets to form a union, I said. But the initial charge stuck, and I was fired. Lugging my typewriter and my bombastic leaflets, I walked into the Depression—all gloom off the Willis Avenue Bridge. It was winter, a time of desperations—and loving . . .

I shared all of it with a girl named Friede, whom I had met at a crusading May Day Parade. She was in a Greek toga, sandaled. She was *saftig* and pretty and virtuous. Russian-born, she was sixteen, and studying to be a pianist. She liked modern composers, like Varese. She came to my apartment one night. My wind-up phonograph played scratchy bits of a broken Brahms requiem. A novel by Stendhal was on the floor, pushed there suddenly. Cheese, crackers, and wine . . . black candles burning, the wind blowing up the cloth curtains . . . and the Italian neighbors in the courtyard were calling out, saying nice words in Italian to each other . . . and there were yards of her soft hair bunching into my pillows, and it was love, all tenderness and marveling magic.

Friede's father owned a fat little grocery store in Browns-ville, and she came laden thrice a week with assorted things from her father's bulging stocks. I wrote a poem, published in *Poetry Magazine*, to honor her father's house. A month later I converted her two brothers to total Trotskyism, for I had also been expelled from the Communist Party.

I had spoken up freely one night to say that Stalin was ruining the revolution—and out I was. I has been fired by the City for agitating and by the Communist Party for the "purity" of my revolutionary ideas. But I took along four communists,

133

all garment workers, who, by joining the Trotskyist ranks, swelled it to 156 members in all of North America, just one continent on the road to world revolution. We were visionaries with great programs, if few members, at our grimy offices at 84 East Tenth Street, a street given over to pool parlors, Bowery bums, and artists. It was a street for talking and sharing our antipathy for the communists, a street with squat little houses and stores balanced evenly between bohemian antics and poolroom bedlam.

Across from us, the fabulous anarchist, Carlo Tresca, had his editorial office. Often he bumbled by, large-hatted, his black tie flowing, and yelling something about "da bomba business" to us. Hated by communists and fascists, by gangsters in unions, Tresca was killed during the Second World War while walking on Fifth Avenue. It was a political assassination, we thought, with fact and mystery blending.

Our weekly newspaper, *The Militant*, came out every two weeks or every month when we were exacting. I wrote for it on occasion to practice animated social reporting, or I rewrote stories from the capitalist daily papers to fit our editorial needs. It was easy to create dramatic situations in a country going to the dogs; or I proofread the work of others and changed what I did not like. And when the paper finally rolled off our flat-bed press, I folded it, pasted on the addresses of our thousand universal subscribers, and sold it at our street meetings.

One rain-soaked, wintry night, in 1932, I attended a communist rally at which Louis Engdahl, a professorial looking leader of the Communist Party, was discussing the coming fate of Germany. Engdahl still had Stalin's illusions: Hitler would last only six months—the communists would force him out. "Be assured, comrades," Engdahl assuaged his huge audience, "the Nazi swine will rule in the grave by the end of 1933. They are being put in by the international capitalist masters of fascism. We must expose the social-fascist nature of the Socialist Party leadership . . ."

It was pure communist idiocy, and I said so when I finally managed to get the floor. I was quaking, but I spoke out angrily: *"You* will rule from the grave, comrade communists — not Hitler. Communists, the socialists, and all those opposed to Hitler must join ranks. We should forge a real united front. Stop this prattling about socialist leaders being *social-fascist.* It is a meaningless word, invented by Stalin. Stop your divisive tactics, Comrade Engdahl . . . ," I finished yelling, as the cat-calls came from Engdahl's front-bench claque.

Engdahl, fuming, yelled back at me, "You Trotskyists take your lives in your hands when you come here to make counter-revolutionary speeches. I am not responsible for anything that happens to you when you leave!" It was at least an invitation to beat hell out of me . . .

When I left the meeting, I stood at the rainy, windy, crowded entrance. I sold *The Militant,* shouting, "Get the truth about Germany! Let us fight Hitler and not each other, comrade communists." I was anxious about Germany, about Anna and Pop in Hamburg. Pop had written to me a week ago to say that Hitler had made gains even in Communist-controlled Hamburg.

Then it happened, Engdahl's invitation to my slaughter. Three leather-jacketed communists jumped me. My papers went flying. One foot went to my mouth, another to my groin. The out-going crowd merely made a circle to egg on their comrades. It was a murderous circus. A foot went to my mouth again. I managed to get up once, to take a boxing stance, stupidly . . . The next round of kicks, with six arms also flaying at me, sent me out. I woke up in St. Vincent's Hospital. Three teeth were gone and my testicles were hardly in a masculine shape.

135

A socialist dentist, not sympathetic to my politics, but to my poetry, gave me a free dental bridge to span the opening in my upper jaw; and a doctor sympathetic to my politics, and not to my poetry, did all the restoration necessary for my testicles. It was a baptism in Stalinist violence; it was communism in action. We were the gentler folk, the people of ideas. We could talk, and we talked to everybody. Men should use their ears, not their fists, we said. But that hardly helped us when confronted by the communists out to shut us up at every street meeting. Hitler was in power, and he was remaining in power. It was Walpurgisnacht in Germany.

There was murder, too, on Avenue A and Seventh Street, one Saturday night in August. It was our usual street meeting. I stood by the soap box, bareheaded. A small American flag was our major prop—by law. A mob of communists were going through their usual disorders. It was always a riot when they came. They could not listen, they were frightened of our criticism, for we accused them endlessly of allowing Hitler to come into power . . . and then the bricks came down . . .

Two lay dead after dozens of bricks fell, all thrown from a roof across the street, but the two, ironically, were communists. Soon it was discovered that the brick-throwers, too, were communists . . . and it was to years of blood, fists and knives, of bricks and blackjacks, of terror within a terrible time . . .

It was also a time of love and hunger mixed together. We tried to get food, to get on relief, to find jobs. Once as I watched a city-hired snow shoveler faint, I dashed to the foreman to beg for the job. The snow shoveler, hired at fifty cents an hour by the Department of Sanitation, died on a pile of snow. An ambulance came from Bellevue Hospital, and soon I was shoveling snow. It was all dead ends. We were being sucked up into the universal poverty, into the deepening darkness.

136

Those Days Will
Not Return

§

There were to be years of cockroachy tenements, a backdrop
for slowing up some of our senses and quickening other instincts. Six of us lived, always hungry, always on the verge
of moral dissolution, in a railroad flat on Slavic-Jewish
Seventh Street off Avenue C, a flat that we had parlayed
through charity, Jewish kindness, human trust, and guile.

I had seen the red-lettered "To Let" sign banging in the
winter wind, one of the thousands within our deadened eyes.
For a little money we could have rented anything then:
marble mansions or Park Avenue duplexes. For the unemployed, unhoused, were living in the city parks and along
the brackish rivers in their poverty-created architecture of
tents and crates, boxes and trucks, caves and cellars. But
we were fastidious revolutionaries. And we were expert at
taking in sad landlords with empty apartments and no tenants.
Our simple lies, for we had to specialize in delicate duplicity
to live, sounded like every virtue right out of the Gospel . . .
and I talked piously to the old Jewish landlord as he stroked
his gray-brown goatee prudently.

"What do you do?" he asked in Yiddish.

"I am a poet now. Last year I was a drawbridge engineer."

"A po-et? *Oy vey!*" sneered his suspicious wife.

"So he's a po-et. I'm a carpent-ner, nu?"

"Where do you work?" asked his wife. "Do you drink
a lot?"

"No," I said to the last query. I paused about the work question, then said, "Roosevelt's W.P.A. hasn't reached me yet, unfortunately . . ."

"So call him up," said the wife. "Will you pay the rent every month?"

The carpenter-landlord said, "I know, it's bad times, so everybody must die a little bit. You know how long it took me to buy this stupid tenement? For forty years I'm a carpent-ner—and now, suddenly, when no one has money, I'm a landlord. Can you pay rent?"

"I have fourteen dollars," I said. Our rent was months overdue for a flat at Fourteenth Street and Avenue D, a slum within a slum. A week ago we had been evicted. "I can pay you immediately!"

Our furniture was in the snow-piled street facing the Con Edison powerhouse. My five friends were guarding it in shifts. At night we had slept over the grating, in the snow, getting heat from Con Edison. With a pushcart and many trips we'd have a home again after a week in the streets. The city's garbage trucks had constantly threatened to remove our wet beds, the snowed-on books, our broken pots filled with snow, and the colonial chairs I'd bought during my drawbridge-job days.

We had collected money in a panic. Each of us had borrowed quarters and dimes, nickels and pennies, until the six of us had promoted the total of $14.00 . . . and the new landwas asking, "And who will move in with you, that girl?"

I had come by with Friede three days ago to ask about the rent.

"Only six of us. No women."

"Six people? What kind of people?"

"An unemployed Greek, a busboy, an elevator driver, a playwright, an artist—and I. Just six little people . . ."

"A lot of little people," said the landlord.

138

"Some little people. *Ba-hemas!*" went the wife. "All right—give the money and move already."

"We are *not* Bohemians," I protested, handing over the fourteen dollars.

We moved in, six flights up.

Six months later we were again threatened with eviction. The poor landlord had not received another cent from us, and Kaldis, our unemployed Greek, soon to become a labor organizer, and later an excellent artist, said to me:

"Look, that bastard is evicting us tomorrow! Where do we go now? Wouldn't it be better . . ." and Kaldis rambled on into a crooked idea . . . "If he evicts us, it will cost him a lot of money to pay the eviction sheriff, right?"

"At least thirty-six dollars more than he got from us. So what, philosopher?" asked Max.

"So we make a small real estate deal," I said, guessing Kaldis' game. "The sheriff will cost him ten dollars a room for five rooms. If we evict ourselves, for returning the original fourteen dollars, the landlord is richer by thirty-six dollars—yes?"

"And we shall be doing him a *mitzvah*," said Max. "Go to him, Harry. Talk Yiddish with him."

I talked. We were at least thieves, said the landlord's wife. "Po-ets, paint-ners, wait-ners—crooks!" Her husband was gentler, suggesting, "Look, I will help you build a small house on Death Avenue along the Hudson . . . and you can live in that nice little Hooverville settlement forever. But to do a thing like this—*Gottenu!* Okay, here is your old money—and go! Some po-et!"

"Some capitalist system!" I retorted.

"Some bums!" said his wife. "All right, take! Move right away, you bum! Right away, po-et!"

"It's all very sad," I said, taking the fourteen dollars, shaking their unwilling hands, cursing the City, the W.P.A.

139

that had not reached us—and human greed. "We will move immediately . . ."

Kaldis, meanwhile, had found another apartment for twenty-two dollars in rent.

"Are you mad, Kaldis? Twenty-two dollars? We're lucky we got back the goddamn fourteen."

"I need a room to myself—to paint. Poverty brings out the artist in me. Is that strange?"

"You're crazy, so it's not strange. Where do we get another eight dollars?"

"There is a wonderful human agency called the Hebrew Immigrant Aid Society on Lafayette Street," said Max. "They help immigrants. So we're all immigrants again, Kaldis."

"It is fifteen years since I left Lesbos. Ah, rich Lesbos, so green in the Aegean! There I owned some land and a mud hut at least. But now I am a poor American."

"Good for you, Kaldis. We're all poor Jews now. We'll visit the HIAS and talk to the rabbi there about eight dollars," I said, ready to go.

At HIAS, the slender, sad rabbi nodded. His little beard nodded. My best Yiddish was getting warm Yiddish responses. All was heartening and pleasant. Kaldis, big and affable, talked about Mediterranean and Hebrew culture. We had tea from a samovar, and *lechachs,* a brown cake with almonds. Soon Kaldis was talking about Greek values and the rabbi was asking—

"But if you are a Greek Jew, why from Lesbos? Why not from Salonika, where all the Jews live? Mr. Kaldis, are you a Jew, a Turk, or just a plain Gentile?"

Kaldis turned less Mediterranean, remarking, *"Oy vey iz mir!"* which I had taught him on the walk to Lafayette Street. The rabbi was confused. But soon he was smiling, filling our glasses with more tea, and Kaldis put in his clincher, *"Ich bin a Yiddle un ah fiddle . . ."* The rabbi laughed breathlessly.

"He talks now like a Bialystoker, so here is nine dollars. If you get rich, send it back. If not, write me a small poem. *Ziy gezint . . ."*

"Ziy gezint, too, comrade," said Kaldis.

"Be well, rabbi—and thank you for the extra dollar," I said.

A few hours later it was the pushcart again, six flights down on East Seventh Street, and four flights up on East Eighth; we had a home again.

The new apartment, contemporary-rebuilt, had a bathtub in the kitchen, and two unbelievable items—hot water and steam. It was an internally conceived place with French windows which opened on a rotting garden, an English grate which gave the living room a nineteenth-century inner view, and a *Kachelofen,* a German tiled stove. Kaldis, our frantic chef, was happy with it all.

"We are now cosmopolitan," said Kaldis. "If only we had some food."

"We have a dollar left," I said. "Do you want to shop for a cosmopolitan stew?"

"Greek stew . . ." and Kaldis was out with the dollar.

Eating, or planning to eat, had been a fixation of ours. A few days earlier, hunger-maddened, three of us had marched into a pay-as-you-eat cafeteria. They had grown all over the suspicious city. As Max talked to the counterman, Kaldis and I pocketed bread, ham, and cheese. Then we moved in on the pastry, with Max acting as a wandering kibitzer-singer in search of an audience. The counterman loved opera: so Max sang a few bits of *La Forza del Destino* to get us through the last part of the fine, fully kidnaped lunch.

Dinner was usually more harrowing, at a cafeteria called *Life* on Sheridan Square. We came, we took, usually bowls of soup and lots of rye bread — then we waited to be bailed out by any friends we could spot with fifteen cents. Others were doing much the same, feeling trapped in the tiled, neon fastness, with bouncers at the exit, a cop always near the entrance, and all of us in the center waiting to be sprung from this Dantian restaurant that we called *Death-on-Rye*.

At using the telephone for almost free, we were weighted with talent. For twenty cents we bought a pound of nickel-like metal slugs, hundreds of them, at an inventive hardware store. With the slug nickels, we phoned not only friends in New York, but comrades in Minneapolis then leading a truck drivers' strike, and Hollywood — to see what had happened to a script we had written about just such a situation. For light and gas we conned Con Edison. When we could not pay for six months, they put fake fuses into our fuse box, padlocking both it and the meter. We were shut into cookingless darkness. Risking electric shock, we broke their seals, put in proper fuses, and there was light and gas again. When that stratagem eventually failed, we wired in on the landlord and cooked over electric plates. We were so inventive in those days that we paid out less than five dollars to Con Edison, the telephone company, or any other public service.

§

But Kaldis was back from shopping. He was at a large pot putting in various vegetables, the stewing meat, separating each level with wood from an egg box that he had dragged along . . . and soon all of it was stewing, the wood simmering juicily as it broke up into splintery bits. When Kaldis served it up, two hours later, it was pungent with turpentine flavor.

"We'll die from this ignoble Greek's cuisine," said Max. "It's a hemlock stew, you bastard!"

"It's a resin stew, you ignorant man!"

142

Kaldis was a big man. His spoken language was English after a Greek fashion. Max said he never understood half of Kaldis' radiant agglutination of sounds. I understood even less—but it was an animated speech that ranged in subject from Greek philosophy to Greek art to Greek cooking. That was only part of Kaldis, who was also known as a man of action. He was all shock, his long hair streaming, his hands flying. As the unemployed joined the newly created Unemployed Councils, demanding bread, rent, clothes, heat, Kaldis was organizing the hotel workers into a union along industrial lines. He was after kitchen workers, bellhops, doormen, and elevator drivers to demand better working conditions and higher wages—to go on the first strike of its kind in New York.

Many of the kitchens in the fine uptown hotels were staffed with politically-conscious Greeks; whatever their party affiliations, however, they remained individualistic Greeks—each a leader of men, and therefore not to be led. They chose to remain in their kitchens, dubious about Kaldis' leadership, the economic merits of the strike, and their future in case the strike was lost. To break the static situation, we pulled out Puerto Rican elevator drivers, halting their hotel chariots. Then came the Irish doormen, who contemptuously left their patrons in the revolving doors and marched along to picket. Porters stopped their baggage-carrying; and finally only the Greeks remained, stolid in their individualism and their sacred kitchens.

We had to get them out, or the strike couldn't succeed. To end the impasse, Kaldis and I and a very tough Trotskyist named Robins (who later was Trotsky's guard when Trotsky was hacked to death in Mexico) went in for some direct action. At a plush Park Avenue hotel, we broke into the crowded kitchen at noon. A hundred waiters, cooks, saladmen, chefs, and helpers maddened by the lunch rush found the three of us facing them. Kaldis was shouting, "Out! Every son of Zeus, out like lightning! I am Kaldis, and you are disgracing Greek history—out! Proletariat-of-Greece-in-America, off with your black jackets! You white-hatted sons of Dionysus, out of the kitchens! If not . . ."

He held a huge butcher's knife, waving it like a baton, about to conduct a session in slaughtering. Robins was swinging a crowbar, and I had a sizeable meat cleaver. Soon the chefs dropped their tall white hats: the waiters took off their black jackets. Lunch was halted, and the diners were left hungry while their food burned in the emptying kitchens. By the time the police arrived, the kitchens were one vast smell of blackened filet-mignon, seared T-bone steaks, overdone roast partridges, with assorted dishes still burning brightly on the stoves. That afternoon, feature stories in the newspapers completed our work by building us into fearless Greek gangsters armed with cleavers. All the hotel workers went out, and the strike was won. After that, many of us ate and drank on the house in the kitchens of unionized hotels. We lapped up filet-mignons, drank Scotch as waiters, chefs, and busboys hailed our programs for winning over the kitchen proletariat in white hats and black jackets. Soon we had dozens of gently-maddened Greeks entering our Trotskyist ranks, and each Greek comrade came with all of his peculiar gifts intact. Besides, in Greece, the Trotskyists were much stronger than Stalin's pedestrian hosts of words and violence. We had a language for talking about revolution, at least in the kitchens and the cafeterias of New York.

§

By 1935, Roosevelt's W.P.A. finally reached us. Kaldis went on the Art Program as a lecturer on classical Greek art. Max became a prop man on the Theater Project, Friede

144

was a federally sponsored musicologist at the Music Library, and I did research and writing for the Writers' Project. At last, we were leaving the Depression, about to do over the frantic mind and the sickened body of the nation. And Friede and I, after five years of homeless love, were finally able to set up house on Morton Street . . .

Writers' Project

§

It was love in two furnished rooms, most Greenwich Villagey, on Morton Street. It was high-ceilinged, with a kitchen and a dripping bathroom which we shared in equal drips with three tenants. We had a piano for Bach exercises. One down payment, and Friede was playing—overfast arpeggios and rough rondos, for piano music, to her, was merely an adjunct to musicology. Three missed installments and the piano company, hardly concerned with musicology, was threatening to move the piano back to its warehouse. Instead, we moved in the night from Morton Street to East Ninth. Six friends, a station wagon, and out we were, our piano spirited into the unknown. It was the fulminating, acid poet, Spector, whose relative had sold us the piano: and so we had a friendly advisor saying, "If you pay my cousin another installment, it's the end of your career as a revolutionary poet! Don't you know what Lenin said 'Expropriate the expropriator!' In this instance, my cousin!"

This was mandatory to keep the friendship of the world's most acid-blooded poet, though my Hebraic conscience equaled Spector's energy for expropriation. After that, Spector insisted, as we drank wine in the early morning in my new but quite empty apartment, "What are you going to use for furniture, young poet? You've got a bed, at least, but you need chairs, tables, rugs, book cases . . ." And he

147

rattled on, envisioning another installment-buying raid. By morning, with the bottles finished and Spector gone, I said, "Friede, I can buy some cheap pine wood to build what we need. The piano is enough expropriation for this century." And we left it at that to think of love. We had a bed, at least. Two weeks later I built tables, a Dutch-type cabinet, book cases, and some awkward benches. We told Spector and Lenin to go expropriate themselves! We now had decent surroundings to house our newness. There were white walls for paintings our artist friends soon contributed; a drawing by Attilio Salemme, a primitive Greek scene by Kaldis, and some large canvasses by a neighbor who occasionally used our apartment as a spontaneous gallery.

We learned to cook, to know ourselves better, to play between political chores, to love . . . and gentleness for us was occasionally awkward. I had my father's voice, for emotional giving; but I was in a political movement that bred anything but gentle thoughts. I had, for instance, never heard a Stalinist purr nor a Trotskyist become kittenish. I had at least two heads and two hearts; one for politics, always violent, another for love—and both fused and con-fused, goaded on by my ego's convolutions. When I was not meeting late into the Trotskyist night, we were off to a con-cert of the avant-gardes; percussive experiments from Satie, Stravinsky, Milhaud, Honegger, and Varese; and then, home to the long circling room that was both bedroom and parlor, overlooking a little garden where we watched early morning pigeons bolt about; and, later, lovely children came echo-ing laughter and nonsense. And love was there, in our first spring within these walls, breaking into imagined gardens that made up our first real home.

Friede's knowledge of music was enormous. She was writ-ing an article for *The Kenyon Review* about the development of Russian music since the Revolution; at twenty-one her scholarship was self-taught. I had met her when she was sixteen, and since then there had been no emotional or sexual digressions for me, though I was in a political movement where sex, as a permanent activity, often replaced the *permanent revolution.* One learned Trotskyist said to me when he finally quit, "I came in for sexual opportunism, not for revolutionary idealism. I've had almost every girl in this sectarian organization . . . and now I'm joining the Liberal Party."

But Friede's peasant loveliness erupted in my blood and created a constancy that was almost fatal to me, years later, when we parted. She had every gentle nuance of touch and voice—and I was immersed and enveloped in her erotic image. God and Marx, were we romantics!

We had all the emotional tokens, and we did not need a marriage certificate to make us man and wife. But my mother, in religious shock at our pagan ways, offered me five hundred dollars—if Friede and I went through a religious ceremony.

We talked about it dreamily. We could get a shack in Woodstock with the money. We'd have summers and springs with artists, writers, musicians—and Woodstock's more exciting flora and fauna. We debated, time and again the nature of idealism and materialism. Idealism won out. No shack, no artists, no flowers, no birds. My mother kept her five hundred religious dollars dangling before us for years, but we went our pagan way, wedded to love's purities.

But there was comedy, too, within our little purities. Friede was studying with a short, improper composer who specialized in a vast array of percussive sounds: African drums beating in the evening, garbage can covers falling in the early morning, manholes over sewers rattling all day, excavating drills within your living room—all of it, sounding together, made into neat and exacting compositions for small orchestra. The composer was usually sartorially splendid, from his tidy little beard to his large patent leather shoes. But suddenly he took to being in the nude when Friede called for her lesson. He would apologize, "You're rather early, my dear. I haven't had time to dress completely . . .," and he'd pad off past his huge stacks of percussive compositions. Friede, annoyed, finally arrived ten minutes late. It was the same—he was still nude. This time, he reached for Friede rather than his clothes. She, built like a Russian peasant, picked up two of the composer's massive percussive scores and let them fall on his head, for her last lesson in avant-garde composition.

§

The Writers' Project of the W.P.A. was America's first capitalistic-socialized experiment in researching, writing, and publishing histories of the fancies and folklore of our nation. More often, we were, ourselves, the history and the folklore—researching in our own backyards, into our own origins for sources. We were supervised by Henry Alsberg, the national director, and a staff of professional editors who did the final work on our enormous encyclopedic compilations about a country called the United States. We began with state histories and guides, then progressed inwardly toward local and intimate books involving studies of birds in Staten Island, churches and synagogues in New York City, and the number of potholes on New York's streets.

I researched, tongue in cheek and pencil in hand, and wrote at the 42nd Street Library for twenty-three dollars a week. I sat in the North Room and worked on, among other things, a maritime history of New York, a labor history, and a skiing guide.

Our assignments came out of a weekly grab-bag. One junior newspaperman, a poet in his own eyes, at least, had been assigned to copying down street names in the Bronx, for a new street map of the region. For weeks, notebook in

150

hand, the poet wandered disconsolately about the borough. Exhausted by the deadening of his spiritual side, the abject wandering poet came to his supervisor orating, "If you don't take me off that mundane project, I'm going to commit suicide! I, who have dedicated my whole life to poetry, prefer death to a new street map of the Bronx!" His sole published work, then, was one small poem — an ode to a goat in the Bronx zoo.

Another writer, though assigned to do research in Staten Island, assiduously avoided his assignment. When he was about to be fired, he broke in on his supervisor. He held up a letter from his doctor and begged, "Please don't send me to Staten Island, sir! There are mad dogs all over that place. And I *can't* cross any body of water — and it's almost two miles over to Staten Island. Please don't send me to my death!" The supervisor opened the letter from the writer's doctor, and read: "This man has a 100 percent case of hydrophobia — fear of dogs *and* water. Please assign him to some other project."

A writer of German descent was sent out to do a book about the brewing of beer. Having tasted long and studiously at every New York brewery, he was soon employed as a brew-master making beer for a bootleg gang operating over in Newark. Another writer, a teetotaller, was asked to do a study at Bellevue's alcoholic ward. En route, he stopped at a bar for a few experimental drinks. When he finally arrived, dead drunk, at the alcoholic ward, he was locked in. A week later, with a book full of notes about alcoholism and its treatment, he was free to leave. But he returned for further data, and continued his own experimenting. By the time he amassed all the material he thought pertinent, he was a confirmed alcoholic.

It was a job that was not uninvolved with politics. The shenanigans of several hundred hacks on the New York City project made it more of a Leftist five-ring circus than

151

a fertile field for thought about research and writing. The communists, who were in the vast majority, had flooded the project with half-authors who had published only in their minds. There were also writers from the *Daily Worker,* which was written in a specialized prose understandable only to party members. All of them used the project to write propaganda leaflets summoning the workers of the world, at least those in New York, to various ramparts—for cultural insurrections. Or they pulled sit-in strikes, demanding the removal of various supervisors, especially Harold Rosenberg—for opposing their cultural barricades-in-progress. The communists wanted physical domination over the Writers' Project, to sponsor Stalin, red picnics, proletarian literature, full-assed and half-assed proletarian dancers, and to fire all the Trotskyists and other dissenters. On strike, they sat in the officially darkened project building which they relit with red candles. Singing red songs, they established nocturnal dictatorship over the covered typewriters. In the workaday morning the police, with brown polished nightsticks, evicted them from the federalized precincts of poetry, prose, and propaganda.

My first pink slip which I, along with the others, received in 1937 was like a death warrant. Here it is:

June 21st, 1937.

WORKS PROGRESS ADMINISTRATION
FEDERAL PROJECT NO. I
FOR THE CITY OF NEW YORK
235 East 42nd Street, New York, N. Y.

TAG No.

311925 HR

DISMISSAL NOTICE   265-6903-830

NAME ROSKOLENKO, Harry

PROJECT No.

ADDRESS 51 E. 9th St., Manh.   Jr. Newspaperman
CLASSIFICATION

You are notified of the termination of your service with the WORKS PROGRESS ADMINISTRATION FEDERAL PROJECT NO. I FOR THE CITY OF NEW YORK at the close of business July 15th, 1937. Under the rules of the Administration it will not be possible to pay you for any time after that date.

Your final check will be ready at usual time and place.

Date July 21   Amount _____ Approximate Time _____

Reason for Dismissal: REDUCTION OF QUOTA.

IF IN NEED, WE SUGGEST THAT YOU APPLY AT THE HOME RELIEF STATION NEAREST YOUR HOME AFTER YOU HAVE RECEIVED YOUR FINAL CHECK

ASSISTANT DIRECTOR.

F.P.-NYC-230   SIGNED   TITLE

152

Within a week, the pink slip was rescinded, and I was back.

The communists, then, had Richard Wright. He had gone along like a good party member, believing in "Self-Determination for the Black Belt." In an anthology called *American Stuff,* edited by Harold Rosenberg and containing a project collection of the nation's best writing, I had a poem alongside a selection from Wright's work-in-progress, *Native Son.* My poem was attacked by the communists in their project paper, the *Red Pen.* I was accused of insulting the memory of Karl Marx.

All I had done was to use satirically Marx's insulting phrase about the peasants, "The idiocy of rural existence . . ." I had completed the poem by suggesting some over-all idiocies in the City, with my final line reading, "The City creates, but is unkind, another doom."

In a cafeteria on Third Avenue one morning, I sat having coffee with Richard Wright, who was liked by the non-communists, and John Cheever, Lionel Abel, Philip Rahv, and Claude McKay, the Negro poet. "I won't demand that you be sent to Siberia for 'insulting' Marx's memory, Roskolenko," Wright said to me with a laugh. But there were others in the cafeteria who felt differently. "Marx-hater!" one hard-core communist shouted across the room at me—and then he spat on the floor. It was standard behavior to spit, then throw punches. But I ignored the spitting insurrectionist and headed for the library and a day's writing.

I was stopped under the Third Avenue El by the traffic. A flopping drunk bummed me for a quarter. I turned him down, saying, "What's wrong with a nickel?" He took it quickly enough, but then demanded a dollar. I tried to laugh him off, but he hung around, still demanding a dollar. I stared into the street, ignoring him completely.

It was summery and hardly a day to work at the library.

153

I decided to go to Coney Island instead—as soon as I managed to cross Third Avenue and get away from the drunk. Sunbeams shot through the El's tracks, splashing serried lines into my eyes. I saw the beach and the ocean an hour away . . . and then I was pushed violently by the drunk.

I sprawled, hitting my head on a cobblestone. A taxi went around me. I lay there, half out, bleeding from my forehead. Many feet came running . . . and I saw legs, hands, faces . . . and one of them was Richard Wright's. They were lifting me up, balancing me. I was all right, soon enough, after a drink at a nearby bar.

"Did you trip over your poem?" asked Wright, buying me a second drink.

When the second cuts in the Writers' Project came, people were thrown out from Left, Right, and Center— Negroes as well as whites, as if to blend equality with federal grace. One August morning I was again pink-slipped, but three days later I received a letter, which said, among other ego-warming things. "We have also found, however, that full evidence concerning your creative work for this project had not been submitted. The quality and quantity of this work has been examined by us, and it is our decision that on both counts your work is, at this time, of unique value to this project. Your dismissal from this project is accordingly rescinded."

Richard Wright had received similar pink slips along with Lionel Abel, Philip Rahv, Harry Kemp, Claude Mc-Kay, Vincent McHugh, Helen Neville, and Charlotte Wilder, a sister of Thornton Wilder . . . and we demonstrated against this "cultural barbarism." Others, less fortunate than us, were pink-slipped permanently, and we joined their violent sit-ins and sit-outs. Furriers and garment workers, Bowery bums and Broadway actresses, in proletarian loyalty, joined the picket lines of our literary

154

ranks. Cops on horses patrolled outside the Project building on 42nd Street. Traffic was blocked as we united for culture at twenty-three dollars a week; and, as we marched against Roosevelt's cultural economies, the cops charged.

The horses reared into panic as imaginative communists stuck pins into them. The communists wanted a riot, and they got a fine one, with busted heads and shrieking women. It was a newspaper photographer's holiday. The communists were out to get their own men back into the project — not us. Nevertheless, within three days, many were taken back, to add to the infinite political glories of the Works Progress Administration.

Soon the glory *was* even greater. Suddenly, without official clarions, a few of us were told by the administrators, "We have just brought into being a Creative Section for the good of American Literature. Please stay home and write your first book. Come in once a month with a poem, a story, or an essay — and you'll be paid . . ."

Richard Wright finished *Native Son,* and startled the world with a Zolaesque study of a Negro killer. I equaled him in violence, at least. My first book was a profane explosion about my wandering, driven years: the rot and the raw and the singing things. It was ninety-four pages of poems which I called *Sequence on Violence.*

Lewis Mumford, critic of our cities, wrote an introduction that flattered me beyond the book's covers, "Here is war, the defeat, the frustrations of our times: the 'lacerated images' that stalk the dweller in cities and accompany him on his farthest excursions; the 'thunderous days' that carry disaster. The quick terror, the lean excitement of these poems proclaim Roskolenko the very voice of the modern city: the inevitable commentator on 'those bandaged years.'"

Suddenly I was a poet with a book, proclaiming my version of Hell and being paid for it by the United States Government.

Portraits:
Characters
and Some Gentlemen

§

The Trotskyist membership was a peculiar breed of men and women—heroic, though proletarians-by-proxy only. We had a sensitive tea-leaf reader, two fat ex-gymnasts (a man and wife team), a table-tennis champion who had broken his right hand when he smashed the table instead of the ball, and an abortionist looking for work. There was also a group of dentists and doctors who helped establish us financially by bringing along some of their rich patients and friends, brokers who had lost faith in Wall Street, well-kept actresses without plays to act in, and a wandering clergyman gone briefly agnostic. To give us a vital proletarian flavor, there were a few real workers, the huge muscled kind that Hugo Gellert painted on the walls of the old Co-op Cafeteria on Union Square—now Klein's bargain basement.

Sympathetic intellectuals came from everywhere and everything—including some from analysts' couches, which they got up from to join picket lines. Their names are now nationally known as writers, editors, architects, trade union-ists, sociologists, and historians. To them, our promise of world revolution meant personal salvation through deep orgies of self-involvement. They practiced an esoteric brand of universalism. They hated mass-art, which they called *Kitsch*. They were for surrealism and abstraction. They loved James Joyce and Picasso. Diego Rivera, having come to Trotsky's aid in Mexico, was temporarily enshrined in our intellectual pantheon.

Our biggest catch of fish was straight out of *Time, Life,* and *Fortune;* editors and writers who came from Luce's word-wading pool to dive deeper into our depths. There was Dwight Macdonald, who had come to *Fortune* from Macy's necktie counter after four liberal years at Yale. Macdonald was gifted and studious. He wrote enormous searching tracts about the nature of the Soviet state, about party discipline and theory, about bureaucratic collectivism, though most of his work was not printed. Once, during a fracturing polemic regarding whether the Soviet Union was a "worker's state," Trotsky wrote about Macdonald, then taking minor issue, saying, "Everyone has the right to be stupid now and then, but Comrade Macdonald abuses that privilege . . ."

Macdonald, during debates, was all over the place, spluttering angrily when he had objections to express. One of our leaders, James P. Cannon, had earlier suggested that Macdonald would be "happier as a sympathizer than as a member." Macdonald sported a goatee, fine wool tweeds, and a blue workshirt, for better proletarian styling. Nature and man had conspired to give Macdonald the voice of a North American screech owl, the beard of a Russian revolutionist, and the iconoclastic mind of a *Fortune* magazine writer. This gave him an international flavor, but it was not enough to make him a proper Trotskyist to the leadership. He left to edit the excellent magazine, *Politics,* this time in pursuit of anarchism, and emerged finally as a true social critic.

Then there was Edmund Wilson, who had denounced the communists in disgust. I called on him one afternoon at his office at *The New Republic,* to bring in a book review and to get another book. In my hands I held Dylan Thomas' first book of poems, sent to me by a mutual friend, Henry Treece, then doing a book about Thomas.

Wilson, our most eminent literary critic, read my review, his bunny-like shape wobbling between his desk and my chair.

"You write like a Russian. Were you born in Russia?" he asked.

"Nyet," I answered.

I talked about Dylan Thomas' poetry. Wilson was bored. I said a few more excited things about Thomas and mentioned that Treece's book, appraising and lauding Thomas, would soon be out. Wilson was bored.

I tried another tack. I read a few lines. Wilson was still bored.

I shoved the book under his nose.

He was forced to turn a few pages. He got half interested. Then suddenly he sat upright: "My God, this is real poetry! Who *is* he?"

Wilson had warm responses for the downtrodden Trotsky-ists, preferring our morals and literary values to that of other radicals exercising in the proletarian literary zoo. Besides, he was not a fellow-traveler with literary blood on his hands. He was independent, original, and scholarly. The fellow-travelers were anything but that as they served Stalin in the name of liberalism. When they broke with Stalin they served us and others under the same liberalism. It was their kind of a political disease, and we made the least of their ardent confusions.

Of those who came bearing us their talents, James T. Farrell stood out for the energy of his typewriter's wrath. He gave pages and pages to pamphlets, outdoing *Studs Lonigan* in realism to help Trotsky emerge honorably from the judicial proceedings held by the John Dewey Commission investigating Stalin's charges against Trotsky.

Jim had a shy way about him when he was not drinking, but when he was in his rye and beer, he turned all Studs Lonigan with a savage South Side delight.

Before I left for the Pacific in World War II, Farrell attended a farewell party for me. It turned into a gruesome wake as Farrell upended the sexy, posturing hostess, called her husband four kinds of a green cow, and punched three peaceful guests—for not going off to the war. It made me happy, in the doom of early morning, to go off to fight the less taxing Japanese in New Guinea. Farrell came with me in a taxi to Pennsylvania Station; by the time we got there, Farrell managed to get the names and phone numbers of all the guests; and as he shook my hand he said, with a cigarette hanging from his mouth, "I'm going to call all those nice proper bastards and bitches at once and apologize. What in hell time is it?"

"It's five o'clock. It's a Sunday morning in early September, Jim."

"That's fine. They'll sleep better if I call them now."

"Wait till noon, when they've slept." I said.

"I don't want to keep those bastards feeling bad until noon . . ."

As I left for the train, Farrell was in a phone booth telling one of my party friends to go to hell again.

§

When I returned several years later, no longer the Marxist malcontent, Farrell asked me, after a lunch, "What do you want to do, Harry?"

"I'd like to write," I said.

"How about starting with the *New York Times Book Review?* After that bit of prestige, everything will open up. . . ."

He was on the telephone at once, calling the editor. Jim

160

would have called God, if he'd had the phone number, to ease you into something you wanted. Droll, driven, he once said to me with sly laughter, "Zola wrote 47 novels. I want to do 48 better ones . . ."

§

Arrivistes and activists, poets and pedants, saluted the Trotskyists with money and words, and we made the most of their genuine offerings. There was a beautiful lady who came with another beautiful lady to help one of our fund raising rallies—to frolic for us at the Irving Plaza. They did a few risque dances, satanic in black leotards, prancing like two professionals. One was Eleanor Clark, the other Mary Mc-Carthy, both going through a cultural transference for Truth and Trotskyism. They could have made the chorus line at Minsky's Burlesque down the block.

We reached out individually, as well as en masse, for membership. Harvey Breit, a promising poet and critic, was my self-elected assignment.

We went for a bike ride, sixty miles into New Jersey, to spend a talking weekend at a Trotskyist nature camp. Uphill, downhill, on the flat, we cycled wearily. Trucks raced between us, breaking into our dialogue on Marxism. When I thought I was making a point for Trotsky, bang would go an exhaust—and the point was left fusing into carbon monoxide. I tried again. We cycled on, with Breit, obviously not a cyclist, near exhaustion. Between the raging trucks, the carbon monoxide, and my Trotskyist harangue, I almost made a new member. . . .

Worn-out, we stopped for a late lunch. It was wine and cold chicken under a tree. Nearby was a collection of salvaged junk, mostly old cars. The summer sun was burning on the body of an ancient truck, painted red. Its name, U.S. IRON WORKS, was still visible. Two potato farmers were

161

digging in the ground not far from us. The scene looked like America the Exhausted.

Breit was arguing quietly, his rich low voice analyzing my ideas, "But won't Stalin and Trotsky meet one day? Won't they meet in a full circle of political ironies?"

I choked off that ghastly thought quickly. If they did, God help the world!

We joined the traffic again, plunging into the mechanical madness. By the time we reached camp, Breit was walking his bike, unable to continue. Soon we were in the swimming pool, to gather up strength for more arguments.

"What you Trotskyists need are a lot of six-day bike riders," laughed Breit. "Then you'd have a mass movement, in your permanent revolution."

Won't Stalin and Trotsky meet one day . . .?

The ideas of both met, and fused, years later, in new and old countries that I was to visit. It was Stalin's murderous way, and Trotsky's more theoretical one—and I was to see the results of it all, in time . . . but Breit and I argued on then, revolutionaries swimming, waiting for a dinner bell to sound.

Mavericks and Marxists

§

The painting of Diego Rivera's gigantic, revolutionary fresco at Rockefeller Center focused our attention, for a while, on the question of art in politics. Rivera's work was doctrinaire and afforded no problems in itself, but it gave rise to speculation in general. How *should* our painters paint? Within what confines must our writers write? After reading Max Eastman's *Artists in Uniform,* I felt democratically anarchistic about the contents of an artist's canvasses and a writer's notebooks. But our American Trotskyist leaders wanted their artists and writers to remain solidly in uniform, as agile servitors doing for Trotsky what Stalin's "creative" hosts were doing for the Russian dictator.

In objection to this strait-jacketing, I wrote a long letter to Trotsky, using my adopted party name, Ross, and got a long letter back.

Dear Comrade Ross:

Your letter poses very important problems which do not, however, admit, in my opinion of general and categorical solutions suitable in all cases. As an organization, we have as the point of departure not only definite political ideas but certain philosophical and scientific methods. We base ourselves on dialectical materialism, from which flow conclusions not only concerning politics and science, but also art. Still, there is a vast difference in our attitude toward these conclusions. We cannot, to any similar degree exercise the same rigorous control over art, by the very nature of this activity, as over politics. The party is obliged to permit a very extensive liberty in the field of art, eliminating pitilessly only that which is directed against the revolutionary tasks of the proletariat; on the other hand, the party cannot assume an immediate and direct responsibility for the declarations of its various members in the field of art even when it accords them its tribune. The maintenance of these two rules—the preservation of the liberty necessary for individual creation, and the non-transmission of the responsibility for all its roads to the party—is especially obligatory in those cases where it is a question not of theoreticians in the field of art, but of the artists themselves: painters, men of letters, etc. In addition, the party must be able to distinguish clearly the line where generalization in the field of art passes directly into the field of politics. Without making any concessions in principle, the party must, however, confine itself in the case of artists to rectifications, firm but tactful. Marx expressed this idea in a jocular phrase about Freiligrath: "Poets are queer fish." *(Die Dichter sind sonderbare Käuze.)* Lenin applied different criteria to Bogdanov the theoretician and professional politician and to Gorky the artist, in spite of the fact that for a certain period of time Bogdanov and Gorky were closely associated in politics. Lenin proceeded from the standpoint that by his artistic activity and his popularity, Gorky could endow the cause of the revolution with benefits far exceeding the harm of his erroneous declarations and actions, which, moreover, the party could always correct in good time and tactfully.

Viewed from this standpoint, philosophical activity lies between art and politics, closer to politics than to art. In philosophy, the party itself occupies a distinct militant position, which is not the case—at least not to the same extent—in the field of art. Objections to the effect that by the "dogmatization" and "cannonization" of dialectical materialism, the party prevents the free development of philosophical and scientific thought, do not deserve serious attention. No factory can work without basing itself upon a definite technological doctrine. No hospital can treat its patients if the physicians do not base themselves on the established teach-ings of pathology. It would be sheer folly to permit dilletantes to experiment arbitrarily in the factory or in the hospital, on the pretext that they consider themselves "innovators." Innovators must first prove their right to influence practical technology and medicine. The party must be especially vigilant toward these "innovators" who only warm the stale critical dishes, or toward those who are still in the period of investigating, with uncertain results. But least of all does this signify that in the sphere of philosophy the party can act as if all questions have already been resolved for it and that it has nothing to expect from the further development of scientific thought. It is not an easy matter to find the correct political line in this field. It is acquired by experience and by its flexible leadership. Just as in artillery fire, the target is usually hit by a series of shots which fall far and then short of the mark. It is needless to point out that the question: How do the philosophical views of a certain person or a certain group refract themselves in the field of politics and of the organization?—always has a tremendous significance for the elaboration of a correct control of the party. Thus, Lenin fought mercilessly against Gorky in 1917 when above all other considerations stood the necessity of a revolutionary overthrow. On the other hand, it must be considered as the greatest shame that the Stalinist bureaucracy is transforming Barbusse the *novelist* into a leading *political* figure, in spite of the fact that it is precisely in politics that Barbusse marches arm in arm with Renner, Vandervelde, Monnet and Paul Louis.

I am very much afraid that I have not given you a satisfactory reply to the practical questions put to me. But what has been said explains, I hope, why I could not give such a reply which required a concrete knowledge of the situation and the personal conditions. Just the same, perhaps these brief considerations will at least partially help in the working out of a correct policy in this complicated and responsible field.

With communist greetings,

L. Trotsky

The contents of the letter, which I was not shy to quote, were embarrassing to our leaders, and we went briefly democratic in the arts.

§

Michelangelo painted the *Holy Family* in Florence for Pope Julius II, but he soon quarreled with his patron about the design of the Pope's sepulchral monuments. Four centuries later, Diego Rivera went to work for the Rockefellers on a fresco enshrining American culture. Sitting high on a scaffold at the entrance to the RCA Building, the Mexican artist dominated the City itself as he mixed paints and instructed his assistants in the preparation of plaster for the fresco — and what a fresco it was!

Dressed in blue dungarees, I modeled as an American worker. The huge fresco had all the sainted models of dialectical materialism: Marx, Engels, Lenin, Trotsky, as well as lesser theorists and activists. There were James P. Cannon and Max Schachtman, the American Trotskyist leaders, as well as Jay Lovestone and Bertram Wolfe, the right-wing communists, who had formed their own anti-Stalinist party. The fresco was an enormous pageant of propaganda art — a spit in the eye of the Rockefellers and the dazed tenants of the massive building. Rivera, his fat face radiating disdain, spat a great deal himself. One afternoon a man wearing a top hat stood directly under the scaffold and got a mouthful of venomous Rivera spit on his hat. Then another. Those of us up on the scaffold laughed at seeing a capitalist turned into a spittoon. Irritated by Rivera's good aim, the man stepped hastily aside — and we saw that he wore a sign saying: "Rent Your Tuxedo from Harris." He looked up at us and shouted plaintively, "Hey! I'm a paid-up Trotskyist!"

Every evening there was a party at Rivera's apartment on West 13th Street. He was a grand host, loud and spluttering

166

in a variety of languages. He was at his heaviest in those days: 300 pounds. Cartooning capitalism by day on the scaffold, he continued his savage social sallies until late in the night: "Every day thousands of American peasants come through Mr. Rockefeller's small city. They see. They learn Marxism from my painting. In maybe two years, a big revolution in New York, no? Maybe in one year, yes? President Roosevelt soon ask me to Washington to paint even bigger picture. Then all the country explode in big revolution, comrades."

When the fresco was completed — it exploded. The Rockefellers had lost the momentarily liberal view they'd had when they commissioned it. The fresco was insulting to all. Michelangelo had at least celebrated Christianity, but Rivera was celebrating Communism and not the Rockefeller institutions at all. One night the fresco was covered up — and we acted . . .

We splashed Rockefeller Center with violent demonstrations. Rivera led one, his enormous bulk saluting the astonished onlookers. Rivera, who loved to paint revolutionary Mexican peasants on horses and burros, now had capitalist police on horses following him. It was the usual cop-and-comrade chase for the press. Rivera eventually went off to a corner and sketched the proceedings. He took the Rockefeller money and proceeded to paint some smaller propaganda frescoes for Jay Lovestone's organization, as well as dozens of portraits for lady capitalists bearing *mucho dinero*.

For my blue-dungareed services, Rivera did a small portrait of me. He also gave me a wine skin, with some old tequila still in it, and a serape that smelled of manure. "It is from Pancho Villa," Rivera told me sentimentally. "He stink then, maybe, a little bit. Take it, comrade, for the revolution's sake."

The Spanish Civil War came with a bang to shock almost everybody but us. We had been forewarned by Trotsky, years

167

before. And now we were emotional spectators, reacting to it verbally by accusing Stalin's red legions of trying to dominate the democratic and republican cause in Spain. It was solely *their* cause, proclaimed the communists. It was to be *their* victory, too, they insisted. But, it was *their* defeat, and *ours,* in a few years when a million Spaniards and a good many foreigners had been killed. The Trotskyists were for the P.O.U.M. in Barcelona—a strong alignment of Spanish anarchists, socialists, and independents—and I volunteered, heady for it, prepared to die for the P.O.U.M.

But, it was difficult to die, just then. For one thing, I had to get to Spain. I was without passage money, and the Trotskyists had no ships.

To enlarge our influence here, we Trotskyists had joined the Socialist Party, which had contributed less than the Gibson Girls to the sociology of the day. We simply danced like Bolshevik ballerinas into their pink-hued china shop and announced that we had the key to every international situation. In less than a year, with the Spanish Civil War still raging, we destroyed the Socialist Party's courteous liberalism and its old-maid political practices; then we charged, bull-like, out of their now dismembered political china shop. It was an old communist tactic; join 'em, then talk and walk 'em over to you. Our gain was almost one thousand gullible young socialists, but it did not get me on a boat to Barcelona. I would sell my large library, I decided. I would part with a thousand books on politics and poetry, and sail away to the civil war. . . .

§

One night, as Friede and I were drinking red wine from Rivera's wine-skin—misdirecting the spigot and getting wine all over our clothes—I became insistent in my unstable table-talk. "I've got to go!" I told her.

"Must you get killed to prove your dedication? If the Franco Fascists don't kill you, the Stalinists will. Please don't ever say that again — please!" begged Friede.

It was woman talk. I passed the wine-skin to her, saying, "Love means sacrifice . . . if not, a man is a coward. Do I love the cause — yes! Do I love you — of course!" and I stroked her . . .

"Love means living, not dying," she said. "How many American Trotskyists have gone — two, three, four? Symbolically, you're there, Harry."

We had more wine. I was here, not there . . . and Friede was saying, "Isn't it too late to die for Trotskyism? How much of a Trotskyist are you really now?"

She had been questioning me on that recently; the non-subtle rhetorical question that summed up the nights and days and years I spent at endless meetings. When I'd come back, way past midnight, stupefied from smoky rooms and continuous talk, bringing back more political pamphlets, books and newspapers, she would wake up to kiss me, then say, "Darling, take a shower. You smell like a second-hand cigarette factory. God, how can you stand all that bellowing? What great decisions did the gallant Trotskyists come to tonight? Are you for defending the great Soviet Union in case it's attacked? How long are you going to go on with this half-way attitude? What about Red Fascism?"

I seldom answered her sallies. I showered instead — and we lay listening to Purcell's *Dido and Aeneas* unwind on the phonograph. I unwound with it. Friede joined in when Dido lamented —

> Whence could so much virtue spring?
> What storms, what battles did he sing!

And I laughed, as Friede, no longer listening to the record, asked, "And are you, my dear Aeneas, sailing for Spain again? Ah, communism! Ah, fascism! And, ah, love!"

In answer, I sang to the record—

> Come away, fellow Trotskyists,
> Your anchors are weighing,
> Civil wars have no delaying.
> Take a boozy bed tonight
> With a nymph on East Ninth Street.

I forgot Spain for another night. It was easier to go to bed with Friede, to forget Barcelona's capture. Aeneas and I were alive, Dido was not stabbed to death . . . instead we rolled with the buoyant tongues of love.

A year later I volunteered to join the Finns, when the Soviet Union attacked Finland. The Finnish Embassy, all protocol, answered me, "Unfortunately, we are not allowed by American law to accept your offer to help repel the invading Soviet armies. If you should come on your own, you will lose your American citizenship . . ." However, a schedule of ships to Finland was enclosed, "should you care to come as a tourist." I was too much in love to be a tourist.

What was love like then? It hurt with a panic's madness when I had once left Friede for five months to help the West Coast longshoremen during the 1934 strike. I wrote, talked, walked, contributing to the labor press. Often, with only a dime left, I could not write to Friede. It meant bread and cheese. I slept at the houses of friends in the cities; I slept, too on the Pacific beaches, camping there with blanket and roll, washing in the sea, making a fire from debris that had piled up for a century on those wild beaches. Thinking of Friede, I hugged closer to the burning debris, thinking the fire was Friede embracing me . . . the terrible longings of love so far away.

Love kept me from heroism in Spain and Finland. Why

die? Death was forever. Instead, we had Purcell's music. It was a more appropriate accompaniment to poetry than to politics. I was about to end my phase of political pathology. I'd had almost ten years of denunciations, of fraudulent purity, of anger and malice, of days and nights emptying my stentorian voice against Stalin's violence. I was a member of an almost memberless club. In ten years we had collected a few thousand people for an imagined revolution: in-casts ana out-casts, moral saints and amoral cretins, triflers and tragic people living for a specialized vendetta. With our dogmas and funereal sermons, we were also approaching the anteroom to an asylum. But I was no longer a potential patient for the inner recesses of Trotskyism and Marxism.

Trotsky had just written "Their Morals and Ours," a pamphlet praised by his followers. With others, I dissented. Trotsky, the great critic of fashions in revolutions, made a classical restatement of Bolshevism regarding ends and means and moral stances. To me, suddenly, it was another form of Stalinism — the honest flavor gone from the exiled pamphleteer. It was a brilliant essay — for the continuation of Stalinism by Trotskyist means.

You couldn't be half a Marxist, I used to say in jest, and still be a full Trotskyist. I had finally found a copy of Karl Marx's anti-Semitic book, *On the Jewish Question*. It was rather late in an idealist's day to read it — almost 1939. It was too dangerous for the Russians to publish — but Hitler had read it, and used its many malices. I also discovered that Marx's father, Herschel, a lawyer, had changed his name to Heinrich, to be more Prussian; and Heinrich, to add cultural status to his Prussianism, had left Judaism and been baptized a Protestant in 1816. This was four years after the Emancipation Edict, giving all Jews in Prussia full equality. Obviously, Heinrich or Herschel Marx wanted to be even more equal — a legalized Christian. I learned, too, as I began uniting loose

171

ends in Karl Marx's background that prior to Heinrich all the men of the Marx family for 150 years, had been famous rabbis. Heinrich had emerged as a Prussian lawyer and his son, Karl, as a Jew-baiting Red Prussian.

I read from another book: "Without Marx there would have been no Lenin, without Lenin no communist Russia. But, indirectly, Marx is also responsible for all the other totalitarian states, since all of them, rivals of Soviet Russia though they may be, are at the same time imitations or variations of the Soviet model. . . ."

When I read that, by Leopold Schwarzschild, author of *The Red Prussian,* I went on divesting my idealism. When you bolt, it is not sudden. It takes years, unconsciously, in objective and subjective preparation. My education, with its halting fleetness, had given me something on the savage run, and I had lived as an involved political man, registering my objections to so many ugly aspects of modern life. But, I was a poet, too, I said to myself.

Karl Marx had wanted to become a poet, and did not succeed. Hitler did not become an artist, either—and both wallowed in their over-all hatred for Jews. It provided something for my reflections . . . and I read on, from Marx. "Money is the jealous God of Israel, before which no other god may exist." Eighty years later Hitler read this, and more. "What is the secular foundation of Judaism? Practical needs, egoism. What is the secular cult of the Jew? Huckstering. What is his secular God? Money."

I read on. Marx had turned into Mephisto. "The social emancipation of the Jew is the emancipation of society from Judaism." Jews were "Yids" to Marx. He called Ferdinand Lassalle, an opposing theoretician, "The Jewish nigger." When anti-Semitic pogroms broke out in Moldavia and in Russia, Marx, despite the written protest of his collaborator, Engels, ignored them.

172

When I talked this over with my friend Max, he said, "All the socialist and communist leaders and theoreticians have always been natural anti-Semites. It's part of their good-fellowship. What do you expect, humanity from these all-leveling bastards?"

Many years later, Max, an indefatigable researcher, found a statement by Trotsky (Lev Davidovich Bronstein) offering up his piece of self-hatred. During the Russian Revolution, when a delegation of Jews called on Trotsky to protest some Bolshevik anti-Semitism, Trotsky answered, "Go home to your Jews, and tell them I am not a Jew and I care nothing for the Jews and their fate."

Their fate? Ah, yes, Jews were rich, were vulgar, were loud, were *sharp.* So were Armenians, Greeks, Arabs, Yankees, Germans, and Frenchmen. The fate of Jews—to be themselves. The ghetto, with its rude, tribal familiarities, unfortunately had no finishing schools and English governesses. If you could not stand diversity and difference, you developed fatal fancies of racism. Sameness and blandness made you acceptable. But I had expected a human view from the Marxists, at least. The Russian Marxists, instead, had signed a pact with Hitler, and Hitler had signed one earlier with the devil. I was ready to bolt from Trotskyism, Marxism—and their interior programs for better intellectual pogroms.

Voyage from Lilliput

§

It is rather belated, now, to describe some of the Trotskyist leaders; but since they were part of my formative political years, they belong here as a parting profile of a leadership that was blinder than the led. I was, obviously, one of the led.

Like Tammany Hall's political prophets, we had an Irishman at the head, followed by Jews, Swedes, Hungarians, and Litvaks. They were brilliant and myopic, totally dedicated to Olympian oratory and flamboyant writing. And like some admen of Madison Avenue, they had similar craft illnesses; their overpasteurized sectarianism had curdled them into ulcerous, angry men. They overdrank cheap whiskey, smoked endlessly, quarreled daily, and had too little money for their basic appetite, world revolution, which made the making of ulcers a Trotskyist *spécialité de la maison* . . . and now, sitting on the dais, at the national convention, they were settling the sins of many comrades, including my own burgeoning treason. In Moscow, we would have been executed; but here, without state power, we could only be expelled into the outer darkness.

Stacks of the Internal Bulletin, our sacredly mimeographed discussion organ, lay on a large table facing the leaders. Twelve of us, belonging to one of the groups contesting with the leadership, had declared against "defending the Soviet Union in event of a capitalist attack." We sat way

175

in the back, near the rickety stairs. We had made some equally
angry speeches, hours ago. We had said, among many other
tight, descriptive allusions, that the Soviet Union was
"bureaucratic, inhuman, a prison camp, a continent wide
ruled by proletarian czars; that it had pushed back socialism
a hundred years by its interior crimes, its mass executions
and deportations; that it was in the nature of the one-party
proletarian dictatorship to be violent and murderous. Stalinism was the norm; and Trotskyism, if it ever took power,
would lead to that, if it led anywhere . . ."

One of the more likable leaders, Arne Swabeck, was
answering us. Swabeck, a middle-aged Swede from the
Middle West, had a grandfatherly way. If you were broke,
he bought you a meal. He talked quietly, which set him apart
at once. He said, "Comrades, does that mean that you are
leaving us if we do not adopt your anti-Soviet views?"
Swabeck leaned over for a milk container to nurse his ulcers.
Ten other milk containers faced ten other leaders. Someone
had suggested renting a Jersey cow — to save money. A few
mixed their milk with rye, to last the session, which ran
sixteen hours a day for a week. As they talked, belched,
coughed, and spit, it looked more like a hospital for assorted
disorders than a national convention for a future world order
. . . and Swabeck continued, fortified with another gulp of
milk, "As Trotsky says in Internal Bulletin Number Three,
and I quote: 'Comrades James Burnham and Joseph Carter
have placed a fresh question mark upon the class character
of the Soviet state. The answer which they give is, in my
opinion, completely erroneous.'"

Swabeck leaned over, sipped again from his milk, then he
said, pointing his finger at me and others, "And you, Harry
Ross and Max Glee, and you, Dan Eastman and Attilio
Salemme, as well as the others of your anti-Soviet ilk — the
differences that you have with Comrade James Burnham's

176

views are minor. But all of you must give up your anti-working class views regarding the worker's fatherland, the Soviet Union, if you wish to remain here. As long as private property and the means of production and exchange are still nationalized, the Soviet Union, despite its Thermidorian stage, must be defended . . ." and Swabeck sipped again. As he put the container down, Swabeck fainted dead away.

Somebody said that Swabeck was dying. Another called out that Swabeck had merely fainted from hunger, having given his last dollar away. A third said, out loud, "Trotsky's ideas about the Soviet Union would kill anybody — anybody but Stalin!" Somebody smacked the last speaker and yelled out "Traitor! Traitor!"

Swabeck, revived, lay down on a corner bench. A girl ran out for sandwiches. Swabeck sipped from another container of milk, this one even more fortified. The national convention resumed.

The next speaker was Max Schachtman, the second in the tight command. An orator with a college degree, learned and fastidious, whimsical and linguistic, he specialized in after-the-funeral orations. When Stalin killed a well-known Trotskyist, Schachtman, as the historian, supplied the sentimental marginal notes as he breathed a purple fire of scorn on assassin Stalin's head. These funerals from afar, held between some Bronx and Brooklyn hall on a Sunday night were a sort of permanent Trotskyist wake for us. They were calendar days of mourning in German, French, Russian, and Yiddish, with Schachtman usually switching from Lenin to Bartlett, to score a linguistic point of arrival. And now, picking up where Swabeck had left off, Schachtman said, his index finger encircling us, "There are those who say that Stalinsim is the result of the one-party rule. Like Bukharin, I believe in multiple parties — one party in power, the others in jail!"

177

"Bukharin's in jail now, if he's alive. Shame!" we called out. "When have you started to serve Stalin?"

More tumult. More milk drunk. By error, one container held buttermilk. The drinker spit it out. Chairs were edging in hands. Violence was natural now, for some of us were leaving *Mother Soviet Union* for *Father United States,* symbolically. But Schachtman, undaunted, went on by the hour, hammering away at us from his Marxist and Bartlett lexicon of contempt. It was a graduating class in political egotism as improbable parables and historical nuances were trotted out in defense of Trotsky's thesis regarding the inviolable sacredness of the Soviet Union. A year later, Schachtman, forgetting this speech, adopted most of our views and split openly from Trotsky.

Now the biggest milk-drinker of them all, James P. Cannon, took the oratorical floor. He was the Big Bertha: taller, more sardonic, with more bad whiskey than good blood in him. Now he sipped from a collectivized milk container. He had once worked with his hands, and the memory gave him extraordinary status. He also had trade union contacts, especially among the truck drivers of Minneapolis; and that made Cannon esteemed. We had once led a great strike there, and it was considered Cannon's victory. There had been another great strike, in Akron, among the rubber workers; and that, too, was on Cannon's side of the proletarian ledger when Cannon and Schachtman eventually contested for power . . . and now Cannon was summing up his guidance, his angelic conceits regarding the imminent world revolution, and Stalin's removal from power—any day.

Once, in 1937, Cannon had asked me to go to Mexico to be one of Trotsky's proletarian guards. I had turned down these noble class-conscious honors. Instead, I covered Cannon, then also "working" on the Writers' Project. We met in the morning. I took his research assignment, went to

178

the library, and Cannon went off to the Trotskyist head-quarters, on University Place, to make a small world revolution.

Cannon's political grapeshot now turned on James Burnham, splattering him full-face. He yelled, "You are a professor of history, Comrade Burnham, but what sort of history are you trying to teach us here? Is it Marxist? No! Is it Trotskyist? No—I say again. It is Burnhamist trivia to suit your ideas about 'the managerial revolution.' If you insist on denying that the Soviet Union is still a worker's state, you will be expelled as a dangerous mongrel from our ranks!"

Burnham, neatly cool in all sorts of woes and weather, argued back academically, his classical Oxford training hardly up to Bolshevik polemical practices. Someone called him the "Walter Mitty of the left." That was most unfair. He was also a history professor; therefore, his proletarian credentials were suspect. His hands were not, never had been, never would be—dirty. Besides, he did not have ulcers. It scored against him. He was sartorial. He had never worn overalls. He wore hundred dollars suits. He went to the theater, too. He was writing a non-Bolshevik book, *The Managerial Revolution*. He was looked upon as a Wall Street customer's man shopping among the Trotskyists for economic conceptions. But by the time the national convention ended, Burnham, caving in, repeated all of Cannon's attacks against us—the twelve holdouts. And it was a burlesque of tribal indecencies, soon enough, when Cannon, with typical Bolshevik grace, forced Burnham to make the speech expelling us from the organization.

For a small organization, we were so serious we couldn't tolerate each other's views. The Trotskyists were split like a watered pea soup, with every member a cook, ladling out his thin factional concoction. But none of us would make

179

history, except as eccentrics and fetishists. The grim garbage buckets of socialism, Russian style, had overflowed the theoretical kitchens, and the most sensitive thing any of us could do, I finally said aloud, was to shove all the soup, all the theories, and the whole kitchen, down some incinerator — and walk away.

We had hordes of monotonous talkers, with styles that made an interjection impossible; and the rousing rhetoricians, all fancy, signifying the party line; the class-type lecturer, who knew his Marx, Engels, Lenin and Trotsky, and bored you to a dialectical death. Trotskyists had to be talkers — if nothing else. And, not oddly, we Trotskyists mistook arrogance and faith in Trotsky's beautifully written programs for superior political virtue and political intelligence.

We walked away, down three flights into the late night, after Burnham's expulsion speech. When leaving I had called out to the most likable professor gone temporarily Bolshevik in style, "Recant, Burnham! What Zinovief did for Stalin, in recanting, you're doing for Cannon. Recant, Burnham!" I left forever the sad little red building at 116 University Place. I looked about, as we came into the late night, much as if I had never known these surroundings; a lighting-fixture factory, a small Chinese laundry, an auction store, a bowling alley. All of it now seemed representative of politics: the outer darkness, dirty laundry, second-hand belongings and games. I was out of it all at last.

It was a frightening emotion. I felt clean, but expected more shock to ride through me. Max and I were feeling some peculiar elation, and we went to a bar to tie-on an old-fashioned American drunk. We would start our re-Americanization with that — and then go on to make millions. Others who left, like Dan Eastman, the son of Max Eastman, went home to glory in newly-found pacifism. Attilio Salemme, after a brief stay in an asylum, went back to art and emerged as a

180

wonderful innovator. They, at least, had something; Max and I, that night, had only the bar to mirror our emptied selves in the glasses and bottles. For once, we did not know what to do with the days and nights ahead of us: we were without Party programs and schedules. I would sell my huge political library, I decided, and read other books. I gagged over the tenth drink.

I called Friede, explaining, embracing her over the telephone. She said, "Come home, Harry — shouldn't we celebrate with a drink?"

§

A week before, my father had died. I stood, half choked before his grave in a Brooklyn cemetary. My mother, lamenting, anguished, was ready to join my father. I held her left arm. My sister Edna and my brothers — Bill, Mike, and Herschel — were crying naturally, without inhibition. I was tearless, hardly the good son of the good man in the grave.

I touched the spot where my father had struck me twenty years before. Figuratively, it was still a live wound, and I was bleeding now. When the blood came, I felt less ashamed. I was trying to feel love. It lasted a moment, and I was lost between love and remorse, numbed to nothing. . . .

Where was my love? My brothers looked at me in anger. Herschel, the oldest, the most successful, said to be worth millions, stared at my empty face and turned away. He had tears at least . . . and I thought, "Love is hard to find, even among Jewish families." Once I had read in T. S. Eliot — or was it Ezra Pound? — that "Jews are joined together in the womb by intense familial love . . ."

When my father was sick, I had visited him often. His left arm pained him then, he said. He smoked a hand-rolled cigarette quietly — and I recalled, over his soft warm smile, that I had taught him to write his name so that he could be-

181

come a citizen. We sat, hunched over the kitchen table like tea-drunk Talmudic scholars, and I would spell out my father's name slowly. I would say *B-a-r-n-e-t-t* and he would always say *B-b-a-a-r-r-n-n-e-e-t-t-t-t* — by the hour. After that I wrote his name out in large letters, which he copied like an engraver making a hundred dollar bill. Ten citizenship lessons later, we were in an officious-looking building awaiting a swearing-in ceremony. With a clerk and a judge acidly looking on, my father signed his way into American citizenship — almost a quarter of a century after his arrival on Ellis Island. But he was giving up his citizenship. The pain was really in his heart, and he was saying, "I'm dying, son." I had cried then and held him to me for his 78 years of Russian and American misery, the farmer and miller who'd left a village in the Ukraine to enter the needle trades. . . .

I remembered the factory on Greene Street from the summer I had been ten. What singular ugliness in which to live out a life. My father had left five hundred dollars to be spent on the funeral. It had gone into a box, a hole, and a prayer. There were no wills, no deeds, no estates. The *mitzvah*-man, the doer of deeds, was dead. The caged man of Greene Street and Wilson & Company was truly caged. And I remembered the day of the Triangle Fire . . . and my father telling us that it was near his factory. My mother had cried a lot, had called the land *America gonev*. It had stuck to me.

My father had known how the land flowered in the Ukraine, and once he had said to my brother Herschel, "Buy a small green place in the country so I can die there. Let me see something green, Herschel."

I remembered, once, when I had to write an emotional, angry letter, and my father was advising me: "Say it strongly, morally, and leave nothing out. If you do you are betraying yourself. Take the letter to the post office — and then you have

182

a choice—mail it back to yourself or tear it up . . ." He laughed warmly, then added, "And tear the stamp off, because you may want to write another such letter . . ."

But Greene Street was a black and gray street of factories, of men at heavy pressing irons. And my father was dead, killed by the street . . .

§

At the bar, with Max, I had my eleventh drink. I was summing up in dialectical terms my political contributions. They were 3,500 days and nights of grotesque time; three teeth kicked out and my testicles stomped on; but I had made twenty converts to a revolution that would never be made, happily. I had written hundreds of Agitprop poems to celebrate the class struggle, as well as articles for *The Militant,* and *The New International,* which James Burnham co-edited. I was doing my moral bookkeeping, in a garish fashion, distilling the ten years. When I finally arrived home to Friede, acceptably drunk, I was the pained lover waiting for more atonal dedications on her piano.

The shower was sobering, and we made love—it was our world again, not a political cosmos. The night was arrested between us, and tomorrow was another time. I had returned to myself, the poet still.

The Writers' Project was over. Jobs would be easy to get, we were told. They were not. To eat, my library went to the Fourth Avenue bookshops. Marx, Engels, Lenin, Trotsky, and Kropotkin, all soon lay on other dusty shelves, to be fingered by strangers. I went through my books with hate, filled up valises, emptied the valises at shops, and never argued about the price . . .

Meanwhile my brother Herschel plotted a future for me in the Democratic party. He had talked with William O'Dwyer, then an assistant district attorney. O'Dwyer was a politician with a future in the corrupting City, and I could become his secretary, said Herschel. It was all very simple for an ambitious man, turned totally American, to ride along with an ambitious politician. I finally met O'Dwyer at a Democratic clubhouse in Brooklyn. Sweatily he shook my hand, which I wiped clean against my coat. After two hours of being with him and his fellow Democrats, I knew that a job with them was impossible. "They're a bunch of ambitious incompetents," I told Herschel. "They sicken me."

I went home, to drift into myself.

But within a month everything became stranger. I went to Prairie City, Illinois, to help a publisher, James Decker, with a small press print an anthology of modern British and American poetry that I had edited. Friede wrote me while I was there; the language of the letter was strange, brittle and inconclusive. It was even signed with *love* at the end. A week later I was back in New York, and I knew that Friede had committed adultery. I don't remember her words . . . she said something about loving, now, a South American composer.

Stunned, I listened again to Friede's confession. We had not been married but it seemed to me, nevertheless, adultery. And the woman who'd committed it was alive before me, talking now of music and a new love . . . talking also of projects with her South American composer. It sounded so commercial and sickening. It meant money, eventually, for her; she was suddenly ambitious, she told me. When she said something about projects one more time, I lashed out at her with a fist.

She fell at the street entrance to the house. She lay bleeding, unconscious, and I carried her up the four flights. I bathed her wounds. I phoned her brother Ben to tell him. I phoned a doctor. When both arrived, I left. The police could find me when they wanted me – if she died.

184

It was the death of nine years. Now there was the terror of being alone without Friede's magic. It was a world suddenly without her music, an end to all the intimacies — and my senses were dead. Love had been assassinated ...

Friede lived — and so did I. It was late in 1939, and the war had begun in Europe. In a cold flat on Jane Street, I became a temporary recluse to finish another book of poetry. The New Deal was enlarging its values, awaiting war production to ease American industry back to its pre-1929 glories — and I became a pacifist and an amoralist in connecting sequences.

At night there were nymphs all over the Village, in cheap bars and cheaper cafeterias, awaiting expectations. Easier than whores, and more delightful, they were soon in my bed. In the morning, nameless, they went off after a cup of coffee, and I went back to my poetry.

Why be moral when you'll soon be rich, or dead, we said. It became whiskey, poetry, and bedding down. It was 1940, and even Saint Augustine would have relapsed. In my private apologies, making the flesh-bound rounds seemed an orderly way of trying to forget Friede and the coming slaughter.

Doldrums, Decadence –
and Some Bastards

§

"I am a conscientious objector," I wrote to my draft board. They were unmoved; they were in the body-drafting business and I was excellent physical material, they said, after a casual medical examination. But I was a conscientious objector, I insisted belligerently, and read them some of my anti-war poetry.

Did I perhaps belong to the Quakers? No! To the War Registers League? No! To Jehovah's Witnesses? No! To what did I belong? I belonged to myself, I explained. I was one individual objector belonging to nothing but my private objection to killing. Were they, the draft board, frightened of poetic objectors? England, under attack, was not. There was Stephen Spender, an objector in a fireman's blue uniform, putting out fire-bomb fires in London. Would I do that? Of course – everybody should put out fires. "But a war," I added, "is not at all like a fire."

"It is so like a fire," said one dour member, "and we are all firemen now. The world may soon burn up, Mr. Roskolenko. Are you in favor of the whole world burning up?"

I offered to donate my blood, not spill it. I had, out of hunger, been forced to become a blood-donor over the past year. Every six weeks I went to a little store on Second Avenue where they took 500 cc's of my blood and gave me

$35.00 for the experience. Off I'd go to a restaurant to gorge myself into strength again.

On my fifth visit to the draft board we had a mild scene. A gentle English teacher, a member of the board, said "I understand 'The Song of the Shirt,' which is all the poetry that I know of a social-minded nature. But your poetry is obscure, in flight from reality. Is it for the literate masses in the colleges or for your former political friends? Who did you want to impress, the literary critics?"

I expressed some doubt about the critics, hours later, over Scotch, after the teacher had bought one of my books. I lectured to him until early morning about man's hope, our world of woe, the need for more morals than we had, and my occasional obscurantism. Both of us were soon too drunk to understand either my militant pacifism or his illusory patriotism, but by the time the sun came up, I had won a small victory for one man — myself. I was accepted as a conscientious objector.

When a friend of mine heard the story of that night, he passed it on to a *New Yorker* short story writer. The writer had me punching the drunken English teacher on his nose for objecting to my imaginative poetry — and I was, in the story, drafted as a result. If I could carry out a full frontal attack on an English teacher, in defense of obscure poetry, I was more of a soldier than a conscientious objector.

§

I was no longer a valid conscientious objector on June 21, 1941, the day before the Soviet Union was attacked by Germany, its spiritual ally until that midnight. The rumors of Nazi barbarism were no longer unverified press stories. The human statistics of mass slaughter were believable. Appalled by the Nazi death factories like Dachau and Buchenwald, I finally wrote a letter to the draft board on Saturday, June

188

21, stating that I was no longer a conscientious objector, that I was ready to be drafted, and for the Navy, I hoped. I had, I said, been a sailor . . .

A few days later, I was back at the draft board. How did I happen to know that the Soviet Union would be attacked on June 22, the day before I wrote my letter?

"It was a coincidence," I said, "an accident of timing."

"You're a communist," they said.

"You think that I knew in advance that the Germans would attack—that I have a secret code? Okay, so I'm a Russian spy. Put me in the Russian Navy, and let's get it over with."

"When your name comes up," said the dour member of the board, "we'll put you in the American Army."

"Look, I'm an experienced sailor. Why the Army? I'll *volunteer* for the Navy. Let me be a goddamn sailor!"

"With your background, you can't volunteer. You'll have to wait to be drafted. Next, please."

I had waited since 1939 for *some*thing; through two years of doldrums and odd jobs, I had been homeless and hungry most of the time. Real jobs had not yet materialized; and without money, apartment or clothes, I was an orphan to my many friends. Those who had jobs housed and fed me from their marginal groceries. Each night it was dinner at a different house, then sleep, later in a makeshift bed. Max was among those who fed me; David Ignatow, the poet was too. I shoveled snow, delivered parcels, addressed envelopes, worked for the Census Bureau, moved furniture, painted apartments, wrote occasional book reviews for the liberal weeklies—the lot. The dozens of job-seeking letters I wrote were enthusiastically or politely answered. Robert Morse Lovett, a literary friend, then the acting commissioner for the Virgin Islands, wrote that he would make a job for me soon—"to run a trade school for wayward boys and girls on

St. Croix." It was never built because Lovett was fired for alleged radicalism. I wrote again—this time to Harold Ickes, Secretary of the Interior, offering to go to Alaska, Puerto Rico, the Canal Zone, anywhere laborers were needed. Ickes answered by asking me to file for Civil Service, "In event that a job opens up in America's colonial vineyards."

Charley Harrison, who occasionally fed me, was then feuding, as a journalist, with Harold Ickes. It was blood all the way in the liberal magazines both wrote for. Over the phone, after I'd made some lame defense of Ickes' stewardship, Charley sneered, "Look, he's just another liberal sonofabitch who can't write worth a shit! He's at the end of his long rope with the Roosevelt administration. The only thing Ickes needs is another piece, to hang himself in public. Do you like *Yiddishe* Sauerbraten? Good! And what else do you like? Who doesn't? So bring some svelte literary dame . . . Yes, only the very sad telephone each other—to keep from dying. Are you dying? You're only hungry, poet. Look, I haven't written a book in years. Why not? Ask my analyst, Dr. Edmund Bergler. He says I have a writer's block when it comes to my own creative work. Sure, I can insult Secretary Harold Ickes, which is creative enough—but that fucking novel—I'm blocked. I sit, gin in hand, for days. I write four and a half words finally. I rewrite them, and add another twenty words, all beautifully typed. Then the block sets in— and I talk with Dr. Bergler. You're not blocked? You're just hungry? Go make money! Go to Madison Avenue! Go to Washington! Go see your rich brothers . . . And who are you laying these nights? Still carrying the half-lit torch for Friede? Get another lamp, Diogenes! See you on Friday at exactly fifteen minutes after six P.M., *chaver*. The hell with our Interior!"

A telephone call from Charley was as extended as a visit. Often, when Charley could reach me through a friend who had a phone, he would call at two in the morning — to talk about jazz, Faulkner, E.E. Cummings, Hemingway, Celine, Trotsky, styles of prose — and wind up saying, "I'll meet you at the Hickory House in thirty minutes. You're sleeping? Alone? Man, you are slipping down the cosmic drain . . . In half an hour, poet!"

That summer, I innocently went to a charitably-sponsored colony for writers, artists, musicians, and poets-on-the-bum; not so much to write another book as to eat again without having to depend on the largess of Charley and other friends. I'd heard, from Harvey Breit, that the place had a French chef. And since Mrs. Eleanor Roosevelt had sponsored me, out of political politeness, I was soon gamboling over the colony's woods, lakes, French kitchens, and American bedrooms with a handsome lady sculptor. Her husband, an Australian scientist, had driven her up one Sunday; after hurriedly meeting the colony's assorted esthetes, he said to me before departing, apparently because I happened to be standing there, "Mr. Roskolenko, I appoint you a discreet committee of one to take care of my wife's intellectual needs. She's a bit rough, cobber, but all bitch! Do see if you can manage to keep her sculpting, Mr. Roskolenko — and thank you, chum, for any occasional private errands of mercy . . ." He drove off.

His wife turned out to be an impressionable pagan in the nearby woods, and to deserve her soulful vigor, I worked hard, when I was not equally pagan, on my new book. Housed in a nineteenth-century salon called the Belfry Room, with white, carved woodwork and samples of Hudson River School paintings, I lived in a strange world of poetry, French food, and other sensual services. Often it was love in the afternoons, and my poetry just went to hell.

Soon we turned the colony into our private habitat, as we went from our bedrooms to the lakes and the woods. We were normal, we agreed. The other guests were anesthetized freaks, we said in bed, or on the pine needles. When you've hungered too long, every vulgarity riots in you, we agreed again.

Many of the guests became known, understandably, as *artist colony bums.* They were the thin *creative* ones—all bones, bad teeth, high flushes, bad liquor, precious poems, bad novels, worse music, and poor painting. The good ones, somewhat fatter, seldom returned for a second visit to the endowed colony; for ugly charity it was, despite all of its fumbling about for spiritual certitude. Later, the creative ones formed little cliques in New York, to re-create in their colonized minds all the vintage values of those summers.

When Trotsky was murdered in Mexico late that August, the Australian's wife and I mourned in the woods. A man she knew had worked with Diego Rivera, Trotsky's benefactor, and had done, said the sculptor, "A mile of murals in Mexico City . . ." and so we mourned, making a wake in the pines to bless Mexican murals, imagination, history, conscience and fertility—our pasts suddenly quickened by the death of my former, adopted, political father. Trotsky had been my literary conscience, too; for his style now meant more to me than his bolshevism. Trotsky had become a shortened hero out of time . . . and he was dead. Later, our private wake done with, I walked to Lake George, sixty miles away, taking two days more to grieve over my affinities and affections for the murdered Old Man. The wounds of my stripped Marxism were still there. But my rebellions, I thought, had ended; and I was ready, when I was finally drafted into the Army, for a chance at American-bred heroism.

It came, soon enough. The day the Japanese bombed Pearl Harbor, I had a job pitching toy trains in a Washington, D.C., bargain basement for the oncoming Christmas. Excited, suddenly freed, eager to get back to New York,

I attacked the toy trains. One hugely planned collision sent all the cars circling on ten separate tracks. Then off the large exhibition tables they hurtled! Down the aisles! Toward the girls selling Virginia hams! Past the section manager went cabs and cabooses — and within ten minutes I was in my room, packing for Union Station.

Soldiers, sailors, and marines were entraining with duffle bags, rifles, and bayonets. Suddenly they were in a war. So was I, off to the United States Army, 252nd Coast Artillery, Fort Hancock, New Jersey. It was close to the Navy, at least; for we were as much Coast Guard, as we were ancient Coast Artillery. We had mine-layers, for the inner harbor defenses of New York; minesweepers, for the outer waters; ocean-going tugs and PT boats, as well as 16-inch guns mounted on flat cars. Fort Hancock looked exceptionally warlike despite its 1918 equipment.

In charge was forlorn-looking Colonel Orr, formerly from a cavalry unit on the Mexican border. He was bow-legged, from a long love of horses; and cantankerous, because he hated the 16-inch railway guns that had been forced on him. On Saturdays, after the pomp of the morning parade, he was all leader, as short as Napoleon, and quivering with self-importance. He stood before the massed regiment, his circling right hand enveloping the faraway world at war, which was somewhere behind the Statue of Liberty; and he said, regularly, weekly, monthly, words that we inscribed on our pulsating temples, "In a few months we shall be in Europe with our 16-inch guns. Whoever says they are obsolete is obsolete himself! The 252nd was at Ypres, at Verdun, and on the Marne in 1918. Men, we shall be there again!"

There was always proper applause.

§

Four months later, I was a corporal. I had been a confused basso in the regimental chorus for a month, an enterprising

193

editor of the base newspaper for another quixotic month, and on the losing swimming team by the fourth frantic month. We were, despite our energy, looked upon as old men holding down the fort on the spit, walking guard in the snow and rain, while waiting for German spies to come up from submarines always reported a few miles away. Like our equipment, we were ready for 1918 in 1942. If we were ever really going to become warriors, we'd have to transfer to a nobler fighting outfit, join the paratroops or go to O.C.S.—at any rate, get out of this old man's home on the sandy, windy beaches of Fort Hancock.

Six months after induction, I was in Fort Benning, at Officers' Candidate School, to become, they thought, an infantry officer. I saw myself, when the Second Front started, at age 36, a second lieutenant slogging in the mud of Flanders —and I had an immediate antiseptic revolt against the infantry, Officers' School, Georgia's red clay roads, Georgia itself, night marches, and the tactical problems involved in fording Georgia's Chattahoochee River under enemy attack. I was as mobile and as maritime as a porpoise. All I needed was seawater and a ship, I repeated to everyone.

I was a sailor, not a soldier, I said when I talked this over with the commandant of the Officers' Candidate School. He recalled, in answer, a night march he had been on with my training regiment. Since I was the shortest man in the regiment, I was in the first squad, to hold down the pace for the forty-mile march. Unfortunately, I loved walking, and terribly fast. Ten miles later, with most of the men falling all over themselves, the commandant drove up in a jeep, and said, "Will you put that little sonofabitch way in the back before he wrecks the regiment! He's been forcing the pace up to seven miles an hour and the march calls for four, goddammit!"

Now, as I saluted him in his office, he looked at my

194

broad, soldierly feet. I stood at ease finally, and spoke up—to be put on a ship, to be a sailor. In three weeks I would graduate as a second lieutenant, I said. I had corresponded, meanwhile, with the National Maritime Union, the War Shipping Administration, and the Army Transport Service. I had seven years of ship discharges and maritime licenses, I told the commandant. "Our ships need sailors and officers, Sir. The convoys to Russia, the sinkings near Murmansk, the Battle of the Atlantic . . ." and I went on, writing a battle scenario about the terror of the sea. "It's the draft board's fault, Sir. I don't want to be commissioned for the Infantry. I want to go to sea—and the Army Transport Service wants me as a Second Officer!" My early soapbox training was still useful.

The commandant swore, then said, with bookkeeping accuracy, "You cost the school at least four thousand dollars in training fees! What are you going to do about it, Officer Candidate?"

"I'll pay you back from my future sea pay. In installments, Sir . . ."

"Who wants your goddam installments? Go join the fuckin' sailors! And get the goddamn fuckin' hell out of here!"

I saluted briskly—and got the fuckin' hell out.

§

Two weeks later I was at Fort Mason in San Francisco, taking a much-needed six weeks' refresher course with the Army Transport Service. Commissioned a Second Officer, I wore two gold stripes and lived graciously on per diem while I studied piloting, dead reckoning, celestial navigation, and Mersig to equip me for the floating war in the South Pacific. I was equipped, too, with a yearly salary, over six thousand dollars. A war of conscience, for man, had finally ended the Depression for me.

My first free weekend brought me to Kenneth Rexroth's cosmopolitan apartment, to relax from the A.T.S. cram course. At Rexroth's I relaxed, danced Russian dances, drank red wine and listened to Rexroth talk himself red-purple on anarchism, poetry, mountain climbing, Chinese script, Jewish cooking, German sorrow, Jung's mystique, Ezra Pound's treason, and the fact that the Bible should be illustrated—for its eroticism.

There was a plump green-eyed girl with me, a bit taller than me, an all-rounded esthete involved in dancing, singing, painting, sculpting, modeling, acting, and fornicating—all seven of the fervent arts. But she was really a legal secretary, practicing an eighth art that at least gave her a salary. She and I had met two nights before at a dance studio opposite the off-limits *Iron Pot* saloon on Montgomery Street. I had heard bacchic dance music—Palestrina. I heard the delicate thud of dancers. I followed the sounds up three flights into a studio. Dancers in black leotards were thrusting about in Greco-Graham antics. Degas had called his ballet dancers *rats*. To me they were cats, with strong legs, ample thighs, and desirably round buttocks—all they needed were tails streaming from their enhancing leotards. They suffered for years as they exercised, turned thin, took stupid jobs—to hang on as part-time dancers ennobled by occasional bits of choreographic ecstasy. I had seen them around the Trotskyists, the ballerina-rats . . .

The green-eyed girl and I left, an hour later, introduced by my pretense of enough knowledge of choreography to make me a dance critic for *The New York Times*. Her name was Isabelle, and she and I floated happily down the curving stairs, into the *Iron Pot*, our hands locked. We had a similar language, she said over beer. She liked arty talking, she said over another beer. We liked walking, we said, leaving hurriedly. We loved dancing, we said, dancing freely at a folk dance place. We would definitely love each other, we said. . . .

I had not seen Rexroth in years. Now he was wearing a long mustache, Prussian style; his hair cropped like a Junker industrialist. But he was a poet in his endless declarations, standing at a mirror as he spoke, hoping to make the mirror react metaphysically. He talked about love and hate, much as he had in 1928, saying, hoarse and harsh, "Harry, I'm the most hated poet in the United States! The illiterate communists, the literate upper bourgeoisie, the whole damned literary country hates me! They hate you, too, Harry. Those effete poets! We are their natural enemies. None of them fuck, except each other . . ." and he finished declaiming, "We've satirized America's singing screech . . ." and stopped staring at the mirror long enough to sit down to the spaghetti dinner his wife Marie had put before us. "I'm a universalist!" he said at the table. "I've exposed the sham of our literary criticism!"

I had more wine to balance the heady dialogues of denunciation. Rexroth, slopping his spaghetti, hardly looked like a cosmic literary warrior out to cut queer throats, or undeserved reputations. But later, he really began to hate—it was a long list, including Ezra Pound, T.S. Eliot, Carl Sandburg and Robert Frost. Then, as a reflex to his theme of hatred, he talked happily of the High Sierras, where he went camping with Marie every summer. Occasionally, to get the pure mountain feeling, he said he went to sleep on the kitchen floor, rolled up in his sleeping bag . . .

Isabelle and I had more wine. We were in love. I hated nobody now. Only the war was hateful. But death was some other day. It was after tomorrow, in sòme future explosion at sea. And we danced on, remaining indecently alive. I finally took her home from Rexroth's illuminating renderings. . . .

Months later, Rexroth wrote to me in New Guinea,

197

"For days I've been walking up and down before the dancer's house on Union Street—to see her. She never answers my bell. She never answers my notes. She must be afraid of me . . . but when I land on her, you can feed yourself to the wallabies. Enjoy the war! Love, Kenneth."

But in San Francisco, in 1943, I enjoyed Isabelle. I was trying for an acceptable standard of morality with women. With Friede, it had been nine years of acceptable constancy, until adultery had murdered my instincts for loving only one woman. Love easily became sex after that. Why distinguish it? It was in the American brain. And like many citizens, I was a vagrant sexual bastard, I finally concluded. But in Isabelle's little wooden house on top of Union Street, I suddenly wanted the rest of my life, if I lived after the war, to become orderly. One bed and one girl. It was passing noble, my father's way. It was an *idée fixe*, as desperate as the need to breathe under water . . . for we who were about to sail to the fighting seas wanted daily letters saying that we were loved.

It was six weeks of love in Isabelle's little house. Below was the Embarcadero, with freighters, transports, and battle-wagons marching out to sea—and Isabelle and I stood by the shaded window in the foggy morning, staring into the em-battled Pacific. Which ship would be mine, one morning? Nearby Alcatraz loomed up with its imprisoned criminals. Once, in 1934, I had interviewed Tom Mooney there, for a labor-angled story about his political imprisonment. I had been taken in by his wallowing martyrdom. Soon I would sail by The Rock and wave from a troopship to the gangsters, the murderers, the con-men. I had not become one of those Americans. I recalled Cherry Street, and the other Americans of my violent boyhood. What were they fighting for?

I looked back into the large living room. A Sibelius symphony was playing. Isabelle was making coffee, and then we planned to take off across the Bay for a game of tennis.

I wanted to play at everything in a rush; her green-green eyes shone with little delights as we walked through the hilly city ambushed on the Golden Gate. Discovered by the Spanish, settled by the Mexicans, founded on gold, wrecked by fire, it engaged all my strident senses. The women were prettier; the men were tougher. The vistas joined hill and street in larger naturalness. My eyes stared on until they drowned in the mist that would, soon enough, create a new emotional memory—the ship to take me to the war beyond the gray mist.

We played tennis. We swam. We walked through the Muir Woods, hugging the giant redwood trees. We felt holy and happy, joining twigs, leaves, and branches in the silences that the newness of love made. Isabelle had known another man six months ago, an Army captain now in England. She was not in love with him, she said; had only slept with him. Her "only slept with him" defined the new America: there was a war on. We kept walking, our hands on promises, to squeeze from the flesh what some words meant and others did not mean.

It was to make the war easier for me, later, in the thousand letters that Isabelle and I exchanged, and the nude photographs of herself that Isabelle sent to me. Once in Finchaffen, New Guinea, I used a nude photograph of Isabelle in order to join a strange kind of club, to make my occasional nights ashore happier, when I was not on the endless ferry run taking high octane and diesel oil between Milne Bay and the advanced air bases up the New Guinea coast. The strange club had only one entrance fee—a nude photograph of your girl. We pinned our nudes on the wall of a shack made of kunai grass, and we sat and drank steaming beer in 120 degrees of sweating, filthy heat. It cooled something. We stank with jungle rot, then showered, when the hourly rains

199

bombarded us. The red earth, mud one minute, steamed up to dry into a fine dust that clogged our eyes and our nostrils . . . and we drank the beer, gazing at dozens of nude all-American girls: the wives, mistresses and friends of the sergeants and the officers of this stimulating club, *The Petroleum Unit Thatched-Nudist Society*. There was only one taboo — no nasty cracks about the redheads, the blondes or the brunettes. Some were skinny and tall, others were fat and short; some had inspirational thighs and dream-like breasts, others were less heroic as they drooped in bulbous poundage. Isabelle, high-breasted, in a Graham dance-stance, was always decently praised. We were very proper bastards, we agreed.

But one morning, the club burned up and three lingering members were killed. A Jap plane had dropped bombs over Finch; and tents, shacks, and corrugated huts went up, burning with a mammoth fire into the jungle . . . and all the nudes were gone. Isabelle was my token sacrifice to the flames. I had been away, piloting a small tanker to Hollandia. When I returned, the oil dumps were still blazing . . .

§

And now, Isabelle, in her wooden house, was saying over the coffee and a different symphony, "I'll send you a nude dance photograph, darling."

She was at the foggy window watching a troopship pull in.

"It's this one," I said painfully. "They told me yesterday, Isabelle."

She was crying above the music, joining the private echoes of the tears that sounded in my heart, bouncing with fright.

I had packed, unseen, the night before. We had gone to Julius's Restaurant a few block away. The Coit Tower flashed its lights for the new mariners. We ate silently, then returned to the house on hilly Union Street to make love. It was always lewd, occasionally gentle, more often with a touch of rape, always orgiastic, never in the sweetness of acceptance, always on the verge of the first forced pretense of acceptable rape. It was the way she wanted it; and after that, I knew a few things about one woman.

She stared at the troopship in disbelief and cried on, saying between tears, "You should have told me last night, darling."

I liked her tears. I was gentle. I had written poems to her. War was like love. Love was like war, all enmeshed—a tangle of weirdness making our emotions hardly stable. Who wanted stability to die? What was it like to swim among sharks? I had been taught that. Make noise! Splash! Stab with a knife! Hit out with oars! Et cetera. How did one swim when a tanker, carrying oil, blew up? I knew—swim under the oil until you're out of the oily circle. What to do when you're bleeding to death? "You just die," said one comedian in the class at the end of the six weeks of training.

Isabelle walked down the long stairs with me. I lugged my Val-Pac, she my Bach records. At the taxi she cried some more. We kissed again, made promises, talked of marriage . . .

The war was past the harbor, somewhere in the Pacific, on some strange islands in Melanesia and Micronesia . . . and the taxi took me to the troopship.

"When the Bottle's Bloody Empty, Pet"

§

We crossed 8,000 miles of the beleaguered Pacific, to the war. With screeching sea birds alighting on the poop deck, it was a panicked excursion under our own steam. Blacked out, unescorted by destroyers, our wireless silenced, we imagined Japanese subs in every dark swell riding the night ocean. We sped at 20 zigzagging knots on the converted liner, once the *S.S. Republic*—a ship familiar to me in 1926 when I made the Hamburg run on it as a seaman. The old brass nameplate was still emblazoned amidships, but it had turned as sea-green as we felt. When the ship's alarms called us to battle stations just before the sun came up every morning, we stood aligned, counting out, much as if some of us had disappeared in the night to join the strident waves. We sweated in the cold and the heat, awaiting a real alert, the ship attacked, to chuck depth charges onto the submarines down below. We listened to radio music and the news. We were always winning in the Middle East, in Africa, in the South Pacific—the waters we were in at the moment of the broadcast. When a real alert finally came, it was for Japanese planes coming at us. We fired all over the sky but hit nothing, and the planes made off to the north. But now, with our position known, we waited for more savage attacks. We were carrying several thousand worried soldiers and hundreds of heroic-looking marines; and the rumors of forthcoming battles quickened all our sleepless nerves in the endless nights as we lay near the clambering nets and the lifeboats or took to the willing Red Cross girls who completed the transport's cargo of flesh.

On the twentieth harrowing day, we rendezvoused with a group of destroyers—and off went the marines and a thousand soldiers. We learned later that the marines had invaded grisly Tarawa, to make up the huge mounds of the dead; and the soldiers had gone to invade Finschhafen, for an easier time. We went on, our destination still unknown.

At night, unable to sleep in the airless holds, I slept above on Mae West style life jackets. It was pneumatic with fancies. When the rains plowed in, I went back to the stinking holds to fall into a coma. Men were snoring and blowing wind, clothes were drying, crap games were going, deals were being made—the holds had wars of their own making. Two days before reaching our now-known destination, Sydney, a French destroyer joined us to convoy us to Australia.

I'd had a long boyish affair with Australia; a wild dream of sailing the raging Pacific, when I was eight; then a real attempt, some years later, to go there with a Marconi-rigged schooner. But now, I really was in Australia. We were berthed in Punch Bowl, a staging area a few miles from Sydney, to continue our training until we headed North to New Guinea; then farther, to the Philippines and Japan— the geographical heart of the war. But in Sydney's beery atmosphere, we soon had interim battling. "To hell with the bloody Yanks!" said some Australians. They laughed, had another beer, stopped for tea, stole what they could, and the curious war went on. We, the Yanks, needed their labor force; for the Army Transport Service was short of ships and had, in some dreamy manner, arranged to build its own small ships in North Sydney's many boatyards. They were midget tankers called Y boats, sixty feet long with only a few feet of draft to enable us to come in close to the invasion beaches of New Guinea and the Philippines. Our dream-swept blueprints also called for F.S.S.'s — Fast Supply Ships. These were made of plywood from stem to stern and lasted, if not sunk by enemy action, only two pulverizing months. We had the plans but not, as yet, the mystically conceived small ships.

In a few weeks, gallantly if not soberly, we started building them. We hired rum-drunk Australian carpenters, beer-logged blacksmiths, gin-soaked steel workers, and a few teetotalling, tea-drinking marine engineers, fitters, mechanics, plumbers, and riveters. They were mostly "the bloody drunken lot who can't get into the bloody army," as one permanently boozed-up Australian gate-guard called our labor force. I became a security officer to keep the wild Australian boys from making off with the machinery, motors, and lumber that we had piled up behind heavily-guarded lockers.

In the "working" boatyards and gear shops, it was always "cuppa time" or "smoko time," with the Australians looking you whimsically in the bloody eye. The workers, always in leaning and resting positions, smoking cigarettes or at cups of tea, told you, with fastidious down-to-earth Down Under emotions, "Mate, you can bloody well go to hell! I ain't doing a bloody bit of fucking bloody work until I finish me bloody cuppa tea, mate!" But, somehow, thousands of "cuppas" and "bloodies" later, we had built some of our plywood armada for Invasion Day, many drinking months away.

We were liked and not liked. We were loved and we were unloved as the "invading Yanks" who were, said some pithy-minded male Australians, "Over here and overdressed, overpaid and oversexed . . ." To this, at the fighting saloons, we often answered, "You're underdressed and underpaid, undersexed and under General MacArthur . . ." and then the boozing fists circulated. The functional reason for these beer battles was simple: girls. Thousands of departing Australian soldiers had left lonely wives and girls behind. But soon the lonely females had "their Yanks." They were bedding down together all over Sydney. At the overpopulated pubs, where the Yanks and "their sheillas" celebrated their English-speaking union in various American and Australian accents of love, the war games went on.

I wrote daily letters to Isabelle, occasionally a poem, to soar and soothe me through my lonely evenings. I was waiting to do everything for the United States of America, I told her. My letters to Isabelle were private inspirations to my hope, for a new America, a new Europe. But occasionally I departed from that patriotic stance and took to the streets of King's Cross, Sydney's superimposed Greenwich Village, where the sheillas were patriotic right into their panties. Office girls crowded in front of the hotels, especially the swankier *Hotel Australia* on Castlereagh Street, after work, hoping to be picked up by an American officer but happy, just before the pubs and the restaurants closed, to get a restless buck private. By the time the war ended, ten thousand girls bore bastards. The sheillas, nevertheless, made all of us better soldiers and sailors, and we got fat on the beer and playing.

Harold Rosenberg, the American critic, had sent me the address of a famous American poet stationed in Sydney with the Johns Hopkins Hospital staff, shipped en masse to Australia. The famous poet, Rosenberg said, would make things cultural more so, should I be trapped within Australia's beer parlors. We had many things in common besides prosody and George Saintsbury. We were Jews bearing invisible crosses—and I bore mine with grim laughter; but it was hardly that one drinking afternoon in the *Hotel Australia* bar. Some of us were talking about Palestine and the

206

war in the Middle East. I said that I believed in Jewish statehood. A group of second lieutenants from Alabama, with too much love of beer, interrupted; "Jews and niggers are the same!" said one. Another, drunk all the way between the head and the bar, wobbled over to me, saying, "You're another Jew bastard!" I said, not yet drunk, "And you're a drunken bastard!" A friend with me, Tommy Poore, a second officer, interrupted one of the four racists from Alabama, saying, "Gentlemen, I've got a Jewish wife, so what does that make me?"

"It makes you a converted Jew bastard!" said another prophet of a second lieutenant from the state of Alabama.

"Well, in that case, I'd be an Irish sonofabitch if I didn't clobber you, you miserable shit of Alabama ectoplasm!" And the beer, and the mugs, and the boys from Alabama, and the two of us were soon clobbering our way into a race war. No one won—and all of us lost.

Oppressed by the scene, I finally sent a note to Famous American Poet. Then another note. No answers. I hung around bohemian pubs, asked famous Australian men of letters about the American poet. Finally one said, after investigating for a week, "He's gone north—he's up in New Guinea fighting the bloody mosquitoes!" We went to a private club and drank until morning. We talked literature—and it was steak and eggs and beer for breakfast. We drank until noon—and it was kangaroo steak and beer for lunch. We drank until dinner—and it was more of the same, with red-haired barmaids, ample and high-bosomed, waiting to take us "'ome for a sleepo."

After this inspirational encounter, I took to reading what the Australians had written. There was Christopher Brennan, a minor metaphysical poet; Henry Lawson, a folk poet who had created some of the national aspects and attitudes in his book, *While the Billy Boils;* Adam Lindsey Gordon, who had done it earlier, in *Bush Ballads,* to get away from English influences. And, to add more foam to my beered-up reading, I completed my introduction to Australian literature with "Banjo" Patterson, who had written the lyrics for *Waltzing Matilda,* Australia's hobo ballad turned national anthem. It had appeared originally in *The Bulletin,* Sydney's major weekly—a mad, angry, rousing, often racist, yet engaging arbiter of Australia's floating morals, politics, and wool prices, as well as sober art and simple poetry. But *The Bulletin* was more often profane and violent than poetic. It was acutely nationalist, crying alternately "Keep Australia White," and "Back to the Bush, Boys!" Nationhood meant land, farms, huge flocks of sheep. It gloried in its appeal to the *outback*—a place back of beyond. It was an ulcerous, cancerous magazine of suspicion. To the insider it was known as *The Bully.* Jews, fresh from the horrors of Hitler, on arriving in Australia, were called, by many, *Refujews.* But there were other refugees, the disfranchised aborigines. Kept in the outback, with few allowed in the cities, the aborigines were a dying people. I saw them at Botany Bay, throwing boomerangs for an occasional shilling; thin, spindle-legged, ancient-headed, they grinned to be accepted.

Almost the size of the United States, but containing only the population of New York City, Australia had six major cities spread along its coastlines; but, inland, for almost 2,000 miles, it was a vast no-man's-land of salt bush and deserts, inhospitable to man—a dead heart. This dismal geography had created the Australian personality, a mixture of half-energy and a full-leaning do-nothing posture; and much beer was needed to keep the posture mobile in the pubs around Sydney. Australians gambled along with their drinking; there was a game called two-up, a penny toss, and there was soccer, tennis, yachting—and many anti-English games, and then there was horse racing. It was their attempt to soften the inherent anger of the land and its people ... and little did I then expect, with my initial experiences, and my brief antipathy, that I was later to make Australia my home — to become a willing propagandist for Australia's many joyous eccentricities.

I still had a job, of course, in the building of our plywood fleet. On my nocturnal security rounds, I walked about with an armed guard. I examined the boats we were working on, to see if the keels were still there. I counted our stocks of marine engines, outboard motors — "the lot" — to see how much of the lot was still American property and not Australian by right of "pinching." One night they pinched. A locker had been broken into. Two large propellers for our double-enders were missing. The guard, all beered-up, had not heard. I phoned the captain in charge of our unit, but he was partying for the night with a sheila at some unknown address.

Angrily, I said to the beery guard, "Your compatriots are not Allied patriots on dark nights. The guy who got the two screws is wrecking the A.T.S. invasion — the bastard!"

"I wouldn't rightly know, Sir," said the guard, staggering back to his gate.

It was thievery, I rightly knew, and I spent the night on a tarpaulin guarding the locker. I was so proudly American, I caught cold by dawn. . . . In the morning, dirty and unshaved, I reported the theft. It went through normal channels — to nowhere. Some Australian yachtsmen, unable to buy propellers because of war shortages, now had two propellers.

A week later, a 600-HP outboard motor, worth several thousand dollars, disappeared; taking off, said a lanky Australian marine engineer, "On its bloody own — my oath!"

On his tenth "My oath!" I said, "Mr. Adams, only two of us have keys — you and I."

"Do you suspect me, you bah-stud?"

209

"You, your cobbers, your Premier—and every Australian from age three up, chum."

"Well, then, let's have a beer, mate."

It was impossible not to love them, if you could afford it.

§

From a bookseller, I accidentally got another clue to Famous American Poet's military whereabouts. A girl, Laura, at the old Macquarie Mansion on Elizabeth Bay, knew F.A.P.

"He's gone to settle the war in New Guinea," she said when I phoned. "How? Well, he's writing a book of jingles in the jungles of the fuzzy-wuzzy. The book's about everybody jingling, jangling, and free-versing in America—from your Walt Whitman, that nice old man with the gray beard and the sly pose, to that awful Mr. Ezra Pound. But would you like to call around for tea and some littry frippery?"

I came by. She was awesomely attractive. She was tall and talkative. She was married, but her husband was with the Royal Australian Air Force in England. She had, also, "been a bit intimate with F.A.P.," she said. "How can you refuse a supplicating poet?" She offered me Scotch, not tea. She was English, "Stuck here by an accident prior to the war; but I can't wait to get back to lovely London. I'm a Pommy. My father was a salvage expert—you know, he took care of wrecked ships for the underwriters. He dived, deep-sea fashion. He died, diving one day. Poor father! . . ." and she was saying, later, over more Scotch, "Would you care to come to my mad New Year's party? We'll drink to winning this great human conflict for Man, God, Politics, Science—and the awful Generals. Do you think I'm treasonable? No, I'm merely a cynical newspaper reporter currently covering the courts, the theater, the scandals, the shortages, and the thievery here . . ."

210

I broke in. The propellers, the outboard motor, all of it made her laugh. She pointed to lovely Elizabeth Bay with hilarity, "Look out there! Do you see that yacht with two propellers? Well, they're yours, chum. That yacht was pulled out of the water a week ago for just exactly that bit of 'repair work.' "

As I was about to leave, she said, "Oh, just a mo." Another drink was pushed in my hands, to help me through her next round—the horror of the times, and "My husband's been seeing quite a bit of Dylan Thomas; that is, until six weeks ago, when they bunged Dylan into an alcoholic ward. They don't expect Dylan to live this time, what with all the lovely beer and spirits going down his lyrical stomach. Ah, poetry! Ah, newspapers! Ah, *merde!*"

Everything came quickly after that. She hated Australia and said that two times. She loved the English and said that four times. She was upper middle class and said that seven times. She did not like General MacArthur and said that only once. She liked General Eisenhower because he had deferred to General Montgomery, "A great Pommy general!" I was at the door for an hour listening to it all over again in her very lovely English. It was so precise that it cut clearly and beautifully through my American ears. I was seated again. There was more Scotch. She was ecstatic about the Americans, "They are so kind, so childish with their sheillas, so thoughtful about old ladies crossing Martin Place and King's Cross, so immature about money—and such children of nature lost in their nature . . ."

When I left I floated along with the Scotch. She was an actress, at least. She was a poet, of course. She was a most attractive scandalmonger, certainly. She was very pretty: all blonde, blue-eyed, feminine in her tall way. Her brief kiss, mouth open, was opening up Australia for me . . . and I wondered how many more letters I would write, late at night, to Isabelle in San Francisco.

§

Elizabeth Bay on New Year's night was all picture-framed. Sailboats in the coves, Christmas lights, dancing drunks singing *Waltzing Matilda;* and if there was a war, it was on some other planet.

"Oh, look what you brought — two beauto bottles! You are a dear, pet," said Laura, taking my offering. "I want you to meet two great Australian painters, Donald Friend and William Dobell. No, they don't paint the bush, nor wallabies, nor our sheep, nor our land-devouring rabbits. Bill Dobell has some paintings of his in your Modern Art Museum in New York. Donald Friend paints mystical things, himself mostly, I reckon. He's lived in the Orient, so there! And this one's our most waspish wit, Mr. Cyril Pearl. He bites, chum, I warn you. What does he do? Ah, the lovely American touch — a man's profession. He's City Editor. He makes the *Sydney Daily Mirror* what it is — all rag. Say something, Mr. Pearl, to Mr. Roskolenko. Say something, Mr. Dobell, to Mr. Roskolenko. Say any kind of something, Mr. Friend, to Mr. Roskolenko. Ah, yes, drinks . . ." and Laura went off to provide for her twenty guests.

"How do you do, Mr. Roskolenko?" said Mr. Dobell, who was short, fat, and shy in his pleasantries.

"How yer, chum?" said Mr. Friend, who was taller, slimmer and comfortably affable.

Mr. Cyril Pearl was talkatively different. "It's merely the cultural lag, Mr. Roskolenko," he said soon. "Twenty years from now, if Japan doesn't win, we'll be like New York and Los Angeles — all smog, smucks and gadgets. Lovely thought, no?"

212

"Unlovely thought, yes."

"Been in any major or minor battles yet?"

"This is my first," I said.

"And your second front is mostly literary," and Cyril Pearl looked at Laura coming toward us with glasses.

Nearby two American officers were quarreling about General MacArthur. One, a captain in the Marines, was saying, "He's just a measurer of contiguous foxholes. What sort of support did he give us at Tarawa? I was there, Major! We lost more than eleven hundred United States Marines from our invasion force of eleven thousand. God, man!"

"The war's come here to roost," said Laura, taking me to dance. Her long thighs joined my short ones in a calypso movement. We moved toward the bay windows that circled the large room.

"You must come again when the war's over," she said. We paused at the bar for doubles.

"You're a yellow sonofabitch!" said the Marine captain throwing a punch at the Army major. "Fight, you bastard! Fight like you didn't fight at Tarawa, Major! I lost ten buddies there, you bastard!"

Laura separated the U.S. Army from the U.S. Marines, saying, "Please, dear devoted warriors! Any day, the Philippines will want you, gentlemen. Be prepared!"

Pretty soon the captain and the major were hugging each other. Five minutes later they were fighting the Australians.

"Throw the bloody Yanks out!" said Donald Friend, the artist, when the Marine let go a left at him. It did not land. Both fell on the couch and lay there talking about art. The party was getting gregarious.

Men and women came and went. They stopped in for a drink and then went off to other private wars of the New Year. Some of those who stayed were singing *Waltzing Matilda*. It was now a sentimental party.

213

As Cyril Pearl was leaving, warmly aglow, he said, "Mr. Roskolenko, do phone me for lunch before you lose more of your illusions about the noble Australian savage. He's all beer and wattle, chum!" and he was gone.

Others were going too. Time had hurried up. The double Scotches had hurried words, songs, stances, and fights. The Marine was still brawling about Tarawa. A moment later he stood centered and was reciting *The Shooting of Dan Magrew*. Someone pushed him to the door. Another opened the door—and out shot the Marine, rolling down the circular stairs with his tumbling glass and recitation. At the bottom he found two drunken Australians—and they were soon battling again. The place was suddenly quiet. I had an empty glass in my hand . . . and I was listening to Laura easing things for me.

The radio was on. The year's major events were being broadcast. Jap midget subs had once entered Sydney Harbor to try to sink the *Queen Elizabeth* anchored inside the boom. I listened to the Australian year unwind and my own year wind.

I opened a bleary eye to see Laura straightening up, "As my sister's coming over for lunch. She mustn't know that you've slept with me, pet. She thinks it's not proper what with my husband fighting in the London pubs."

Over breakfast, we sat at the bay window, seeing the morning over Elizabeth Bay; flowers, yachts, trees, cricketers, children jumping, people walking by the coves . . . and Laura was saying, "Do you feel guilty about me? About yourself, pet? Do you, really? My God, I believe you. But this is the Day of Resurrection and you have arisen for me, so let us be happy that we've met. You're goodo for me, chum. Nice, strong, sensitive—and you listen. I like a good listener for a lover, pet."

214

"Must I apologize for something I said — or did not say?"
I asked over steak, eggs and coffee. I was almost memoryless.
But whatever Laura had said, apparently, I was about to become her permanent lover. How nice, the prospect! How
lovely, the apartment! What an accidental condition! And
then I thought about Isabelle. I shook my head now, too
dubious about Laura.

"Oh, you have a beauto conscience, I must say!" said
Laura. "There is a girl with green eyes — Arabelle, or is it
Isabelle? There was once a depression. There was a girl
named Friede whom you almost killed. Will you do that to
me if I sleep with my husband? Beauto! Ah, now that's real
love for you! And since you don't like my narrow bed, Sir,
I'll get another, for happier mating, mate. Oh, that horrid
Australian slang! More coffee?"

I was anchored there. I had accepted an invitation . . .

§

Five months later, I was still there. Down at Walsh Bay
we had built some ships. They had gone north, landed on
invasion beaches, delivered medical supplies, and were
blown out of the water with their crews. It was the way the
war went. When a boat was built, we crewed it for death in
New Guinea. It had no other errand.

I had errands. I learned how to open all sorts of liquor
bottles in a hurry: Red Heart Rum, Corio Whiskey, Black
and White Scotch, Gilbey's Gin — 270 bottles that went into
Laura and me and our friends within five months. I counted
them in their empty glory one night. They were stashed
around the walls, in the closets, in bookshelves, on top of
the icebox, under the narrow bed, on the bay window —
bottles of glory that could not, because of embarrassment,
be thrown out. Laura patted them and called them, "Dear

215

little lovely pets that do so much for a war. Such reasonable freedom bottled without bondage. And you are a nice man to get such beauto rations. Tomorrow night we have a party, pet; and the next night, Famous American Poet's coming for dinner. I believe he thinks he can have sexo with me, darling. Poor boy, I must disappoint his lyrical soul. Up in Milne Bay, without women, struth! How hard on his creativity! Here, he was in and out of a dozen beds. When did he find time to write his brilliant, cosmic, ecstatic poetry?"

I was the listener to travail, trivia, chatter and patter; to statements that ended with "pet." Once a week I went with Laura to the Gilbert and Sullivan opera which she covered for her newspaper; and we had to get drunk to listen. We arrived drunk, drank during, and after — to get over the nonsense music. Once I refused to go. She stormed mildly, "That awful Gilbert and his Mr. Sullivan! Do you want me to suffer all alone? You don't love me at all, pet. I have given you my bed, my honor — so you must, most definitely, come to hear *The Mikado,* pet. Oh, that's a very good little boy!"

We had managed, because there was *some* time when we were not drinking or at work, to edit an all-Australian issue of an American magazine and to include, in our literary haze, the hoaxed poems of a non-existent poet named Ern Malley. The poems had been passed on to us by Max Harris, the editor of *Angry Penguins,* and the *enfant terrible* of literary matters in Adelaide. Max Harris had also published *A Second Summary,* a book of my war poems written by the bottle, and I was the subterranean hero on every page of its boozy bleeding. Sidney Nolan, the artist, had illustrated it. That I was alive at all, and not in some alcoholic ward, astonished Laura's tender sensibilities.

It was love, we said. It was love, I said. It was love, Laura said. It was . . .

216

§

Famous American poet finally came down from the North.

F.A.P. had gone after everything resembling a female in Australia.

F.A.P. sat with us at a restaurant, the *Kanimbla,* and sulked.

F.A.P. drank sparingly of the wine and did not talk poetry.

F.A.P. was awkward, distraught, boxed-in, unlyrical.

F.A.P. drank more wine and did not talk shop.

F.A.P. went off after dinner alone.

F.A.P. wrote a famous book, later.

§

It was May now. Again I counted the empty bottles. There were 294. That morning, at the Army Transport Service's installations at Walsh Bay, I had also counted my chances—of living through the war. Up in New Guinea, sober, there was a patriotic and accepted way of dying.

The personnel officer, who crewed our ships, said to me, "It's your neck, man. There's a Y tanker in Finschhafen that I'm crewing in a hurry. You can catch an Army freighter for Finch tomorrow—and in ten days you're in the goddam war. You wanna go?"

As I signed, I asked, "What happened to the other crew?"

"The other crew? The cables went out yesterday. They're dead, man, dead. You still wanna go?"

I nodded funereally, and said, "Yes . . ."

We were saying good-bye over the 295th bottle. I was packing. Laura was drinking, crying tenderly, protesting in lovely English cadences. It was like a ballet, with emotional turns and tearful arabesques. We talked of love again. We were sensitive people, we agreed. All poets were, of course. Bottles sensitized poets and heroes, we agreed again. "Look what it's done for Dylan — struth!" She mentioned other fraternal members of the bottled spirits and said that I was definitely not an alcoholic; "Pet, you only tried to keep up with me. I think you'd rather have had ice cream — and just a bit of rum on top . . ."

I wanted nothing on top, nothing on the bottom, nothing in between — nothing but New Guinea. Laura had been talking for five straight months and lapping at the bottles.

"When is love not love?" I asked. In the last months I had written only occasional letters to Isabelle — and even been honest about Laura, and the second best bed. Laura had done the same when she wrote to her R.A.A.F. husband in London. Oh, we were very honest, all the way.

"When is love not love?" I asked again.

Love was behind the eyes, in the eyes, in the combing of the hair, in the angle of the walk, in the feel of the touch, in the enveloping smell, "And in the Hell," I said.

"When is love not love?" I repeated angrily.

"When the bottle's bloody empty, pet," said Laura laughing. It was empty. There had been 150 days and nights and a minor rape of the heart.

§

I was on the Army freighter the next morning bound for New Guinea. We pulled out of the Wooloomooloo Docks in the rain. There was a hand waving under an umbrella. It looked like a massive hand reaching up to a neon-lit sign behind the Wooloomooloo Docks, advertising beer and spirits. It waved nervously in the fog; a hand detached, saying, "When the bottle's bloody empty, pet . . ."

218

Death Is Tomorrow

§

Finschhafen, or Base F was just another staging area for the forthcoming invasion of the Philippines. It was a vast tent city built on red sand that became oozing mud during the hourly seasonal rains. Massed there were the nervously-geared fighting men of the 32nd Division, khaki legions waiting with their murder machines in the soggy heat and the oppressive rains. The hacked-away areas for tents, grass huts, and equipment depots, including the bulldozed roads, were useless operations as the Army engineers tried to change nature. The kunai grass sprang right back as you looked, popping up so many inches per day, enveloping the metal-wrought military civilization that had invaded this permanent green hell of primitive man.

Deadened by the heat, the jungle humidity, and the hourly rains, the American and Australian soldiers were kept alert by soggy drilling, visiting Hollywood actors, and occasional Japanese raids, but mostly by invasion rumors. Hollandia had been invaded in April. A thousand miles away was Morotai, and the scuttlebut was that we would soon be fighting there. After that came the long watery road to the Philippines and then the Japanese mainland. It was the way the war would go, we said over beer.

I was third in command over an ocean-going, base-shunting, octane-laden ship. The Y 21, under 500 tons, had been re-crewed from survivors. They looked weary, hardly the victors, as they lapped at hot cans of commissary beer — too worn for more than beer and cussing out the war. They were Americans, Australians, Dutchmen, and Indonesians; and as the Y 21 moved out of the cove at Langamach, they fought in their mother tongues. The Australian seamen shouted the loudest, going at it bull-blast with their *bonzers, bloodies, good on you, struth, bang-on, bang-off, wouldn't it rot yous, cows,* and *my flaming oaths;* the Americans answered in a poverty of imagination with their *motherfucking sons of bitches.* No one knew what the Indonesians were saying. We were headed for Port Moresby, five hundred miles down the New Guinea coast, to load high-octane on our water-ballasted tanker. We finally managed, when the beer was gone, to organize the watches. It was typical of the Army Transport Service at war, on a ship, and at sea, at its deepest affinity of patriotism, beer, and efficiency.

My first chore before sailing that morning had been to go to Base F's commissary by truck for our stores — canned goods and beer rations — 24 cans of potent Australian beer per man. The crew used beer as a chaser for fruit juice and pure alcohol. I was invited by a kid-sailor, Bryan, an Australian, to "Have a go at it, Sir . . ." Boilermakers helped to chase away the war.

"It's just normal Allied insanity," said the sour-souled captain of the floating saloon. Captain Shaw, Australian, was skinny and short and sadder than any of us. He almost never smiled; it was something he had given up. He added, "We'll take three days to make Port Moresby. We'll take eight hours to load the three hundred thousand gallons of high-octane. And we'll be back in this inferno within a week."

It was the longest address he was to make to me or to anybody on the Y 21. He had been happier in the Royal Australian Navy, said Bryan, the young sailor; but at one of the New Guinea invasions, Captain Shaw had run his ship onto a reef. Out he went, retired to the Y 21, to his ulcers, angers, and petulance. He almost never slept, drank gallons of tea, took all sorts of pills, and stared with bleary eyes toward Goodenough Island in his spiritual deadening. I tried talking to him during "meals" or when on my watch regarding the ship's unsanitary condition. He merely looked away and said, "We'll be sunk one of these starry nights. Why bother cleaning up this filthy ship?"

The Y 21 had been around New Guinea for a year with similarly indifferent captains and crews. At its launching ceremony, the bottle of champagne had not broken when it was struck, too genteelly, against its sides. Somebody said it was a bad omen. They tried a beer bottle taken from a riveter. That had smashed . . . and so had the original crew, dead within the year, killed in their lifeboats when the Y 21 was under attack. The ship itself had miraculously escaped, and now, re-crewed, its international complement of sailors acted as if they too were ready to abandon the ship, not yet under attack. It was a dying piece of maritime machinery from lazerette, galley, and bridge, to the foc'sle and the scuppers. It was a garbage can afloat. Why bother?

I bothered about everything, especially about rats and snakes. Our main food locker was in the forward lazarette. In the glueing heat and the torrential rains, when we tied up to the oil docks at Langamach, things crawled out of the jungle and down into the lazarette; and the cook, a Malayan, came up with dead snakes, live rats, half-eaten wild pigs — all of which soon had him refusing to go near the lazarette. Our occasional fresh meat we picked up from the small commissary boats chugging around Finschhafen harbor.

At Port Moresby, or at Milne Bay, we tied up to massive mother tankers. Towering above us with their 20,000 tons, anchored under the foothills of the Owen Stanley Mountains, their huge pumps filled our four forward wells as if we were a spittoon. Then away we chugged, at seven knots, to Lae, Finch, Saidor, and Hollandia, wherever the fuel was needed, through the mined New Guinea coastal waters. Our navigation lights burned at night, but when I objected to their visibility's making us a fine target, Captain Shaw said tersely, "The danger of mines and collision is greater than the possibility of enemy action, Mr. Roskolenko . . ."

It was a poor, joyless ship. Its final errand, we agreed, was to *die* – explode. Despite Captain Shaw's sleeplessness, and his constant bridge-walking, all of us expected him to run us aground. Though I was the navigation officer, he would not allow me to set the course; nor would he allow the First Officer, a Scandinavian-Australian named Hansen – tall, bald and anemic – to function properly.

We stood our watches watched. Captain Shaw, napping briefly over charts and tea during some less wearying interludes of anxiety, would, when more distressed, pull out miles to sea, way off the arranged course, to avoid imaginary sandbars and reefs ever-present in his self-imposed terror. At forty-five, he looked twenty years older.

When I wrote to Laura in Sydney, she wrote back soberly regarding the morbid captain and the drunken crew, saying, "I beg you, darling, get off that dying ship. It has the wrong number, too; for 21 makes up the number three, which is fatal for a sailor in a war. Please, please, change ships . . ." And then her letter wandered off into other intimacies. She talked of love. She would divorce her husband, she wrote. She would marry me, she said. "But get off that bloody Y 21, pet . . ."

After each trip, when back at Base F, I was queried by the Army Transport Service's medical unit about Captain Shaw's general condition. Was he bearing up? He was, for a man who wanted death. Mr. Hansen was not bearing up, said Mr. Hansen, who accompanied me once, remarking, "Change the bloody skipper! Give us a bloody resto, chums! We've not stopped in four months for one flaming day of rest . . ." We loaded and sailed. We unloaded and sailed. We were part of the machinery of invasion, ferrying the fuel; others would do the fighting and the dying. We'd stop only when the ship was stopped.

In the interim, there were other ways of dying from the gaseous inferno of fumes down in the pump room.

Every hour, when pumping out our load, an officer visited the pump room to grease the machinery and read the tanks' gauges. Somehow, by common default, it became my permanent job. Down into the narrow compartment I climbed, wearing an air lung; and Bryan, manning the small air pump on deck, would feed me the purer air through an attached rubber hose that leaked badly. I came up, dizzy and toxic, in a gaseous coma until my lungs cleared; and then back I went to read the gauges, to keep the pump running.

One day, after an overdose of pump-watching, I walked ashore into the bush to vomit, and fainted dead away. When I came to, it was not my lungs but malaria that had me puking. After five days of dysentery and vomiting, chills and fever, I was hugging my now skinny body to keep from shaking my bones away. I was in a large tent with other A.T.S. malarial patients, sweating my way through delirium into some manageable mental state. A bed away, in my foggy imagination, was an apparition from the past—James Decker, the publisher, with whom I had worked in the Midwest.

Lying in my sweating, malarial bed, I dreamed about love—to keep me warm during the blanket-covered shaking. And love had four intertwining faces in time with strange ends mocking my fevered dreams. The four women I had known were dissolving: Laura in Sydney had gone to a nunnery for terrified alcoholics; Isabelle in San Francisco to a nunnery for ex-dancers; Friede in New York to a nunnery for ambitious pianists; and in Hamburg, Anna, of my radical youth, was in a concentration camp.

On the eighth day the fever passed. On the ninth day Sergeant James Decker actually materialized. On the fourteenth day, I was an elite member of the Petroleum Unit's Thatched Hut Nudist Gallery, at jungle-enshrouded Langamach; and there, over hot beer, I sat back and stared at a mob of sensualists looking at the nude photos of their wives and girls.

Outside the hut was the towering bush. The almost naked natives who inhabited it were heavily browed, with pierced broad noses and bushy hair matted with weeds and stringed beads. Necklaces of dog's teeth — their negotiable currency — were suspended from their necks. They hung around as "workers" for two dollars a month and food — Spam — to make up our native labor force below the razor-backed Central Mountain Range that rose behind Langamach's many coves and inlets. Their women had been sent into the bush to keep the troops from adding an American strain to the tribe. Whenever a native came into our hut, he would try to steal one of the nude photographs and tie it to his dog's teeth necklace as an additional emblem of universal manhood.

§

I was to return to Finch a year after the war, as a journalist en route to Japan and Indo-China . . . and the changes! My diary, in 1946, read: "The courier plane took off for Finschhafen early one morning. Coming over the Kokoda Trail all was quiet, no bullets whizzing, just a huge mountain range falling away into a brown pastoral.

"At Base F were 13 Americans, guarding a warehouse. Two years ago there had been hundreds of thousands. The

224

kunai grass chapel on S. 11th Street lay on its side, with the crucifix propped up. Half-blurred signs pointed to every city in the world — the games of waiting soldiers. 'New York, 10,000 miles this way!' The familiar two-lane military highway, made of coral, was a disordered roller coaster road now. A steel bridge the Army engineers had put up over the Song River now hung, half destroyed, in eerie dislocation and suspension. The tent city scene was gruesome. Nearby was the American Cemetery with the bodies of 12,000 troops, guarded by 33 teen-age soldiers. It was a dull time for them, caretakers of the war's dead.

"Down at the Army Transport Service's docks, the offices were open, empty, the floors covered with official forms. Two years of rain, grass and dust lay on them. But I found my name on an old roster and I had the impulse to cry . . .

"The scene from the airplane control tower at Nadzab was Daliesque, melting into a plain of aluminum. Bombers lay there without engines, stripped of instruments, with only their garish pictures painted on the fuselage as a reminder. One picture, a lewd nude called 'My Baby' had fifty stripes marked up. This was New Guinea revisited. . . ."

§

On the fifteenth day, I finally reported back to the Y 21. I was ready for every sort of an invasion . . . and Captain Shaw.

Captain Shaw was feathered like a trigger, ready to be squeezed. First Officer Hansen was quarreling openly with him, in front of the crew. "Next trip, and off you go, Captain Shaw! You don't drink, you don't swear, you don't eat the bloody tucker — and you watch every bloody thing that I do. Well, I've had it, *Sir.* After our next trip, I'm going to say everything that I've bloody well thought about you to the bloody Yanks!"

225

Bryan, the kid-sailor, was nodding.

"Mr. Hansen," said Captain Shaw, quivering with an effort at control, "all that I want you to do is what I do — keep this ship alive. Do you understand me, Mr. Hansen?"

The First Officer snapped back, "Yes, Captain Shaw," and then imitating the captain's speech, Hansen bellowed, "The pumps are not working! Must you always eat, Mr. Hansen? We'll be beaching, Mr. Hansen! We're off our correct course, Mr. Hansen! We're going to hell, Mr. Hansen!"

As a perceptive, naturalist philosopher once said, "Never come between a dog and a lamp post . . ." and I did not intrude in this purely Australian diatribe.

No blows, all words, and we were at sea again. This time we went to Aitape, below Hollandia. It was late in September. When a sailor brought my mail on our return to Base F it included a package—a kosher salami five months at sea, sent by my brother Bill. I cut off large slices and handed the first chunk to Captain Shaw. He refused it and turned away. I gave it to Mr. Hansen. He bit, saying, "Bloody good tucker. What is it?"

"Contemporary Hebraic cuisine, Mr. Hansen." I passed pieces to the engineers and the rest of the crew. Two members of the gun crew looked down from their turrets. I heaved slices to them. The ship soon reeked of garlic, with everybody but Captain Shaw munching ravenously away. We finished all five pounds of it then and there.

Morotai had been taken, and all New Guinea was now under our control. From Morotai to Mindanao, in the Philippines, was about three hundred miles. Morotai was to be our most important air base, the jump-off for the eventual conquest of the Philippines. For the Y 21 it was 1500 miles — eight days from Finschhafen. Everything that could go to sea was at sea. As part of the extraordinary armada, the minuscular Y 21 joined the lanes of ships—the battlewagons, cruisers, destroyers, flagships, carriers — and they marched through the waters.

Morotai was still grim on the embattled muddy beaches when the Y 21 pulled in. Nearby in the caves, were Japanese prisoners in shorts staring out from their enclosures. On shore, we found Japanese bodies, waiting not for burial but for nature's destruction to dissolve them. One soldier had grass growing from the toe of his left shoe; the right one was gone; the stomach and the rib cage, a skeletal frame of a recent man; the eyes, distorted by death and the crawling things, were savage sights in his decaying head, where he had been hit. He had, like the others, been left as a carcass as we went on to other military objectives.

We emptied the four wells of the Y 21, took on oil. We went on again. . . .

§

When it happened, I hardly knew. For several days I had been down with malaria again. My fever had gone to 105 degrees, and I was out of my head most of the time. When we were hit, I was vomiting and then holding my head. Blood was oozing. It seemed as if my head had opened up to let in air and cool me; then my right shoulder opened up. I yelled out. It was broken from the hit. . . .

We were in the Western Carolines, off Helen Reef, heading for Palau, supposedly safe from Japanese marauders but not from the reef. Was it the reef? We were too far off to ground; but somebody was yelling that we'd hit a loosened mine. We were hit by something — and sinking.

Bryan was shouting. Bryan was moving me violently out of my cabin, rushing me toward No. 1 lifeboat. He was pushing and yelling something. Whatever he wanted me to do, I tried, vague and uncertain about my responding reflexes. He shoved me to the clambering rope ladder, under the davit of No. 1 lifeboat, to get me down the ropes and into the lifeboat.

The Y 21 had been hit up forward. She was listing. Mr. Hansen had bounced against the pelorus with his head when the ship was hit, said a member of the gun crew. There had been red-blue flames. Captain Shaw, then on watch, had been seen pushing papers and the log into briefcases. He was heard shouting, belatedly, "Abandon ship! Abandon ship!" The obvious was obvious. Everybody was abandoning everything, especially the ship. Who wanted the goddamn ship?

My body was wallowing in fever. My mind was floating on all sorts of waters. I was abandoning my reflexes. I was vomiting on Bryan, who now cursed my clumsy movements against the railing.

I couldn't make the rope ladder stand up under my feet. It twisted with the Y 21's listing, edging away. Bryan, maddened, finally got my feet on the ropes. A member of the gun crew in No. 1 lifeboat, reached up for me. He hauled at me, clawing, and I spilled into the sea.

"I can't swim! The bloody Second's drowning!" went Bryan. "Somebody go for that goddamn Yank!"

I was not drowning, though the oil weighed me down like a great liquid blanket. It was a bath exuding intense relief from my fever. It pleased all of my senses until I began to choke from the oil entering my mouth and nose.

Mechanically, I dived under, to swim . . . and I remembered Rogue River, in Oregon, years earlier. You drown in memory . . . then death becomes easier. But it was not easy, when I came up, to breathe. Malaria, with its own oceans of dread, had its own places of pleasure. Malaria was a boat bouncing in you . . . and all sorts of hands now yanked me from the suffusing dreams, and the oil, into the rolling lifeboat.

I had, in my delirium, expected the oil on my body to

enflame from my fever. I was jaundiced-thin; a ghost within a ghost, capable of nothing, certainly not burning on water . . . and when we were picked up by a Dutch freighter in the heavily trafficked sea lanes to Leyte, I was soon, in my feverish time-sense, back in Morotai and hospitalized. What had taken a week to accomplish were moments made more maddened; I knew very little as I dropped from dream to dream, soaking into nothingness.

I was pillowed on feathers for days; my minor head wounds, and my broken shoulder telling me that *I was out of the war.* So was Mr. Hansen, when I could listen to elementary details, who had a concussion; and so was Captain Shaw, who had been retired to a future in some institution for the mentally derailed.

Eventually, I was flown to Brisbane.

In the hospital there I had a visitor. Laura came up from Sydney for a week to embrace me with many emotional promises.

"Pet, I'll join you in New York after the war ends — promise! I'm going after my visa directly. Does that shoulder hurt you very much? You've gotten so thin, little baby. Was it terrible swimming in that muck, pet?"

Laura would get a divorce. One day, in a year or two, we would marry . . . and I was conscious of many things; how words stood up, fell down, went oblique, drowned themselves in still other words. I was going home, away from the war and into a private peace, the small hero of a small swim in the sea, in oil that was thicker than words, that echoed in the sounds of guns.

Laura was with me now, but I had written to Isabelle in San Francisco. I was a man with two vagrant affections on two continents. I was to marry one, I kept saying in my hospital bed, under the mosquito netting; but, happily for a decision, they were continents apart . . . and when I kissed

229

Laura good-bye at Brett's Wharf and I boarded the *S.S. Lurline,* partly converted into a hospital ship, with its casualties from the Leyte invasion, I was kissing good-bye to an English lady. It was good-bye to manners and mannerisms that make an American, because of his simple directness, suspicious of everything English, especially of English ladies in matters of love.

"See you soon, pet . . ." and Laura left.

The *S.S. Lurline* sailed for San Francisco.

§

I was alive; I was not dying like so many others. Those who could walk sunned their bandaged selves as we crossed the Pacific. They were strapped, taped, gauzed, iodined, doped, fearful, restless, angered; ready for any aspect of life but the last—death. I sat with them in their total dumbness under the shading tarpaulins; or I listened to the sad talkers and their endless sentiments: men from the 32nd and the 24th Divisions, who had walked ashore at Leyte Gulf and had gotten it; and sailors from the ships that fought in the sea battles of Leyte Gulf; men from the *U.S.S. Hoel,* the *U.S.S. Gambier Bay,* the *U.S.S. Princeton,* the *U.S.S. Birmingham,* the *U.S.S. Honolulu;* from assault transports, LSM's, LSD's and LCM's—all who were going home.

One lieutenant, j.g., was bandaged like a mummy, burned from his neck to his knees. He could walk a bit, but talk less—and I fed him with my left hand as we sat together. He was from Georgia; he wanted to be a composer. Mostly we talked just to hear our voices wash into the blueing Pacific distances. We were not dead, but they were dying all over the ship, we heard every afternoon on the crowded sundeck. We sat there in funereal lament when we heard of the dying. They went like wind and rain and dust, jettisoned from love and goodwill in a cablegram sent by the War Department. But

230

the lieutenant, j.g., was alive, and he would be a composer, one day; and I would, perhaps, become a writer.

He died three days before we reached San Francisco. It was like suicide, willed by a mind that would never get to music again. His body, suddenly in the ship's morgue, lay with others on the long voyage back to the coasts of our American memory.

Under the wide Golden Gate, we cheered like madmen. We had come back. Walking ashore to the fog-stained Embarcadero, some of us kneeled to kiss the dirty dock. We kissed the whole world. We were fragmented into hysteria, amid the comraderie, gags and pleasantries of the stevedores. And the Army bands were playing. *Our* war was over—and it was 1945. In May, Germany would surrender. In August, Japan . . . and we who had won everything so democratically would start the new world up again.

The *future* began. . . .

Epilogue
The Future Begins

§

When the war ended, and some of the democratic victors became colony-losers, it began a bizarre profession for me — writing about those countries and their colonies. I was pro-India, pro-Indonesia, pro-Israel — a damn good liberal, I thought. Suddenly I found an acceptable American trade: journalism. In the excitement of postwar liberalism, a journalist could write what he really meant, and I did that. I wrote professionally for political periodicals, critical quarterlies, fashion magazines, slenderly endowed literary journals, and for *The New York Times*. I was a war-made authority not only on foreign policy and politics, but on Australian culture, on New Guinea artifacts, on Polynesian rituals.

I had come out of the war completely intact except for some broken bones and malaria, which had a way of coming back occasionally to remind me of the Pacific. There had been a party for me on my return; there were fifty or so warm-blooded, sentimental friends who varied their affections with thunderous third-act echoes of disaffection. Some were incapable of ending their role as critics; for them, it was not acceptable to agree with anybody on anything. That meant bad taste, as critics. They were sundered by private *Sturm und Drang,* occasionally martyred, but often amused. Like Jewish waiters on Second Avenue, they loved you for your ability to accept the insults they left behind at your overladen table . . . and so friends gathered to drink, eat, but basically to war against the Philistines, and with one another.

At the party, Harold Rosenberg was arguing philosophically with James T. Farrell about Zola and the organic nature of Farrell's Chicago naturalism: "All stock yard dialectics, metaphysical bull—and shot through with fertilizer." Somebody was drunk, somebody was not—and it was an uneven literary battle all the way to the bottle. In a less-embattled corner, Isaac Rosenfeld, the critic and short story writer, was reciting T.S. Eliot's *Prufrock* in Yiddish . . .

> *Lomir geyn otazey, du un ich,*
> *Dort vu der ovnt iz oysgeshpreyed*
> *antkegn dem himl . . .*

George Davis, a shy editor of *Mademoiselle*, for which I was writing articles about Australia and New Guinea, was sitting perplexed alongside of Charles Neider, who had done an exploratory book on Kafka, seeking out all the Freudian symbols. They were listening to Rosenberg's biting, complex, intellectual hog-calling services—while Farrell hugged his whiskey, lost in Rosenberg's reasoned Talmudic destinations. It was a trial, a confession, a statement of values, depending on where you were listening.

Max, now the editor of the Irgun paper, *The Answer*, was denouncing English perfidy to Charley Harrison; and Charley was saying, holding onto two glasses of gin, "I suppose, Max, when you were writing publicity for the Cancer Fund, that I should have been in favor of a little bit cancer, too. I'm against a Jewish State—it means an end to Judaism. The Jews need Gentiles around them to make them better Jews—so I'm for Second Avenue, not for Tel Aviv."

Max was soon saying to Charley Harrison, "Why shouldn't the Jews be needled on occasion? After all, they provided the essential spiritual mystique by creating Christ.

And if that was not enough, eighteen centuries later they came up with a socio-economic God — Marx. And a hundred years later they provided the world with an Einstein; or, if you prefer a more subconscious nuance — with a Freud. What a quartet for modern man to contend with!"

Harvey Breit was joking with Lionel Abel about Rimbaud and the poetry of surrealiste ecstasy, a discussion begun fifteen years earlier; Helen Neville, a fey, talented poet, was trying to toast me a *l'chaim*, which would return me, symbolically, to the living again. After the interruption of the toast, the old feuds began anew, for many of the novelists and critics there had not talked with each other for years. Somebody had slighted someone else in print; others differed about their past politics. Both the oratory and the by-plays of talk were aimed for the balls. It was a New York party, native to itself, with eternal hangovers of envy, chagrin, pique, malice, as well as ardent tokens of love and affection.

In the T.S. Eliot corner, Isaac Rosenfeld was completing *The Hollow Men* in Yiddish . . . *Nit mit a klap nor mit a yomer!*

Charley Harrison, who was overly toasted with *l'chaims* and gin, went screaming into the street after the party, yelling, "Poet! Poet! Poet! Poet!" at me. I had innocently remarked that the title for his best novel, *Generals Die In Bed,* had come from a poem by Sassoon. It gave me a moment of unrewarding scholarship and piqued Charley. "Poet!" he continued yelling out, "Where are your wounds?"

A cop came by the stoop. Charley, in his blue Homburg, looked like an over-ginned member of the diplomatic corps — and the perplexed cop was asking me:

"Did that gentleman call you a sonofabitch?"

"No, just a poet."

"Is that an insult?"

"From Charley it's love and just plain flattery . . ."

Friede had come to the party. Somehow we had, as an aftermath of the war, become friends again; and I was able to laugh at the past, without anger—and we kissed, with sentiment. She had progressed in music. She was now a well-known concert manager, not an unknown pianist. Each of us had given up part of that dubious American word, *creativity*. We toasted quietly to something in between, another *l'chaim* amid the noise around us.

§

In a high-ceilinged, furnished flat on West 90th Street, over a walnut-stained student desk, to the shrieking of a Russian neighbor below me who was always beating his Polish wife — he was short and thin, she tall and fat — I worked on my happier assignments. To the rhythms of my typewriter, the husband-and-wife combat team went through laments, blows, and tirades that usually ended when both went to bed with an empty bottle, their violent language exhausted, and love about to triumph, in Russian.

Above me lived a morbid refugee writer, a playwright without a play produced. On occasion, he tried suicide, to awaken the neglect of his friends and producers. Soon, as a by-product of his instincts for survival, he had a play on in London, and off he went to Mayfair for a season. On his return, still gutted here by failure, he tried suicide again; and again he had a play produced — by a local theater group. He knew many of the celebrated German and Austrian writers in exile — Thomas Mann, Oscar Maria Graff, one of the Werfels, Doblin, Hermann Broch — and when he was not committing suicide — he always called his doctor on time after cutting a wrist — he talked happily of his productive life in Europe, pre-1933.

On my floor, to the front, lived a handsome lady who had many men calling on her talents. When in, and occupied professionally, she tacked a square inch of black paper to her chaste-white door. The would-be lover on her whoring calendar would come back in thirty minutes, and it went on like that, with decent silences, around the timeless clock.

The future was everywhere . . .

My wealthy brothers suddenly took pride in me!

I, the sailoring maverick, the ex-Marxist, the poet, was earning a living, "And from my old typewriter," I heard my brother Mike murmur to my mother.

"Far shraibn verter? Gott tsu danken," she answered, kissing me.

On my mantlepiece, over a bogus fireplace, were dozens of national magazines that I had written for, as well as little quarterlies with my poetry and criticism; but I was now leaving poetry behind. I had lost faith in the fancies. I was embittered by poetry's lack of natural relationship to the people of the United States of America. Poetry was cult-ridden, at best. It fitted in with women's clubs, to challenge an afternoon's admixture of tea and chitchat. It did not soar like eagles. You could not live off poetry, nor with it. Economically, it was a private dead end. Spiritually, it was much worse – dead at the frontals of your eyes. Poets were forced to become the *schnorrers* waiting in the anterooms of the Foundations. Who wanted to support their misery? What begging hands they had!

But I could live as a workaday journalist, and my four books of poetry helped to get me to some editors. I dressed neatly; my hair was not long, not short. And I took to wearing black ties as if to mourn for myself. (During the Thirties, like an adjunct to a proletarian uniform of rebellion, I wore red ties, baggy pants, blue shirts – somewhat not neat all the way.) I shaved daily. My shoes were polished. I drank little and worked hard. But I was thoroughly bored with it all and ready for a return visit to Australia.

237

There was Laura in Australia, and the remembered sensuality of sunny early mornings of the war: the 295 bottles of booze, emptied as I lay, not dying, but drunk with Laura. All of it seemed even stranger now, so far away, so unbelievable in time and desire . . . for Laura had written vague letters about the matter of our marriage.

Her R.A.F. husband had been killed a day before the war ended while on a raid over Germany, and Laura was all conscience and contrition about her emotional trespasses. Then I heard that she was marrying a man who looked like her dead husband. I suffered. I wrote that she was wrong. I phoned from New York. I heard telephonic voices blurr 13,000 miles away. She was not in.

When I returned to Sydney, en route to Indo-China as a journalist, I came by Laura's house on Elizabeth Bay. I stood across the street staring at the windows. I heard sounds — party noises, Laura's laughter, Laura's speech. She was saying *pet* to everybody, including her new husband. I shook in anger! I recognized Bill Dobell, the artist, and Cyril Pearl, the editor. I saw Laura come to the window holding a glass . . . and I went on, that night, to New Guinea, my first stop. Then to Saigon and a new war. The jungle was better than this aftermath of war-love, this seeking, this not finding, this little terror in the skull, this breathless state over the heart, this impatience with my world, this fruitless emotion that mocked everything . . . for years.

Laura was to marry twice, and we were to meet through the years all over the world. We were branches from one lush scrub tree, watered by the same rain, open to the same brutal sun. And it was as if we had never gone from each other, so we called it *love* — not post-war mementoes. For back into the bed we went and back to the mirrors. Yet real love was something Laura, a pure hedonist, could not always experience. She could see nothing in the mirror but herself, and the mirror stared back into Laura's glowing face and she watched herself react, the hedonist above all.

While waiting for Laura, I played out the fragile comedy with Isabelle in New York. Ah, those war-time lies! The language of letters. How simple had my letters made all things! Isabelle now had a flat in the Village, to *love* me for weekends: 48 hours, with Palestrina, steak dinners, and French wine. But there was Arthur, a right type of a man, soon to be a successful lawyer, Gentile, taller, who ate hamburgers all the time and talked about the meaning of *living*. If Isabelle married him they would move to Westchester, buy a house, and lead a cook-out, suburban-hamburger life. She would open a dancing school to teach children of the middle-class Jews in Westchester. She was progressive about Jews, Isabelle had always said.

"But," she told me one night, "you won't convert to Christian Science or the Unitarian Church, which so many Jews are doing . . . and my aunt, that rich-bitch who is going to leave me all the money, objects to you. She's stupidly anti-Semitic, but I want her money, Harry. If I marry you, I get nothing. Besides, you haven't really asked me since that morning in San Francisco, when your ship sailed . . ."

I remembered Ludwig Lewisohn's autobiography, *Mid-Channel*. "Jews and Gentiles mix in bed, but not in the heart nor in the head," I answered Isabelle one night.

"Then let's have an orgy!" she said. Everything was very simple when she talked for sexual stimulation, but it was her neutralized Christianity that finally offended me.

When she phoned one evening to break a dinner engagement, she announced, maturely, and securely, "I'm marrying Arthur tomorrow, darling. I was up all night making and re-making that decision. You do understand why, Harry?"

I understood — why.

"But don't you feel terribly hurt, darling?"

"Just hurt."

"Nothing more, darling?"

"Your vulgarity, fortunately, dissolves my emotions," I managed to say.

"My vulgarity or my marriage?"

"They seem to be related, Isabelle. Are you offended that I'm not dying of love? Is what you're doing called love, Miss Isabelle-cum-Hamburger?"

She was more than offended, symbolically, at least. She raged against me for a while, but then calmed down and said, "I could go on meeting you once a week though. Can't we still be occasional lovers, Harry?"

"I've just found out that I'm still a partial Puritan," and I said good-bye to another postal-fed emotion of the war.

Isabelle was off for Westchester and, with my typewriter, I was off for the world again — if not quite as in the days of trumpets begun as a boy.

§

But what had happened to Cherry Street?

I had gone back often, to look. The changes assured me of the City's growth to suffocation. I remember walking there one Saturday in May — to reacquaint myself with a street, to count the tenements gone, to establish the new — and it was a sad summary of a place as I started from South Street, for a look at the Seaman's Institute. Its pennants still flapped for wayward or onshore studying sailors. The lighthouse on top, a memorial to the *Titanic* disaster, gleamed in the spring sun. Gargoyle finials paraded on the roof. At the entrance, a sailor's figurehead rode over the doors. The Institute had not altered.

I went on, to where Cherry Street began near Catherine. Nearby was Alfred E. Smith's former home: an old house on Oliver Street, unpainted, without a plaque, made unmemo-

240

rable by the crudeness of politics. From there the Brooklyn Bridge swept across the East River.

Two bridges passed over Cherry Street. Under the Manhattan Bridge, the cavernous wine cellars were gone. In the past, idlers and drunkards had been given rations of wine for moving the heavy casks. Now there was only the great mass of stone pediments, a contemporary emptiness. A city project jutted into heavenly gloom, filling in the space where smaller tenements had been. After that it was obelisk housing all the way to Pike Slip; but on the other side of the street, the past still stood — discord not yet revamped — post-colonial dwellings, now unoccupied, waiting to be demolished by the City, and a sign — *No Renting — To Be Demolished — The City of New York*.

The street had been born as a cherry orchard, Sackett's Orchard, but had become known around 1703 as Cherry Garden. Mr. Richard Sackett was a brewer, and there were enough saloons around, even in my time, to attest to Mr. Sackett's original plan for the area. When George Washington moved to the Franklin-Osgood Mansion at No. 1-3 Cherry Street during the first year of his presidency, a joint resolution of Congress stipulated that 5,671 pounds, 2 shillings and 7 and 3/4 pence be spent on refurbishing, cleaning, repairing, furnishing and stocking the mansion. Some of the items read:

	L	s.	d.
Wine & Porter	233	14	4
Champagne Wine	57	15	7
Hay and Straw	11	13	6
Soap	3	18	4
1 Eight day Clock	30	0	0
Spirits for workmen	1	10	6

Obviously, it was a happy street, even then. The mansion

was destroyed in 1856, and the abutment for the Brooklyn Bridge covers its site today.

In 1750, Cherry Street was the northern limit of Manhattan; the farms of the Roosevelt family were adjacent, northerly and easterly. Later the street became as commercial as it was social, with Brooks Brothers and Lord & Taylor opening fashionable stores. In 1795, the common council approved a regulation "to make a good and passable Road from Cherry Street to Corlears Hook." And three years later the council permitted Furman Chessman "to dig across Cherry Street for the launching of a Vessel" on the condition that he "do without delay put the Street in the same Condition that he found it."

I saw Gouverneur Hospital, of Civil War vintage. There I had been by gang-war standards the hero of many private wars. Most of it now only semi-used, the hospital had been turned into a mental hygiene clinic. From here the vista of the Brooklyn Bridge suddenly brought back an older America, another time, the time of my father, the time before the First World War, and the sounds of ships blowing their way out of the piers, going under the bridges — to Europe. I stared on. Soon Gouverneur Hospital bled itself into the May afternoon and died in my eyes.

Where Cherry Street bent to the left at Corlears Hook, and the East River turned north, Robert Fulton had launched his first side-wheeler, the *Clermont*, from Brown's shipyard in 1807. Corlears Hook was named after Jacobus and Anthony Van Corlears, Dutch pioneers who owned all the land around the bend of the East River.

At 303 Cherry Street, the Fidelity Warehouse still bulked up, shocking me with invasions of the past. How those spice smells had tantalized my youth!

Among the leftover slums were new housing projects; modern shambles and old shambles, fusing into an enlarged immigrant world of Puerto Ricans and Negroes. And I did not see one face that I knew, and only some vague smells told me that I had been born on this street.

In 1885 the first real tenements had arrived, as well as the immigrant tenement-dwellers. The Tenement Houses Building Company had erected *model* tenements at 338 and 344 Cherry Street. I remembered the seven-story building at 338, on the corner of Montgomery, as a pigsty reaching up to the sky.

Where I was born, at 362, a grassless, shabby, stone park had replaced my house. Idling handball players were sipping cokes, sweating darkly, to give me back the moments of trumpets—the massive block fights, the gigantic July 4th bonfires, and the bright days of childhood rapture . . . and now the park came up to ghost my feet, to move me like a plunging drunk into every pleasantry and horror in my memory . . .

P.S. 31 was my school. There I had learned enough to run away and there it still was, a gray historical marker on Monroe Street, its roof still caged for basketball games. On its huge door was a chalked-up *Fuck You*, to illustrate the essence of current scholarship. But then, in my own no-less prurient days, we had chalked up a similar language— and I salaamed to the school, content, all-wise, a middle-aged man, a son of America the Beautiful and *America the Gonev*, who had come back to the source, who had never graduated from the school but had run with the seasons. My wild body was now tamed. And I went on again, to where Scammel Street, once on the corner, had disappeared into the garden projects of the Vladeck Houses, turning the area into a grassy series of village squares.

An hour later I stood before the synagogue on Madison and Montgomery, once a Dutch Reformed Church. In its time it was the end of the City; in my time, there had been horsecars and my mother's newsstand. The synagogue, pink-painted, stood out odd and adrift alongside the sky-reaching housing projects. It seemed humped over, a building praying to itself—and I was dreaming back to the newspaper racks and the boxes and the old men who had bought our varied Jewish newspapers. There was my armless mother smiling at the cop who helped her cover up the rack, to keep the rain off the papers . . . My mother, blind her last two years, had died at 87, in a rest home, no longer with her sons, though my affectionate kid brother Bill had housed her until the rest home. I remembered on and on—those watery blue eyes, her blonde hair, her mothering softnesses and charities. She gave to all of the pennies she made at the newsstand; I had taken my own Indian pennies—little loans that were never returned. Here, one Saturday at the synagogue, I had faced the Lions of Judea, the boy and the man turned thirteen years, who had broken every Judaic law and every commandment, who had hallowed almost nothing, had known every sin of man.

When had I prayed last? I had forgotten the language to address God, but I prayed now, mumbling to myself some refrains—*Eli Eli*—*Lomo Azavtoni*. I had done the *forsaking*. A little red skullcap was in my pocket; but it was too early to enter the synagogue. I was entering into my house of prayer in my flesh, impatient for a service to myself—for who would ever mourn for me? I mourned now, contrite, making the moment of this May afternoon another *Yom Kippur*.

Mourn by the river! Cast everything away! And remember the savageries of this street—*O Lord our God, impose thine awe upon all thy works, and thy dread upon all that thou hast created, that all works may fear thee.* The street had died. The synagogue was alive. I said *Kaddish* for my parents—and crossed the street.

I stopped at the corner delicatessen store. A pastrami sandwich and celery tonic. A face suddenly remembered and a face totally forgotten. Greetings. A handshake, words bursting forth, information given. Where was the former owner? He had retired—and so had his son, Lippy Meltzer, who had been my classmate. He had moved away—and I went on, something fogged in the memory, to the Henry Street Settlement. Children's drawings had been engraved on the blue-tile fronting of the Settlement for children's joys . . . many of us had, years before, made the place a place for the wild heart, to keep us from our wayward selves.

The St. Augustine Chapel, once an All Saints Church, built in 1828, graced the other side of the street. In fieldstone and austere simplicity, it loomed up in Episcopalian solemnity, its semi-colonial architecture now in strange juxtaposition to the rest of the once-strident street. There had been another transgressor, who had said, about 400 A.D., when Roman imperialism was dying, that "heart speaketh to heart." My own transgressions walked with me down Henry Street, and across, to the East Side Torah Center. And where I had once drowned cats off Corlears Hook Park, the East River Drive now raced with traffic.

The massive, red-brick building of R. Hoe & Company, where I used to watch intricate printing machinery being assembled, had moved long ago from Broome and Sheriff. The machinery sounds were gone. Once mechanics had tooled rollers for the huge presses. Now Puerto Rican boys ruled the street with new noises and jazz nerves. Spanish sounds had replaced Yiddish ones. I heard a ball game being broadcast over a radio in someone's window. It was a home run in every direction.

At 311 East Broadway was a Ritualarium, a *mikvah*. Once it had been the Arnold Toynbee House; where workers, not anxious to become Marxists, believed that capital and labor were cooperative partners. The building now had other rituals to perform—a *mikvah* for a bride's purifying bath on a Saturday night for a Sunday wedding.

I was making notes on the passing of places, ideas, settlements, and houses, standing in front of the Ritualarium like an impure *melamed*. An old couple came by, past their fourscore. The old woman asked me in Yiddish what I was writing? And where did I come from?

I said that I came from Cherry Street.

"Cherry Street? Are you a Jew?"

"I am . . ."

"Cherry Street? *Es is mer nishtu. Es is aveck gegongen.*" The street was no more — it had gone away.

What was here? I walked on to 273 East Broadway, where a plaque said: "Here lived Meyer London, 1915-1918." A small Puerto Rican boy, sitting a stoop away, offered up the information that Meyer London "was an old man who was once the mayor of New York. He wore glasses so he was an old man, Mister."

The old men were down the street, sitting on stoops; the outdoor people who had nothing to do any more. At Montgomery, off East Broadway, was the old Rabbinical College; and all along East Broadway, as far as Jefferson Street, were schools for studying the Talmud, offices of benefit societies, and collection agencies for Israel. The Bialystoker Building, modern and taller, faced the squat buildings of little *yeshivahs* hanging on to Judaism amid the surroundings of Puerto Rican primitivism; but there was a resurgence of nothing, just the tokens of old age. God was in Seward Park, over the afternoon sun, between the ball players and the sitting people.

I stared at a familiar building, the Educational Alliance, where I had briefly been a boy scout. Ah, those overnight hikes to the Palisades! I was hiking through myself again, going through the woods of darkness . . . and I was swimming in the East River, then floating on a huge log out into the harbor, and a police boat was hauling us back to South

Street. I walked on again, heading for the *Jewish Daily Forward* building. A few feet away, where another *yeshivah* had once been, was the headquarters of the Liberal Party, 2 A.D. It was like Anno Domini instead of Aldermanic District—another transformation and transfiguration impinging on nearby Iglesia Cristiana Primitiva. Glory be!

To the *Jewish Daily Forward* building I had come early in the morning with my mother. My little red cart had been our common carrier, and on it we piled a thousand papers, to haul them to the buyers in front of the synagogue. In my father's time, hundreds of thousands of Jewish immigrants had read the *Forward* for news, gossip, and politics. It was for the working class—advice to the lovelorn, socialistic, a Meyer London vote-getter. Now, with the century having distributed the former cultures of the ghetto, the paper had fewer than fifty thousand readers.

I went on past Jefferson Street, in some explosion of inner wrath, remembering much too much, unable to accept either myself or what I saw . . . the leftovers, the longings, the rituals, in a city changed, a district altered as a cat is altered, the streets gone, and with them the people and the history.

The Chatham Square Library, where I had done my first reading, was still in use. Built for young scholars and older sleepers, it stood on the ground where the British had hanged Nathan Hale. Chatham Square, named after the Earl of Chatham, William Pitt, had once seen British soldiers level a statue of William Pitt, calling him a traitor to England. Now the street had turned in on itself; half left, half gone—all of it in an odd physical perfidy waiting for the City to take it away.

In other parts of the country, and the world, old streets remained; old villages clung to some splendor of the past, believing in an unalterable sequence despite the changes—

unhurt in the all-swallowing of *progress.* But this city was hardly Walt Whitman's *Manahatta,* nor my father's, nor mine any more.

The new Barbarians, circa 1964, were at work on the City . . . and even the symbols of poetry were demolished. Whitman's house on Cranberry and Fulton Streets, where Whitman had set the type for *Leaves of Grass,* was torn down one bright day in June by the Able Demolition Company.

Francis Bacon once wrote, "Beauty is as summer fruits, which are easy to corrupt." And the corruptions, within and without, were of this time, not so much of another time, when I was first on Cherry Street . . . and the street was gone, and the future was with me.